RESOURCE STRUCTURE
OF AGRICULTURE:
AN ECONOMIC ANALYSIS

RESOURCE STRUCTURE OF AGRICULTURE: AN ECONOMIC ANALYSIS

by

KEITH COWLING
University of Warwick

DAVID METCALF
London School of Economics

A. J. RAYNER
Manchester University

PERGAMON PRESS

Oxford · New York · Toronto
Sydney · Braunschweig

Pergamon Press Ltd., Headington Hill Hall, Oxford

Pergamon Press Inc., Maxwell House, Fairview Park, Elmsford, New York 10523

Pergamon of Canada Ltd., 207 Queen's Quay West, Toronto 1

Pergamon Press (Aust.) Pty. Ltd., 19a Boundary Street,
Rushcutters Bay, N.S.W. 2011, Australia

Vieweg & Sohn GmbH, Burgplatz 1, Braunschweig

First edition 1970

Library of Congress Catalog Card No. 70–114570

Printed in Great Britain by A. Wheaton & Co., Exeter

08 015585 5

TO BARBARA, HELEN AND PATSY

CONTENTS

PREFACE

THIS book was conceived at Manchester in an environment which proved to be a stimulating milieu for quantitative economic analysis of the agricultural industry. All three authors were together there and all three owe a very considerable debt of gratitude to Wat Thomas, Professor of Agricultural Economics, for providing consistent encouragement to the attempts made to break new ground by applying new tools to the considerable body of data which had accumulated on the resource structure of the industry. In addition to his positive encouragement for all our research he has also given valuable comments on various papers and reports that have been produced whether as precursors for chapters in the book or as earlier drafts of the actual chapters. The authors would also like to mention Leslie McClements, John McInerney, David Colman and Tim Josling for valuable comments on some of the chapters at various stages of their production.

Cowling started working on the agricultural labour market in 1964 and was subsequently joined in this activity by Metcalf. In 1966 Rayner started working on the demand for tractors in which Cowling co-operated. Later in the same year Cowling and Metcalf started independent investigations of different aspects of the demand for fertilizers and they subsequently co-operated in a published paper. Since then the authors have attempted to integrate these studies of the resource structure of the industry and to tie these empirical investigations to a theoretical structure which is developed in some detail so that a strong base will be laid for the use of this book as a basic text in agricultural economics.

CHAPTER 1

INTRODUCTION

THIS book seeks to examine the resource structure of the agricultural industry and to explain the changing structure over time. The empirical analysis is focused essentially on the inter-relationships between the agriculture sector and the industrial sectors on the input side. That is, we are not directly concerned with resources generated in the agricultural sector and we are not concerned with the flow of agricultural output into the industrial sector. For industrial inputs, specifically, we are dealing with markets dominated by oligopoly structures, as in the case of the tractor, machinery and chemical industries. For the agricultural labour market and the land market this is not the case although there will usually be a greater degree of concentration in the non-agricultural sectors. The factor markets serving agriculture that we will examine will include both these groups and in addition we will examine the provision of research and development, education and extension services to the sector.

The analysis will be theoretical as well as empirical. There is a separate theoretical chapter giving the main underpinnings for the later chapters dealing with specific factor markets. This chapter is essentially based on the orthodox profit maximizing theory of the firm, but the model is adapted to situations of uncertainty and to situations where the instantaneous adjustment of resource structure to equilibrium is not assumed. In addition, the chapters dealing with specific factor markets include sections in which the underlying model of demand for inputs is adapted to the particular situation for that factor market. In addition, the chapter on labour includes estimates of the supply function for agricultural labour since in this case it is a meaningful concept. Such estimates would not be meaningful in the case of oligopolistic structures with administered pricing. In this case it would be interesting to explore the mechanism of price formation, although we have not attempted this.

1

The empirical analysis is essentially based on market behaviour in the post-war period supplemented where possible with material from earlier periods. Largely because of the paucity of information, but also because of the constraints on time, this historical material is essentially descriptive and we have not usually attempted quantitative explanations of market behaviour. The chapters on specific factor markets will often include some econometric analysis and indeed there is a brief introduction to the problems of estimating demand relationships included in the theory chapter. However, we have tried to write up the material on each factor market so as to allow for a coherent development of analysis even if the problems of estimation and hypothesis testing are ignored. Thus each chapter will involve a description of the market and a discussion of the determinants of demand and then the chapter will be ended with an evaluation of the econometric results which are obtained as a result of the methods reported in the intervening sections.

In a similar vein, people with little theoretical background in microeconomics should be able to work through the theory chapter and pick out the relevant bits for understanding the models developed for each factor market. Some parts of the book assume a knowledge of differential calculus but the book can be read by others by simply skipping these sections as they generally only serve to give a rigorous backing to the verbal reasoning that has gone before.

The structure and content of the book as a whole is the product of the endeavours of all three authors—each has contributed something to every chapter. However, particular chapters are the major responsibility of particular authors. Cowling has co-ordinated the work, written the preliminaries and has a major responsibility for Labour (Chapter 3) and Research and Development, Extension and Education (Chapter 7). Metcalf has major responsibility for Chemical Technology (Chapter 5), Land and Buildings (Chapter 6) and Implications of Public Policy (Chapter 9), and Rayner for Theory of Resource Demand (Chapter 2), Engineering Technology (Chapter 4) and Demand for Resources and the Supply of Agricultural Products (Chapter 8). It might be said straightaway that the most well developed areas of empirical analysis are the labour market, the demand for tractors and the demand for chemical fertilizer. Each of these markets has been subjected to careful econometric analysis. To fill in the gaps remaining in the resource picture we have included an essentially descriptive treatment of other markets involving interactions with the industrial sector of the economy. Thus the chapter on Engineering Technology includes a description of trends in the use of various machines together with a qualitative explanation as well as a detailed examination of the demand for mechanical power. Similarly the chapter on Chemical Technology includes some analysis of the demand for pesticides as well as a detailed analysis of the market for chemical fertilizers. The chapters on Land and Buildings and Research and Development, Education and Extension give some documentation of these important areas of resource use but do not attempt any systematic quantitative analysis. An important market has been omitted almost entirely—the market for animal feed. This was quite deliberate in that we wanted to restrict our attention to the interactions between the agricultural and industrial sectors. This is a convenient cut-off in that we then avoid plunging into all the problems of measuring directly agricultural supply relations and intra-agricultural transactions. We have in fact included some extraneous material on the demand for animal feed in developing our indirect estimates of agricultural supply elasticities. It might be useful now to give a brief, chapter by chapter, introduction to the contents of our book.

Chapter 2, Theory of Resource Demand, begins by describing the characteristics of the environment in which decisions are taken in agriculture and examining the motivations of farmers. After explaining and illustrating the concept of an aggregate production function for agriculture and explaining how industrial inputs are priced, a detailed step-by-step analysis is made of the demand function for a current input. The orthodox theory of the firm is developed first assuming a certain, static environment and then these simplifying assumptions are relaxed first to examine the problem of uncertainty surrounding both the price structure faced by the farmer and the marginal productivities of the different resources under different environmental conditions, and second to examine the dynamic environment due to changing technology and lags in adjustment to changes in the price structure. This part gives a particularly detailed account of the process of quality change in inputs into agriculture and indicates how this process can be quantified and integrated into our theory of the firm. Subsequently the peculiar problems of durable inputs are examined and the optimal rules for investment in such resources are examined. The chapter is completed by a brief excursion into the problems of actually estimating the relationships between demand for specific inputs and the relevant prices and other variables which our theory suggests are the determinants of the quantity demanded. In other words this section is concerned with the problems we are faced with in empirical analysis when we are trying to get estimates of the relevant demand elasticities.

Chapter 3 on Labour is orientated round three pieces of empirical analysis, first an investigation of the aggregate supply and demand relationships for agricultural labour giving separate results for the post-war and inter-war periods, second an analysis of the determinants of agricultural wages, describing the process of estimating an industry-level "Philips curve" and documenting the results, and third a model of regional labour supply giving results for a period in the nineteen-sixties. These separate results are introduced in the context of the historical record of large and continuing outmigration of people from the agricultural sector.

Chapter 4 revolves round a detailed analysis of the market for farm tractors in the post-war period. This is supplemented by a description of trends in the use of particular types of machinery and the recent developments are put into historical context by a description of the early moves toward the mechanization of agricultural processes. This chapter and the previous one on agricultural labour obviously show a lot of inter-relationships and should be read in conjunction in order to grasp the whole process of substitution of capital for labour in this industry. The chapter on Engineering Technology is completed by a brief description of the structure, conduct and performance of the agricultural sector of the engineering industry.

The chapter on Chemical Technology (Chapter 5) follows a similar format to the one on engineering, being focused on the demand for a particular set of chemicals—those used as fertilizers by the agricultural industry, being essentially nitrogen, phosphorus, and potassium compounds. The chapter is rounded out by some documentation of the use of pesticides which include a wide range of inorganic and organic chemicals and where innovations are quite frequent. Because of this latter fact a section of the chapter is devoted to an analysis of the process of diffusion of innovations although the subject matter is relevant to the uptake of new engineering technology and new crop varieties as well. The supply side of the chemical industry is described and government intervention, which is of major importance for fertilizer demand, is discussed.

Chapter 6 on Land and Buildings looks at the competing demands for land for urban and agricultural uses and examines the movement in agricultural land prices over an extended period. Some documentation is made of recent investment in farm buildings and variables are suggested which may be relevant to an explanation of building investment.

Chapter 7, Research and Development, Extension and Education reviews the limited information on these sectors contributing resources to the agricultural industry. Most of the data refers to the public sector with only very fragmentary evidence for the private. In addition to aggregate expenditure figures, the chapter again discusses the innovation and diffusion of new technology, this time with reference to new crop varieties. A model of decision-making under uncertainty is also discussed from the point of view of selecting among different crop varieties with uncertain yields. The chapter is rounded out with a discussion of the problems of attempting cost–benefit analyses of public intellectual investment.

Chapter 8 brings together the studies of different inputs and examines the resultant changing resource structure of agriculture over the post-war period. There is some discussion of the interaction between the demands for different resources followed by the derivation of an aggregate supply elasticity for agriculture from the estimates of the demand elasticities for the different inputs with respect to the product price, i.e. agricultural output price. This section includes a theoretical discussion of the problem of generating short-run and long-run equilibrium supply elasticities from the short- and long-run demand elasticities. The chapter is completed by some discussion of likely future developments in resource structure and technology.

Chapter 9 focuses attention on the impact of public policy measures on resource use. Direct and indirect public policy measures impinge very significantly on the factor markets serving agriculture. The first sections of the chapter attempt to evaluate the impact on these markets of the agricultural policy instruments adopted by government in the post-war period. This is followed by an analysis of the impact of various measures of macro policy on specific factor markets.

CHAPTER 2

THEORY OF RESOURCE DEMAND

THE aim of this chapter is to put forward general hypotheses which can explain why the aggregate demand for a resource varies over time. In later chapters we turn these general hypotheses into specific hypotheses which explain the demand, by farmers, for particular inputs over the post-war period. That is, the general hypotheses indicate the type of factors that are likely to have influenced the demand for any particular input; we then attempt to measure and test for the influence of these factors. The theory put forward is expressed in the form of a demand function for an input: the demand for an input is assumed to depend on the magnitude of various determining factors or variables. In addition, we attach to the function a hypothesis about the qualitative influence of each variable on demand—the direction in which we expect demand to change given a change in each variable, whilst holding the magnitudes of the other variables constant.

The aggregate demand by farmers for an input is simply the sum of the demands by individual farm-firms. Hence, firm theory, which explains the behaviour of the average firm, forms the basis for deriving a demand function explaining aggregate behaviour. To develop the appropriate theory, we first look at some relevant features of the decision-making environment within agriculture. We go on to derive demand functions explaining the aggregate demand for an input and conclude with a note on the method used, in later chapters, to test and measure demand functions. However, as a starting point, we define some concepts which are used in the rest of the chapter.

I. Some Concepts and Definitions

The activity of production may be defined as the process of combining and co-ordinating materials and factor services (inputs) in the creation

6

of goods and services (outputs). The *production function* is then a concept which relates how the output from a production activity is dependent upon the quantity of inputs combined in that activity. More specifically, it is defined as the technological relationship which shows, for a given state of technical knowledge, the maximum possible level of output for any given level of inputs. We should note that inputs and outputs are *time flows* of measured physical quantities: that is, they are measured over a given time period. We may further distinguish stocks of goods, which are either the source of input flows or the result of output flows. Stocks are measured as physical quantities at a point in time. The term *productive resource* (factor of production) is a stock concept and a resource is the source of an input flow.

In agriculture, we can associate a single discrete production period with a production activity—for example, the period of time required to grow a single crop of wheat. We may then distinguish between those resources which provide an input flow—a flow of services—for a single production period only, i.e. the resource is completely used up within the production period and those resources which provide an input (service) flow over several periods. The former are called *current* or monoperiod resources—for example, most fertilizers; the latter are denoted as durable or polyperiod resources—for example, capital goods such as machinery. The fact that a current resource is generally bought to provide an input flow to the production function for a single production period whilst a durable resource is bought to provide a service flow for more than one period leads us to derive separate demand functions for the two types of resources.

II. The Decision Milieu in Agriculture

II.1. TRADITIONAL CAPITALISM, ATOMISTIC COMPETITION

Agriculture is one of the sectors of the U.K. economy in which traditional capitalism is still prevalent, particularly as the private limited company is essentially a form of traditional capitalism in the sense that there is no divorce between ownership and management. The essence of traditional capitalism (entrepreneurship) is that the functions of risk-taking, reward-receiving and decision-making are carried out by the one individual (or by the family acting as a unit). Thus the farmer typically combines ownership of the firm (although not necessarily of the land) with management of the firm. As manager he therefore makes the decisions determining the success of the firm; as owner he receives the rewards of success. Also as the owner he carries the risks of the firm which arise because as manager he has to make decisions on the basis of an imperfect knowledge of his environment. We can therefore visualize that the farmer is orientated toward balancing, in some way, the possible rewards of success with the degree of risk involved.

The number of entrepreneurs in agriculture is large and the size of individual farm-firms is small in relation to the size of the industry. The structure of the industry therefore represents atomistic competition. Consequently we can regard individual farmers as price takers, in the sense that they cannot significantly affect the prices of their products or inputs. On a localized basis some collusive activity may be undertaken by farmers' co-ops, trading groups, etc. The extent of this is not significant enough to affect the argument, however. Hence we can regard farmers as being *quantity planners*: that is, they plan, independently of each other, the level of their output under given price expectations. More precisely, they plan the level of their inputs and via some concept of the relationship of output to inputs (their implicit production function) they plan output.

II.2. UNCERTAINTY IN THE ENVIRONMENT

The production of farm commodities requires that inputs be committed for some time period (of varying length) before any output is obtained. Hence if product prices are determined by market forces, they will be unknown to the farmer when he plans production. Product prices are therefore liable to be uncertain particularly as the individual farmer cannot forecast what the aggregate supply of any commodity will be. Thus he has imperfect knowledge of the planned output of other farmers; also, the influence of extraneous factors on supply—such as weather and disease—cannot be forecast. Even if aggregate demand is fairly stable from one production period to the next, aggregate supply is liable to change and therefore the farmer faces an uncertain market price.

Uncertainty also surrounds the production function of the farm-firm for any production period. Firstly, the influence of extraneous factors on production cannot be accurately forecast and, secondly, the farmer has imperfect knowledge of his production function. Hence the planned level of output, for given input flows, is unlikely to be exactly realized and the farmer is aware of this.

II.3. TECHNOLOGICAL CHANGE LEADS TO A DYNAMIC ENVIRONMENT

Technological change may be described as the discovery of new production techniques. In this sense, most of the technological change that impinges on agriculture is developed outside the industry—by industrial firms and government research agencies. This research and development leads to new technology both for the industries supplying agriculture with inputs and for agriculture itself. Thus new processes for producing agricultural inputs are discovered; also, new agricultural inputs are developed and existing ones are improved. Often quality improvement in an agricultural input is a result of the development of a new way of producing the input.

This technological change causes relative prices and potential production costs in agriculture to continually alter. Farmers are thus faced with the problem of adjusting their resource structure to meet the changing circumstances. In addition, they face the problem, in each production period, of evaluating the new technology and deciding whether or not to adopt it. Consequently, we may describe the decision-making environment in agriculture as being dynamic—one which continually poses new problems to farmers.

II.4. GOALS OF FARM-FIRMS: FARMER OBJECTIVES

Economists have traditionally assumed that decision-makers follow maximizing behaviour patterns in relation to some goal(s). However, in recent years it has been suggested that the decision-makers in firms do not attempt to maximize anything but instead follow "satisficing" behaviour—that is, they seek a course of action that is "good enough" in relation to some criteria, such as a minimum level of profits.†
Satisficing models have a psychologically richer basis for explaining behaviour patterns than optimizing models and may therefore provide

† For example, see H. A. Simon, Theories of decision-making in economics and behavioural science, *American Economic Review*, vol. 49, June 1959, pp. 253–83.

a better description of individual decision-making. Drawing from psychology theories, satisficing models assume that the motive for action stems from drives and that action terminates when drives are satisfied. The conditions for satisfying a drive are specified by an aspiration level which can adjust as the result of experience. However, the satisficing approach necessitates a far more complex model for predicting behaviour than the optimizing (maximizing) approach and, so far, has proved non-operational for deriving predictions about the *aggregate* behaviour of firms. So, for predicting the aggregate behaviour of farm-firms, we rely on a maximizing behavioural assumption for explaining the behaviour of the representative (average) firm.

It would, perhaps, then be a truism to say that farmers attempt to maximize their utility (subjective benefit) from the owner-management of their farm-firms. It seems fair to assume, from our earlier discussion of the traditional capitalistic organization of agriculture, that utility maximization for farmers is closely associated with some form of profit maximization. Thus, profits provide the means for personal consumption and the means to build up the asset value of the firm— and are the key to future wealth. The testing of personality theories in psychology provides evidence that entrepreneurs are strongly motivated by the drive to achieve, and profits are looked upon as a measure of success as well as being a monetary reward for endeavour.†

We will initially assume on the above basis that farmers are profit maximizers. This is not to say that the sole motive of farmers is to maximize profits, but that profits are an important consideration— important enough to allow us to substantially explain aggregate farmer behaviour on the basis of this assumption. This leads us to postulate that farmers will vary their use of inputs, in response to changes in their environment, in the way predicted by profit maximizing theory. However, we shall also postulate that although farmers are profit seeking, they are cautious in adjusting to the dynamic environment when it comes to changing their use of inputs. In effect this means that where there is technological change, the adjustment of resource use, in a profit-seeking direction, to a given change in the environment (such as

† See, for example, J. W. McGuire, *Theories of Business Behaviour*, Prentice-Hall, 1964. It should be emphasized that there is a cultural aspect involved here: not all societies recognize a successful man as one who makes money.

a price change) takes time and the longer the time period considered the more complete will be the adjustment that is made.

Profits, defined as total revenue minus total opportunity costs, are a flow concept and we will take them to be measured over the production period. For a current input, which is bought by the firm, the opportunity cost is the price paid for the input; for a current input supplied by the firm to itself, the opportunity cost is the price for which the input could be sold. The opportunity cost of the input (service) flow from a unit of a durable resource, which is owned by the firm, is the implicit rental of the input—usually measured as the market value of depreciation over the period. In addition, the opportunity cost for all inputs includes the interest foregone by not lending capital funds tied up in the input.†

Finally, we might briefly consider if other variables as well as profits enter the utility function in an important way. Thus farmers may elect to maximize some combination of profits and leisure. Particularly on family farms, this may lead to a lower labour input and a consequent divergence in the use of other inputs—such as labour substituting inputs— from that predicted by profit maximizing theory. However, leisure may not be in direct conflict with profits: the amount of leisure being of less importance than better quality (more expensive) leisure. A leisure objective is not considered in our analysis but it may be an important consideration for other analyses of farmer behaviour. A second possible consideration is that farmers might prefer some loss in profit in order to maintain some desired level of liquid assets (cash) and to avoid borrowing to the level which would maximize profits. This is considered later on to some extent when we consider a capital funds constraint on the demand for inputs.

III. The Aggregate Demand for an Input‡

Our analysis of agriculture's demand for an input is based upon three relationships. Firstly, it involves the physical concept of an aggregate

† For a full discussion of opportunity cost measurement see R. G. Lipsey, *An Introduction to Positive Economics*, 2nd ed., ch. 19, Weidenfeld & Nicolson, 1966.

‡ In the rest of the chapter, it is assumed that the reader has some elementary knowledge of production theory. A lucid verbal and graphical introduction to production theory is given in C. E. Bishop and W. D. Toussaint, *Introduction to Agricultural Economic Analysis*, Wiley, 1958. A mathematical treatment is given by J. M. Henderson and R. E. Quandt, *Microeconomic Theory*, McGraw-Hill, 1958.

production function for agriculture; secondly, it involves the relationship between agriculture and the industry supplying the input, and,
thirdly, it involves the way farmers change their demand for the input
in response to economic forces in their environment. The first two
relationships are important, in our context, only as far as they affect
the third. Hence, we first deal briefly with these two before going on to
derive theoretical demand functions, firstly for a current input and
secondly for a durable input.

III.1. AN AGGREGATE PRODUCTION FUNCTION FOR AGRICULTURE

The production function concept indicates that there is a physical
constraint on the level of output which is obtainable from given levels
of input flows. We may visualize each individual farm-firm in agriculture as being constrained in its decision making by its own production
function.† We can then conceive of an aggregate production function
for agriculture as being the aggregate of these individual firm production functions. However, this conceptual aggregation procedure raises
several theoretical difficulties.‡ One particular difficulty concerns the
uniqueness of the aggregate production function. If the aggregate
input flow of a resource were the same at two points in time but the
distribution of this input flow amongst firms changed, then this function
might not be unique or single valued. In this situation, the flow of
aggregate output might be different at the two points in time even though
aggregate input flows had not changed. However, this difficulty is
bypassed in our analysis, as a result of our assumption that farm-firms
vary their use of inputs in a similar direction (profit-seeking) in response
to a change in their decision-making environment. In other words,
firms are presumed not to change their demand for any particular input
in an opposite direction to each other, and therefore a change in demand
by firms leads to a change in the aggregate demand for the input.

† Farms are multiproduct firms and we should therefore speak of a relationship
between product combinations and input flows. Here we will consider output to be the
value aggregation of individual product flows.

‡ See, for example, A. A. Walters, Production and cost functions: an econometric
survey, *Econometrica*, vol. 31, 1963, pp. 66, especially pp. 8–11 and the references
contained therein.

In view of the above discussion, the aggregate production function may then be regarded as being that of the "representative" firm with input and output flows being multiplied by the number of firms. To predict aggregate behaviour, we may then apply firm theory to predict how the representative firm acts within the constraint of its production function. Two hypotheses concerning the production function of the representative firm are important with regard to the demand for an input. The first is the hypothesis of diminishing marginal productivity: this states that if successive increments of one input flow are added to a fixed combination of other input flows, the addition to product— the marginal physical product (M.P.P.)—will eventually decline. From this hypothesis we can see that the opportunity for the representative firm to increase its profits, by increasing the input flow of one resource, is constrained by how quickly the additions to product decline as the input flow is increased. The second hypothesis concerns that of resource interaction. Two resources are defined as technical substitutes when output can be maintained by reducing the service flow of one and increasing the service flow of the other. But we also postulate a diminishing marginal rate of substitution between the input flows of two substitute resources. This hypothesis states that if we substitute one input flow for the other, whilst maintaining output constant, then the quantities of the second input flow which we can save or withdraw become successively smaller and smaller as we substitute them by the first input flow in successive equal increments. This therefore suggests a constraint on the extent to which the representative firm can profitably substitute the use of one resource for another. Thus, if output is to be maintained, the opportunity for substitution becomes less and less the greater the substitution already achieved. Hence, both of these hypotheses suggest that the production function imposes a constraint on the extent to which the demand for an input will change following a change in economic forces. In other words, the size of any change in the demand for an input will partly depend on how quickly the marginal physical product of the input declines and partly on the decline in its marginal rate of substitution with other resources. One final point is that two inputs may be technical complements, which means that output cannot be maintained by substituting the input flow of one resource for the other's input flow but that they must be used in combination. It is possible, however, that at low input levels, resources may sometimes serve as technical complements whilst serving as technical substitutes over a wider range of input combinations. For example, a tractor requires a man to operate it but, in general, the use of tractor services tends to substitute for labour services over the wide range of possible input combinations.

An Example†

An example of an estimated production function for the representative firm in U.K. agriculture is given by Rasmussen.‡

He estimated the production function by the equation:

$$V = 1 \cdot 702 \, X_2^{0 \cdot 078} \, X_5^{0 \cdot 314} \, X_6^{0 \cdot 283} \, X_{10}^{0 \cdot 508} \qquad (2.1)$$

where V is the value of output; X_2 is the value of rent and rates, X_5 is total tenant's capital (machinery, etc.); X_6 is the value of labour; and X_{10} is the value of purchases (seed plus feed plus fertilizers plus sundries). In fact this is the estimated equation for mixed farms: four equations were estimated with farms classified into four types by their main product. The equations were estimated by cross section analysis of farm accounts. This production function, because of its algebraic form, conforms with the two production function hypotheses discussed in the previous section. For example, the hypothesis of diminishing marginal productivity can be illustrated by the marginal product equation for labour:

$$\partial V/\partial X_6 = 0 \cdot 283 \times 1 \cdot 702 \, X_2^{0 \cdot 078} \, X_5^{0 \cdot 314} \, X_{10}^{0 \cdot 508}/X_6^{1-0 \cdot 283} \qquad (2.2)$$

Thus as the labour input (X_6) is increased its M.P.P. falls.

Secondly, we can see that there is a resource interaction effect in the production function—resources can be substituted for each other to maintain output. The hypothesis of a diminishing marginal rate of substitution can be illustrated by considering, for example, the substitu-

† The reading of this section may be omitted without disturbing continuity.
‡ Knud Rasmussen, *Production Function Analyses of British and Irish Farm Accounts*, University of Nottingham School of Agriculture, 1962.

tion of tenants' capital for labour. The marginal rate of substitution (M.R.S.) of X_5 for X_6 is given by:

$$- dX_6/dX_5 = (\partial V/\partial X_5)/(\partial V/\partial X_6)$$

$$= \frac{0\cdot314 \times 1\cdot702 X_2^{0\cdot078}\ X_6^{0\cdot283}\ X_{10}^{0\cdot508}/X_5^{1-0\cdot314}}{0\cdot283 \times 1\cdot702 X_2^{0\cdot078}\ X_5^{0\cdot314}\ X_{10}^{0\cdot508}/X_6^{1-0\cdot283}}$$

$$= \frac{0\cdot314\ X_6}{0\cdot283\ X_5} \tag{2.3}$$

Thus, as tenant's capital (X_5) is substituted for labour (X_6) the marginal rate of substitution between them progressively declines.

III.2. SUPPLY CONDITIONS AND INPUT PRICES

We now discuss the way in which input prices are determined as this influences our approach to the analysis of the demand for an input. In particular, we are concerned with the question of whether or not the aggregate demand of farmers for an input partly determines its price—even though an individual farmer cannot significantly influence the price he pays for an input. The answer to this question hinges on the supply conditions for the input and so we now look at the supply of resources to agriculture.

As discussed in Chapter 1, inputs supplied from industrial sources to agriculture generally have predetermined prices. This arises from the oligopolistic market structure which characterizes the relationship between the suppliers of these inputs and farmers (the buyers). In addition, most input supplying firms tend to export and/or supply goods to the non-farm sector, so that changes in U.K. agricultural demand may have only a small impact on their cost structure. Hence prices to farmers tend to be "sticky" and unresponsive to farmers' demand in the short run and disequilibrium largely takes the form of changes in sellers' inventories. This means that we can regard the prices of these inputs over a short time period, such as a year, as being un-affected by their aggregate demands within the same time period.

The relationship between supply structure and aggregate demand is, however, more complex with regard to the non-industrial inputs used in agriculture—labour, land and intra-agricultural inputs.† The prices of these inputs are to be partly explained by forces within the agricultural sector itself and this necessarily leads to a more complex model for explaining changes in the demand for these inputs. For example, in an analysis of the demand for labour in agriculture we need to explain both the quantity of labour hired and the average earnings of labour if both are simultaneously determined.

As far as this chapter is concerned we will develop an explanation of the aggregate demand for an input on the assumption that the input price is predetermined. An advantage of this assumption is that it allows us to directly apply the theory of the firm to obtain predictions about the aggregate demand for an input. This theory can then be used empirically in an analysis of the aggregate demand for an industrial input. Finally, in Chapters 3 and 6, which deal empirically with the demand for labour and land, the theory is extended to incorporate the way in which, for each of these inputs, aggregate demand influences price.

III.3. DEMAND FUNCTIONS FOR CURRENT INPUTS

A current resource was defined as a resource which provides an input flow for a single production period only. The resource stock, if applied to production, is thus completely used up within the period. Hence, the demand for the input flow, over the production period, of a current resource is measured by the quantity of the resource which is bought for the period. In order to develop an explanation of this demand, we first derive a demand function for an input using profit maximizing firm theory. We then go on to consider how the uncertain and dynamic aspects of the decision milieu in agriculture affect this demand function.

(a) *Certain, Static Environment*

As a point of departure, we assume that the representative or average firm in agriculture has perfect knowledge of its production function and its product price and also that it attempts to maximize profits over

† Predominantly feed and livestock.

the production period. In addition, we will assume that the firm operates in a static environment—one without technological change. Thus, the firm does not encounter the problem of having to decide whether to purchase new inputs or new brands of existing inputs.

(i) *The demand curve for an input.* Let us first use profit maximizing firm theory to derive an input demand function in the situation where only one input flow—that of a current resource x_1—can be varied within the production period. The production function of the representative firm may then be written as

$$q = f(x_1 | x_2, \ldots, x_n)$$

where q, the flow of output, is dependent upon the input flow x_1 given fixed input flows of the resources $x_2, \ldots, x_n$. To maximize profits, the firm should operate within the region of the production function where the marginal physical product of x_1 is declining. Within this region it should use a quantity of x_1 such that the marginal revenue product of x_1 (M.R.P.$_{x_1}$)—the value of the marginal physical product—is equal to the marginal cost of x_1. From our earlier discussion, we can assume that the representative farm-firm is a price taker: the per unit product price (P_p) and the price per unit of x_1 (P_{x_1}) are fixed to the firm. Hence, the marginal cost of one unit of x_1 is equal to P_{x_1} and the marginal revenue product of x_1 is equal to the marginal physical product of x_1 (M.P.P.$_{x_1}$) times product price. The necessary condition for profit maximization can thus be written as:

$$\text{M.P.P.}_{x_1} \cdot P_p = P_{x_1} \tag{2.4}$$

The profit maximization position of the firm is illustrated below in Fig. 2.1 where the quantity of x_1 that the firm should use is Oa units. In the diagram, the M.R.P.$_{x_1}$ declines with increasing x_1 because of diminishing marginal physical productivity of x_1.

The firm's demand curve for an input shows the quantity of input which the firm wishes to purchase at various prices of the input, while all other factors remain constant. Hence, assuming the representative firm maximizes its profits, its demand curve for x_1 is its marginal revenue product curve for x_1—since it will use a quantity of x_1 to equate marginal revenue product of x_1 to the price of x_1. The demand curve relating the aggregate demand for x_1 to its price is then formed by multiplying the quantity demanded by the representative firm at each price of x_1 by the number of firms, all other factors, including product price, being held constant.

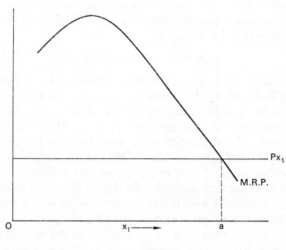

FIG. 2.1

The demand curve tells us that the demand for x_1 is related inversely to its price—if price increases (decreases) demand decreases (increases). From equation (2.4) we can also see that the demand for x_1 is directly related to product price. Thus we can rewrite the equation as M.P.P.$_{x_1}$ $= P_{x_1}/P_p$ indicating that if, for example, product price increases, the profit maximizing firm will increase the use of x_1 until the marginal physical product of x_1 has fallen to equal the new and lower price ratio. Diagrammatically, an increase in P_p would be represented in Fig. 2.1 as a shift to the right in the M.R.P.$_{x_1}$ curve which with P_{x_1} unchanged, leads to an increase in the demand for x_1. In addition, we can see from this equation that if both prices change in proportion—for example if both prices double—the demand for x_1 does not change. Thus the demand for x_1 by the representative firm is related inversely to the ratio of the price of x_1 to product price. Consequently, we can hypothesize that the aggregate demand for x_1 (D_{x_1}) is a decreasing function of P_{x_1}/P_p:

$$D_{x_1} = f(P_{x_1}/P_p) \qquad (2.5)$$

Finally, the extent to which the demand for x_1 changes as a result of a given change in the price ratio, P_{x_1}/P_p, will depend upon the production function. Thus the quicker the marginal physical product of x_1 declines (the steeper the marginal physical product curve) the lower will be the resulting change in demand.

(ii) *Two variable inputs and profit maximization.* We now assume that the input flows of two current resources, x_1 and x_2, can be varied within the production period. The production function of the representative firm may then be written as

$$q = f(x_1, x_2 \mid x_3, \ldots, x_n).$$

The problem of determining the firm's profit maximizing quantities of x_1 and x_2 is solved in two stages. Firstly, to produce any given output, expenditure on the two inputs should be allocated so that cost is minimized. This minimum cost combination of the two inputs is achieved when the marginal rate of substitution between them (M.R.S.) is equal to the inverse ratio of their prices,

i.e. when M.R.S. of x_1 for x_2 $(dx_2/dx_1) = P_{x_1}/P_{x_2}$ (2.6)

Secondly, the optimum level of output is determined within the region of the production function where the marginal physical product of each input flow is declining and is the output quantity at which the marginal cost of output is equal to the marginal revenue of output. Since the firm is a price taker the marginal revenue of one unit of output is equal to product price. The conditions for profit maximization are illustrated in Fig. 2.2 below.

Figure 2.2(a), with the axes denoting quantities of the two inputs, represents an isoquant (isoproduct) map: an isoquant showing the different combinations of the two inputs which can produce a given

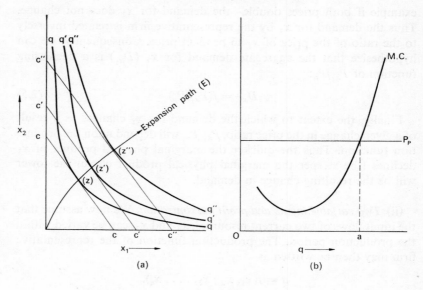

FIG. 2.2

quantity of output. The curves qq, $q'q'$ and $q''q''$ are three possible isoquants representing three output quantities q, q' and q'' with q'' greater than q' and q' greater than q. The curvature of the isoquants represents the hypothesis of a diminishing marginal rate of substitution between the two inputs. The lines CC, $C'C'$ and $C''C''$ are three isocost lines: an isocost line showing the possible combinations of the two inputs that can be purchased for a given cost outlay. In the diagram, it is assumed that the prices of x_1 and x_2 are the same for each isocost line and $C''C''$ therefore represents a higher cost outlay than $C'C'$ and $C'C'$ represents a higher cost outlay than CC. The minimum cost way of producing output quantity q is given by that combination of x_1 and x_2 where the isocost line CC is tangential to the isoquant qq—at point (z). At (z), the slope of the isoquant (dx_2/dx_1) is equal to the slope of the isocost line (P_{x_1}/P_{x_2}). This q can be produced by other combinations of x_1 and x_2 but only at higher cost—such as those combinations where $C'C'$ cuts qq. Similarly, points (z') and (z'') represent the least cost ways of producing the output quantities q' and q''. A line joining up the least cost combinations of the two inputs at each output quantity is called the expansion path. The total cost curve which shows the minimum total cost for each level of output, is then given by the expansion path. From this total cost curve, we derive the marginal cost curve (M.C.) of Fig. 2.2(b).

The optimum output is determined as output Oa units where, with the marginal cost curve rising, marginal cost equals product price.

We are now in a position to see how price changes affect the firm's demand for inputs. To start with, let us consider the effects of a fall in the price of x_1 whilst the price of x_2 and product price remain constant. The response of the profit maximizing firm to this price change may *theoretically* be broken up into two parts—a direct (substitution) response and an indirect (expansion) response. The direct response of the firm is seen in a change in the minimum cost combination of inputs at each output level. If minimum costs are to be achieved for a given output quantity following the fall in the price ratio, P_{x_1}/P_{x_2}, then x_1 must be substituted for x_2 until the marginal rate of substitution (dx_2/dx_1) has fallen sufficiently, along the isoquant, to equal the new price ratio. Thus the minimum cost combination of inputs for producing each output quantity now comprises more x_1 and less x_2. The indirect response results from the fact that since the price of x_1 has fallen there is a reduction in the total cost of producing each output quantity. Hence, the marginal cost at each output quantity is also reduced and therefore output can be profitably expanded until marginal cost again equals product price. The substitution and expansion effects of the fall in the price of x_1 are illustrated below in Fig. 2.3.

Figure 2.3(a) represents the substitution effect. The point of tangency (z_1) of the isocost line C_1C_1 and the isoquant qq represents the original minimum cost way of producing output quantity q. With the fall in the price of x_1 the slope of the isocost lines change. The isocost line C_2C_2 incorporates this price change and the tangency point (z_2) shows the new minimum cost combination of the two inputs in producing q. In addition, the firm's expansion path becomes expansion path (E_2) whereas with the old prices it was expansion path (E_1). The new expansion path represents a lower total cost at each level of output, because of the fall in P_{x_1}. Therefore, in Fig. 2.3(b) the marginal cost curve moves

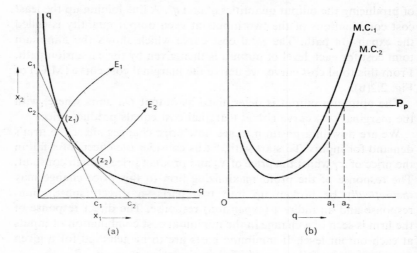

FIG. 2.3

to the right to M.C.$_2$ from M.C.$_1$, and the output quantity which maximizes profits is increased from Oa_1 units to Oa_2 units. The expansion effect thus tends to increase the use of both inputs—but along the new expansion path.

The observable or total response of the firm to the fall in the price of x_1 is the sum of the direct and indirect effects. As a result of the fall in the price of x_1, both the substitution and the expansion responses increase the use of x_1. Therefore, the demand for x_1 is related inversely to the price of x_1. However, the substitution and expansion responses have opposite effects on the use of x_2; as the price of x_1 falls the substitution response leads to a fall in demand for x_2, x_1 being substituted for x_2, whilst the expansion response leads to an increase in demand for both inputs. Consequently, profit maximizing theory of the firm cannot predict whether the demand for x_2 will increase or decrease when the price of x_1 falls. However, if we have some empirical evidence concerning production relationships which enables us to know something about the technical conditions of production, we may be able to state which direction of change is more likely. Thus, the easier it is for the inputs to be substituted for each other in production (i.e. the less the curvature of the isoquants)—the greater will be the substitution response to the price fall. Consequently, the more likely it will be that the substitution response outweighs the expansion response and that in fact, the demand for x_2 will fall.

A change in product price, with the prices of the two inputs being held constant, has also a predictable effect on the demand for the inputs. If product price rises this means that output can be profitably expanded and therefore the use of both inputs will be increased.

From the above discussion, we can see that the representative firm's demand, and therefore aggregate demand, for one of the inputs depends on the level of the prices of the two inputs and on product price. The demand function relating the aggregate demand for x_1 (D_{x_1}) to these prices may be written as:

$$D_{x_1} = f(P_{x_1}, P_{x_2}, P_p) \qquad (2.7)$$

In this function we can expect the demand for x_1 to be negatively (inversely) related to its own price and positively related to product price. From our discussion of the effect of a fall in the price of x_1 on the demand for x_2 we can see that we are not able to predict how the demand for x_1 will change in response to a change in the price of x_2. Thus the demand for x_1 will be positively related to the price of x_2 if x_1 is an input which shows a substitution response to the price change which is greater than the expansion response. On the other hand, where x_1 is an input which shows a substitution response to a change in P_{x_2} which is less than its expansion response, then the demand for x_1 will be negatively related to the price of x_2.

To end with this part of the analysis we should note that profit maximizing theory informs us of one further feature of the demand function for x_1. If all prices change in the same proportion—for example, if P_{x_1}, P_{x_2} and P_p double—then the representative firm does not change its demand for the inputs. Firstly, the price ratio P_{x_1}/P_{x_2} stays the same and consequently the minimum cost combination of inputs does not change. Secondly, although the total cost and the marginal cost at each output quantity has changed, product price has changed in the same proportion. Consequently, marginal cost equals product price at the same output quantity as previously. A demand function which has this property is said to be homogeneous of degree zero. The property may be incorporated into the demand function by writing it with the prices expressed in the form of relative prices:

$$D_{x_1} = f(P_p/P_{x_1}, P_{x_2}/P_{x_1}) \qquad (2.8)$$

Function (2.8) indicates that if all prices are multiplied by a constant (that is, they change in the same proportion), then demand does not change because the constant is cancelled out in the price ratios. Expressing the demand in this way implies that producers are influenced by relative or "real" prices rather than by the absolute level of prices. Thus, if inflation has equal effects on all of the prices there is no incentive for producers to adjust their use of inputs.

If we believe the demand function to be homogeneous of degree zero and write it in the form of (2.8), with demand expressed as a function of relative prices, then we should note that we impose a constraint upon the function. The constraint is that the sum of the separate elasticities of demand for x_1 with respect to P_{x_1}, P_{x_2} and P_p should equal zero.† Consequently, the elasticity of demand for x_1 with respect to P_{x_1} (its own price) is equal in magnitude but opposite in sign to the sum of the separate elasticities of demand for x_1 with respect to P_p and P_{x_2}. These points are elaborated upon and proven in the next section.

(iii) *The homogeneity of the demand function.*‡ Further insight can be gained into the properties of the demand functions which were put forward in the last two sections if we investigate their homogeneity. If a function $y = f(z_1, z_2, \ldots, z_n)$ has the property:

$$f(tz_1, tz_2, \ldots, tz_n) = t^n f(z_1, z_2, \ldots, z_n)$$

where t is a constant, then the function is said to be homogeneous of degree n. Two properties of homogeneous functions that are important to us are:

† The elasticity of demand with respect to a particular price is the percentage change in demand resulting from a 1 per cent change in that price, with all other prices being held constant.

‡ This section is more mathematical than the other sections of the chapter and may be omitted by the general reader. For this reason the main result was stated at the end of the last section. For a discussion of homogeneous functions the reader is referred to J. Parry Lewis, *Mathematics for Students of Economics*, ch. 22, Macmillan, 1964.

(1) If $y = f(z_1, z_2, \ldots, z_n)$ is an homogeneous function it can be written as:

$$y = z_1^n f' \left(\frac{z_2}{z_1}, \frac{z_3}{z_1}, \ldots, \frac{z_n}{z_1} \right)$$

where n is the degree of homogeneity and f' is a new function.

(2) *Euler's theorem.* If $y = f(z_1, z_2, \ldots, z_n)$ is an homogeneous function of degree n, and it is possible to obtain the first order partial derivatives, then:

$$z_1 \frac{\partial y}{\partial z_1} + z_2 \frac{\partial y}{\partial z_2} + \cdots + z_n \frac{\partial y}{\partial z_n} = nf(z_1, z_2, \ldots, z_n)$$

Let us now consider the homogeneity of the demand function that was put forward in section III.3 (a) (i) where only one input flow—that of resource x_1—was assumed to be variable. In this case it was stated that the demand for x_1 was a function of the price of x_1 and the product price:

$$D_{x_1} = f(P_{x_1}, P_p)$$

Moreover, it was stated that if both prices were increased in the same proportion—for example, if they were both multiplied by a constant t—then the demand for x_1 would not change. Therefore, the function is homogeneous of degree zero since:

$$f(t.P_{x_1}, t.P_p) = f(P_{x_1}, P_p) = t^0 f(P_{x_1}, P_p)$$

Therefore, by property (1) of homogeneous functions the demand function can be rewritten as:

$$D_{x_1} = P_p^0 f'(P_{x_1}/P_p) = f'(P_{x_1}/P_p)$$

which is equivalent to the postulated demand function (2.5). Secondly, by Euler's theorem:

$$P_{x_1} \cdot \partial D_{x_1}/\partial P_{x_1} + P_p \cdot \partial D_{x_1}/\partial P_p = 0 \cdot f(P_{x_1}, P_p) = 0$$

Therefore

$$P_{x_1} \partial D_{x_1}/\partial P_{x_1} = -P_p \cdot \partial D_{x_1}/\partial P_p$$

And dividing both sides by D_{x_1}:

$$\frac{P_{x_1}}{D_{x_1}} \frac{\partial D_{x_1}}{\partial P_{x_1}} = - \frac{P_p}{D_{x_1}} \cdot \frac{\partial D_{x_1}}{\partial P_p}$$

Thus an implication of the demand function (2.5) that was put forward in section III.3 (a) (i) is that the elasticity of demand for x_1, with respect to P_{x_1}, is equal in magnitude but opposite in sign to the elasticity of demand for x_1 with respect to P_p. This means that in any statistical analysis of the demand for an input, x_1, where a demand function of the form of equation (2.5) is postulated, this constraint is imposed upon the results.

The demand function that was put forward in section III.3 (a) (ii) has similar connotations with regard to the relationships between the price variables. Here we said that:

$$D_{x_1} = f(P_{x_1}, P_{x_2}, P_p)$$

Because $f(t.P_{x_1}, t.P_{x_2}, t.P_p) = f(P_{x_1}, P_{x_2}, P_p)$ the function is homogeneous of degree zero and can be rewritten as

$$D_{x_1} = f'(P_p/P_{x_1}, P_{x_2}/P_{x_1})$$

which is equivalent to the demand function (2.8).

Therefore, using Euler's theorem, and dividing both sides of the resulting equation by D_{x_1} we obtain

$$\frac{P_{x_1}}{D_{x_1}} \cdot \frac{\partial D_{x_1}}{\partial P_{x_1}} + \frac{P_{x_2}}{D_{x_1}} \cdot \frac{\partial D_{x_1}}{\partial P_{x_2}} + \frac{P_p}{D_{x_1}} \cdot \frac{\partial D_{x_1}}{\partial P_p} = 0$$

That is, the sum of the separate elasticities of D_{x_1} with respect to P_{x_1}, P_{x_2} and P_p must equal zero. Hence, the elasticity of D_{x_1} with respect to P_{x_1} is equal in magnitude but opposite in sign to the sum of the separate elasticities with respect to P_{x_2} and P_p. This result is important with regard to the statistical estimation of the demand function for an input. Thus, if we specify the demand function for the input to be homogeneous of degree zero, and consequently estimate it with the prices entering the function in the form of relative prices, then we force into the results the constraint that the sum of the separate elasticities of demand for the input, with respect to prices, must equal zero. This may be illustrated as follows. Let us suppose that the relationship between the demand for x_1 and the price variables is of the form:

$$D_{x_1} = b_0 \cdot P_{x_1}{}^{b_1} \cdot P_{x_2}{}^{b_2} P_p{}^{b_3} \qquad (2.9)$$

Let us note that we can derive from (2.9) the result that the coefficient b_1 is equal to the elasticity of D_{x_1} with respect to P_{x_1}, that b_2 is equal to the elasticity of D_{x_1} with respect to P_{x_2} and that b_3 is equal to the elasticity of D_{x_1} with respect to P_p. Thus the specific form of the demand function forces constant elasticities into the results.

If, in addition, we specify that the relationship is homogeneous of degree zero, then:

$$b_0(tP_{x_1})^{b_1} (tP_{x_2})^{b_2} (tP_p)^{b_3} = t^0 \, b_0 \, P_{x_1}{}^{b_1} P_{x_2}{}^{b_2} P_p{}^{b_3}$$

Therefore

$$t^{b_1}t^{b_2}t^{b_3} = t^0$$

Therefore

$$b_1 + b_2 + b_3 = 0 \text{ and } b_1 = -b_2-b_3$$

Thus, we may rewrite the demand equation expressed in *relative* prices as:

$$P_{x_1} = b_0(P_{x_2}/P_{x_1})^{b_2} (P_p/P_{x_1})^{b_3} \qquad (2.10)$$

Finally, if we estimate the demand relationship expressed in relative prices then we will be estimating the coefficients (b_0, b_2 and b_3) of equation (2.10). However, it can be seen from the above that estimating the coefficients of equation (2.10) is equivalent to estimating the coefficients (b_0, b_1, b_2 and b_3) of equation (2.9) under the constraint that the sum, b_1 plus b_2 plus b_3, is equal to zero—in other words, under the constraint that the sum of the elasticities is equal to zero.

(iv) *Farms are multiproduct firms.* In the previous discussion, it has been assumed that the representative farm-firm produced only one product. In reality, this is not the case and we may assume that farm-firms adjust the quantities of different products produced in accordance with their relative profitability. Profit maximizing theory says that the quantity of an input which should be employed in the production of each product should be such that the marginal revenue products of the input from each product line are equal. However, the majority of inputs are used in the production of more than one product. Consequently, it is usually sufficient (though oversimplified) in an analysis of the demand for one of these inputs to calculate a weighted average of product prices (with the weights representing the relative importance of each product) and use this average price in the analysis in the place of the product price of the past few sections. However, when an input is so specialized that it is utilized in the production of just a single commodity then, clearly, the relative profitability of products must be taken into account in the analysis. Thus the demand for such an input might be expected to vary inversely with the price of a product which is competitive in production with the particular product that utilizes the input. The demand function for the input would then include not only the relevant input prices but also the prices of the competing products.

(v) *Capital funds constraint on profit maximization.* An implication of the owner-management organization of agriculture is that there are likely to be financial constraints on the size of the farm-firm and on its use of inputs. As in uncorporated businesses publicly subscribed capital is generally unavailable, the main sources of capital funds for farm-firms are past profits and bank loans. Consequently, the farm-firm may not be able to obtain as much capital as it desires. Firms may also voluntarily limit their borrowing because it increases the risk of insolvency.

Firms may thus be unable or unwilling to buy the quantities of inputs which would maximize profits. In this situation, if the availability of capital funds increases, the demand for an input may increase—even though relative prices remain constant. Thus, the demand for an input may be directly related to the level of available finance. There are two possible variables which we might use in the demand function to represent the level of available funds. Firstly, the level of past profits is almost certainly important as representing the level of available *internal funds*. The availability of internal funds is particularly important if firms are unwilling to borrow for then it is only if profits increase and their liquid asset position is improved that they will increase their demand for inputs. Secondly, we can postulate that the rate of interest charged by banks to farmers represents the ease with which credit can be obtained as well as the price for borrowed funds. If we accept this hypothesis, we can go on to use the interest rate to represent the availability of *external funds*.

(b) *Uncertain, Static Environment*

As we have indicated earlier, the decision-maker in the farm-firm does not have perfect knowledge of his decision milieu. On the contrary, he faces uncertainty with respect to the firm's production function and with respect to product prices (and to some extent with respect to input prices). We now want to investigate how this uncertainty affects our analysis of the demand for an input.

(i) *Product price uncertainty and the formation of price expectations.* Our previous discussion has indicated that if farm-firms are motivated toward profit maximization, the level of product price is a relevant consideration in their decision-making. If product price is unknown when farmers are planning production, it is argued that they form a prediction about product price and base their planning upon that prediction. In other words, they choose, for planning purposes, the price which they think is most likely to be realized from a range of possible prices. We can call this price the expected price. It is likely that farmers form expectations on the basis of their experience of past prices. If this is so, then we can postulate that for the representative firm, expected price is related in some way to past prices.†

The simplest hypothesis that relates expected price to past prices is the one which assumes farmers formulate their expectations on the price experience of the most recent production period only. This hypothesis states that expected or anticipated product price for this production period (P_{pt}^N) is equal to the price received in the last period ($P_{p_{t-1}}$). This particular model of the formation of expectations would

---

† Empirical evidence supporting this hypothesis is presented by W. Darcovich, Evaluation of some naive expectation models for agricultural yields and prices, pp. 199–202, in *Expectations, Uncertainty and Business Behaviour*, ed. M. J. Bowman, S.S.R.C., 1958.

often seem to be too naive since it implies that farmers take no account of additional past price experience. In fact, it would seem more realistic to assume that farmers learn that prices are liable to fluctuate from year to year and that they have some concept of a "normal" price. This price would then be related to prices received in several past production periods. For example, we could postulate that the formation of expectations about P_{pt}^N is adequately described by, let us say, a three-year weighted average of past prices, with more weight being given to more recent experience. For example:

$$P_{pt}^N = (3P_{p_{t-1}} + 2\,P_{p_{t-2}} + P_{t-3})/6 \qquad (2.11)$$

A more general model of the formation of price expectations which incorporates the notion of a "normal" price is the "adaptive expectations" model. The essence of this model is that farmers are visualized in each period as "revising their notions of what is normal in proportion to the difference between what actually happened and what they previously considered as normal".[†] This hypothesis may be written algebraically as:

$$P_{pt}^N - P_{p_{t-1}}^N = \beta(P_{p_{t-1}} - P_{p_{t-1}}^N), \qquad 0 < \beta < 1 \qquad (2.12)$$

where β is known as the coefficient of expectations.

The model implies that farmers' ideas of what constitutes a normal price is based on the experience of prices received in past periods. It also relates expected price to past prices in a specific way with more weight being given to the more recent experience in a geometrically declining lag fashion. Thus from (2.12) we obtain:

$$P_{pt}^N = \beta P_{p_{t-1}} + (1 - \beta)P_{p_{t-1}}^N \qquad (2.13)$$

And if we successively substitute for P_{pt-i}^N we obtain:

$$P_{pt}^N = \beta P_{p_{t-1}} + (1 - \beta)\,\beta P_{p_{t-2}} + (1 - \beta)^2\,\beta P_{p_{t-3}} + \ldots + (1 - \beta)^n$$

$$\beta P_{p_{t-1-n}} = \sum_{i=0}^{n} (1 - \beta)^i\,\beta P_{p_{t-1-i}} \qquad (2.14)$$

This means that the greater the coefficient of expectations, β, the

† Marc Nerlove, Distributed lags and estimation of long run supply and demand elasticities: theoretical considerations, *Journal of Farm Economics*, vol. 40, 1958, p. 303.

greater is the weight placed on most recent experience and the fewer are the past prices that have any substantial influence on P_{pt}^N. The size of β is estimated when the demand function incorporating the adaptive expectations model is estimated by regression analysis. The next section illustrates the procedure for incorporating this model of expectations into the demand function.

(ii) *The adaptive expectations model and estimation of the demand function.*† If we think that the adaptive expectations model realistically describes how farmers form their expectations about product price we shall wish to incorporate it into our demand function in a form which is suitable for empirical estimation of the function. We shall illustrate the procedure involved in the situation where x_1 is the only resource with a variable input flow. The aggregate demand for x_1 in time period t (D_{1t}) is, from our previous discussion, a function of the price of x_1 in period $t(P_{1t})$ and product price (P_{pt}). However, product price is unknown to producers and expected product price for period $t(P_{pt}^N)$ is used for planning purposes. We must also accept that our model is a simplified statistical one and we include an error term u_t in the function,

i.e. $$D_{1t} = f(P_{1t}, P_{pt}^N, u_t) \tag{2.15}$$

Further, let us postulate that demand is linearly related to prices:

$$D_{1t} = b_0 + b_1 P_{1t} + b_2 P_{pt}^N + u_t \tag{2.16}$$

In (2.16) the coefficient b_1 is expected to be negative and the coefficient b_2 to be positive. If expectations about P_{pt} are formed in the manner described by the adaptive expectations model we can substitute equation (2.14) for P_{pt}^N in (2.16)

$$D_{1t} = b_0 + b_1 P_{1t} + b_2 \beta P_{p_{t-1}} + b_2 (1 - \beta) \beta P_{p_{t-2}} + \cdots$$
$$+ b_2 (1 - \beta)^n \beta P_{p_{t-1-n}} + u_t \tag{2.17}$$

Next, we lag (2.17) by one period and multiply by $(1 - \beta)$ and obtain:

---

† This section may be omitted without disturbing continuity. It constitutes a digression in the sense that the adaptive expectations model is not used in the empirical analyses in later chapters.

$$(1 - \beta) D_{1_{t-1}} = b_0(1 - \beta) + b_1(1 - \beta) P_{p_{t-1}} + b_2(1 - \beta)\beta P_{p_{t-2}}$$
$$+ b_2(1 - \beta)^2\beta P_{p_{t-3}} + \cdots + b_2(1 - \beta)^n\beta P_{p_{t-1-n}}$$
$$+ (1 - \beta) u_{t-1} \tag{2.18}$$

The last term in $P_{p_{t-1-i}}$ has been ignored in (2.18) because n represents a number which is tending toward infinity and so $n + 1$ also tends towards infinity.

If we now subtract (2.18) from (2.17) and then move $(1 - \beta)D_{1_{t-1}}$ to the right-hand side of the resulting equation we obtain:

$$D_{1t} = b_0\beta + b_1 P_{1t} - b_1(1 - \beta)P_{1_{t-1}} + b_2\beta P_{p_{t-1}} + (1 - \beta)D_{1_{t-1}}$$
$$+ u_t - (1 - \beta) u_{t-1} \tag{2.19}$$

Equation (2.19) is known as the working or estimating equation: it incorporates, in a manner which is suitable for estimation purposes, both our hypothesis concerning the variables influencing demand and our hypothesis about the formation of expectations. The coefficient of expectations can be obtained when we estimate (2.19) by regression analysis. Thus, an estimate of β is given by subtracting the estimated coefficient of $D_{1_{t-1}}$ from unity.

It is worth noting that it is difficult to incorporate the adaptive expectations hypothesis into the demand function if we specify that the function is homogeneous of degree zero and write it as: $D_{1t} = f(P_{1t}/P_{pt}^N)$. We can now only derive a working equation by the above procedure if we are willing to believe that farmers form expectations about the price ratio (P_{1t}/P_{pt}) and therefore that the expectations hypothesis concerns this ratio rather than product price alone. In fact, since input prices are often known to farmers at the time of planning, it would seem unrealistic to force the above price ratio into an adaptive expectations scheme. However, two alternatives are open to us if we specify that demand is a function of relative prices and that expectations are formed about product price only. Firstly, we might have some *a priori* belief about the value of the coefficient of expectations. In such circumstances, we could use equation (2.14) to construct a series to represent P_{pt}^N and substitute this for P_{pt}^N in our demand function. Alternatively, we could assume various values for β and generate, by (2.14), a set of series representing P_{pt}^N. We could then use our regression procedure to select from the alternative series, the one which represents P_{pt}^N the best. Thus we could repeatedly estimate the demand function by regression analysis using each series in turn to represent P_{pt}^N. We would then select as being the most representative that series for P_{pt}^N (and therefore the relevant β) which leads to the best explanation of demand measured by "goodness of fit".

(iii) *The U.K. agricultural support system and the formation of product price expectations.* Over most of the post-war period, the United Kingdom government has operated a deficiency payments (guaranteed price) system of agricultural support. Under this system, guaranteed prices for the major commodities are announced in March/April of each year. In addition, some form of long-term guarantee has been implicitly included in the system since 1947. The form of the long-term guarantee was made explicit by the 1957 Act. Under this act the government undertook each year "to maintain the total value of the guarantees at not less than $97\frac{1}{2}$ per cent of their total value in the preceding year, . . . , and to maintain the guaranteed price for each commodity at not less than 96 per cent of that determined after the preceding annual review".†

Although prices are guaranteed for each successive year, farmers still have to form expectations about most product prices because they have to make their production plans before the guaranteed prices are announced. However, the support system, particularly the long-term guarantee, means that there is a measure of continuity in prices from year to year without wide price fluctuations. Hence, for an analysis of the post-war period a simple model of the formation of price expectations would seem appropriate. In fact, because of the constraints on price changes that are built into the support system, the simplest hypothesis which states that expected price is equal to the price received last period ($P_{pt}^N = P_{p_{t-1}}$) is probably adequate.

(iv) *Uncertainty surrounding the production function.* An element of uncertainty surrounds the production function of the farm-firm because of the influence of extraneous factors, such as weather, on production. Thus the farmer cannot forecast exactly what quantity of output will

† H.M.S.O. cmnd. 109, *Annual Review and Determination of Guarantees, 1957*, March 1957, p. 5.

result from the use of stated quantities of inputs. In addition, the decision-maker in the firm is likely to have only limited knowledge of the production function, even in the average year. As a consequence of this uncertainty and imperfect knowledge, farmers cannot exactly determine their profit maximizing position for the production period even if product price is known to them. Despite this, we can still expect farmers to vary their demand for an input, in response to price changes (known or expected), in a profit-seeking direction. However, their response is unlikely to be as large as it would be in a perfect knowledge situation. Furthermore, if relative prices change, it may take farmers more than one production period, and involve a trial and error procedure, to find a new position on the production function that is optimal.

(c) *Uncertain, Dynamic Environment*

The theory of resource demand, that we have developed so far, suggests that in each production period the aggregate demand for a current input depends on the prices (known or anticipated) which prevail in that period. This theory is essentially a static or an equilibrium theory, because it assumes that if relative prices remain unchanged from one period to the next the demand for the current input will also be unchanged. Thus, it is assumed that firms always purchase an equilibrium quantity of the input. If relative prices change from one period to the next, then the theory assumes that firms adjust immediately to the price change and purchase a new equilibrium quantity of the input. Even if the environment is not entirely static but is relatively stable we would expect price changes to be small and infrequent. In such a situation, static theory is sufficiently appropriate for explaining the demand for a current input. However, because of technological change, farm-firms have to make decisions within an environment where relative prices are continually changing, sometimes by quite large amounts in a short period of time. Consequently, it may not be reasonable to suppose that they are always in an equilibrium position.

In this section, we therefore wish to extend our theory to include the analysis of disequilibrium situations. However, before doing so, we shall consider two aspects concerning the introduction of new technology into agriculture. Firstly, we shall briefly analyse the economic incentives that induce farmers to adopt new technology. Secondly, we shall examine the way in which our measures of the price of an input and the demand for an input should take account of quality change in the input.

(i) *The adoption of new technology.* In an earlier section, we pointed out that new technology enters agriculture via new inputs and via improvements in existing inputs. The distinction between a new input and quality improvement of an existing input may often be just a semantic matter. However, it is convenient for our purposes to make the distinction and to define a new input as one which leads to a change in the available techniques of production. In other words, if a farmer adopts a new input he manages the firm within the constraint of a *new* production function. Thus, the new input provides a set of new services and adds a new input axis to the production function. In deciding whether or not to adopt the input, the firm is faced with the choice of two alternative production functions. Rationally a profit maximizing firm will adopt the input if the move from the existing production function to the new production function is profitable.

In contrast, we may define quality improvement as being a change in the characteristics of the input which leads to an increase in the quantity of services provided by a unit of the input. We need to recognize that an input is composed of a set of characteristics, each of which contributes towards the services being demanded from the input. The services provided by each characteristic need not, however, be perfect substitutes for each other. Quality improvement takes the form of either an increase in the magnitude of a characteristic or the incorporation of an additional, service-providing characteristic into the set of attributes. Consequently, the impact of quality improvement on the production function may be largely interpreted as a movement along the existing production function if the same number of units of the input is used.

An input in which changing quality over time takes place is usually available to farmers, during each period of time, in the form of several, or even many, different brands (varieties). Individual brands are differentiated by their quality characteristics: there may be differences in the magnitude of some of their quality characteristics and/or differences in the total number of characteristics. In addition, brand prices differ

—mainly, we can hypothesize, because of the quality differences between them. It is, however, unlikely that a perfect relationship exists between brand prices and their quality characteristics so that some brands will be overpriced in relation to the attributes they contain.

Because brand prices differ, we can postulate that each quality characteristic has an implicit price—the value placed on a unit of each characteristic by producers. Consequently, we can hypothesize that producers are influenced in their demand for input quality by these implicit prices—just as they are influenced in their demand for input quantity by the price of the input. We recognize now that producers have to simultaneously determine their demand for input quantity and input quality. We may therefore state that just as the quantity demanded of an input depends on relative prices so will the quality demanded also depend on relative prices. Thus the quality demanded will depend on the implicit price of each characteristic relative to each other and on the implicit price of each characteristic relative to both product price and the price of a substitute input. We can also expect that the brand chosen will depend on how "pricey" brands are in relation to their quality characteristics.†

We may expect that producers will demand increased quality of an input in response to changing relative prices. The change in relative prices often occurs because suppliers introduce new brands at slightly higher prices with much improved quality as a result of the introduction of new techniques into the supplying industry. A change in relative prices may lead to an increased demand for a particular quality characteristic, thus leading to quality improvement in that direction. Alternatively, it may lead to an increased demand for a whole set of characteristics which vary between brands but not for those characteristics which are equal in magnitude between brands. Thus, producers often demand increased quality rather than increased quantity to supply the extra services which they require. Finally, it is now fairly obvious that the change in relative prices may lead to an increased demand for both input quality and input quantity.

† A marginal approach to the profit maximizing choice of a brand is given in the next section. For a more complete analysis of the demand for brands see: Keith Cowling and A. J. Rayner, *Price, Quality and Market Share*, Warwick Economic Research Papers, No. 7, University of Warwick, Coventry.

(ii) *Profit maximizing theory and optimum input quality.*† As an example, let us consider a simple production function relating the output of a single product (Q) to two variable inputs (X_1 and X_2), to the qualities of these inputs, and to a fixed input, X_3. Let each input have two relevant quality characteristics (Z_{11}, Z_{12} and Z_{21}, Z_{22} respectively) and let these be quantifiable. Therefore, the production function is

$$q = f(X_1, X_2, Z_{11}, Z_{12}, Z_{21}, Z_{22} \mid X_3) \qquad (2.20)$$

The price of each input, p_i, depends on the particular brand of the input that is bought because price differences between varieties are related to differences in quality characteristics:

$$p_i = f(Z_{i1}, Z_{i2}) \qquad (2.21)$$

Profit, Π, is the difference between total revenue and total cost. Let P_p denote product price and B denote fixed costs. Then:

$$\Pi = P_p.q - p_1 X_1 - p_2 X_2 - B \qquad (2.22)$$

To obtain the first order conditions for profit maximization we set the partial derivatives of (2.22) equal to zero. Differentiating with respect to X_i ($i = 1, 2$) we obtain:

$$(\partial \Pi / \partial X_i) = P_p(\partial q / \partial X_i) - p_i = 0 \qquad (2.23)$$

Differentiating with respect to Z_{ij} ($i, j = 1, 2$) we obtain:

$$(\partial \Pi / \partial Z_{ij}) = P_p(\partial q / \partial Z_{ij}) - X_i(\partial p_i / \partial Z_{ij}) = 0 \qquad (2.24)$$

The change in price resulting from a change in the level of a quality characteristic ($\partial p_i / \partial Z_{ij}$) we may call the implicit quality price of the characteristic. The conditions (2.23) and (2.24) define both the optimum quantity and the optimum quality of the input. Because the number of brands offered for sale is not infinite but usually fairly small the optimum brand may not be available. Consequently, it may be more realistic to set up the problem as one to be solved by linear programming rather than by marginal analysis.

† This section is for more advanced students and may be omitted without disturbing continuity. It is based on A. J. Rayner, Price–quality relationships in a durable asset: estimation of a constant quality price index for new farm tractors, 1948–65, *Journal of Agricultural Economics*, vol. 19, 1968, p. 248.

(iii) *The appropriate measurement of the price of an input and the demand for an input to incorporate quality change.* We wish to use our theory of resource demand to analyse why the demand for an input changes over time. To do this, we shall need a price index for the input to see how its price varies over the time period in which we are interested. If it is to accurately reflect price change, the index should be on a constant quality basis. Thus, if the quality of the input varies over time, actual price changes will be, in part, a consequence of this changing quality. Therefore, we should extract from the change in price actually paid that part which belongs to changes in quality so that the price index then calculated reflects true price changes only. Consequently, in our future discussion, reference to the price of an input implies this constant quality or true price and not the market price of the input.

Our measure of the demand for an input should also reflect the services available from the input. It is obvious that if there is quality change, the quantity of the input demanded is not an accurate measure of the demand for the input. However, an accurate measure of changes in demand over time can be obtained if we can weight the quantity purchased of the input by an index of quality change in the input. If we have an estimate of a constant quality price index for the input then this quality change index may be estimated by dividing an index of market (money) prices for the input by the constant quality price index. This is so because the constant quality price index implicitly represents the price of the input per unit of overall quality—that is, the money price of the input divided by the number of units of overall quality. Therefore, dividing an index of money prices by the constant quality price index gives us an implicit index of quality units. Consequently, a measure of demand which reflects the services available from the input is given by dividing the money values of the input—equal to quantity times money price—by the constant quality price index.

(iv) *A regression approach to the measurement of a constant quality price index and a quality change index.*† The basic hypothesis of the regression approach to the measurement of a constant quality price index for an input is that price variation between brands of the input

† This section is for more advanced students and may be omitted without disturbing continuity. It is based on A. J. Rayner, *op. cit.*

is related to variations in the quality characteristics of the brands. More specifically, we postulate that the price of the ith brand in year t, P_{it}, is a function of k quality characteristics, $z_{1t}, \ldots, z_{kt}$ and an error term u_t,

i.e.
$$P_{it} = f(z_{1t}, \ldots, z_{kt}, u_t) \qquad (2.25)$$

In (2.25), a quality characteristic which is quantifiable may be directly represented as a quantitative attribute by the magnitude of the characteristic, whilst a quality characteristic which is not quantifiable (the quality may or may not be incorporated in an input or may itself constitute the whole of the input) may be represented by a dummy variable. Equation (2.25) may then be estimated by regression analysis. Strictly speaking, we should use a form of weighted regression, whereby the brands as units of observation are weighted by their respective sales.† Let us assume that the equation is estimated as a linear equation:

$$P_{it} = \hat{b}_{0t} + \sum_{i=1}^{k} \hat{b}_{it} z_{it} + u_{it} \qquad (2.26)$$

The coefficient $\hat{b}_{it}$ represents an implicit price in year t for the ith quality characteristic which varies between brands whilst $\hat{b}_{0t}$ represents the implicit price in year t for all those characteristics which have the same magnitude for all brands.

The *average* brand price in year t, $\bar{P}_{it}$, is equal to:

$$\bar{P}_{it} = \hat{b}_{0t} + \sum_{i=1}^{k} \hat{b}_{it} \bar{z}_{it} \qquad (2.27)$$

where $\bar{z}_{it}$ is the average level of z_i ($i = 1, \ldots, k$) in year t. If we compare average prices in year $t = 1$ and year $t = 0$ by the average price index I_{01}^{v}, then this is given by:

$$I_{01}^{v} = \frac{\bar{P}_1}{\bar{P}_0} = \frac{\hat{b}_{01} + \sum\limits_{i=1}^{k} \hat{b}_{i1} \bar{z}_{i1}}{\hat{b}_{00} + \sum\limits_{i=1}^{k} \hat{b}_{i0} \bar{z}_{i0}} \qquad (2.28)$$

† See A. J. Rayner, *op. cit.*, Appendix II.

The average price index is not a constant quality price index since the average levels of quality characteristics may change between year $t = 0$ and $t = 1$ (from $\bar{z}_{i0}$ to $\bar{z}_{i1}$). However, we can obtain a constant quality price index, I_{01}^t, if we substitute the average levels of the quality characteristics for year $t = 0$ into the estimated price–quality equation (2.26) for year $t = 1$, generate a price $\hat{P}_1^t$ and divide this generated price by $\bar{P}_0$,

i.e.
$$I_{01}^t = \frac{\hat{P}_1^t}{\bar{P}_0} = \frac{\hat{b}_{01} + \sum\limits_{i=1}^{k} \hat{b}_{i1}\, \bar{z}_{i0}}{\hat{b}_{00} + \sum\limits_{i=1}^{k} \hat{b}_{i0}\, \bar{z}_{i0}} \tag{2.29}$$

To obtain a quality change index we must accept that the constant quality price index, I_{01}^t, represents the price per unit of overall quality of the input and is therefore equal to the index of average money prices of the input (I_{01}^p) divided by an index of quality units. The index of quality units represents the index of quality change (g_{01}) and therefore this index is given by dividing the average money price index by the true price index.

Therefore
$$g_{01} = \frac{\bar{P}_1}{\hat{P}_0^t} = \frac{\hat{b}_{01} + \sum\limits_{i=1}^{k} \hat{b}_{i1}\, \bar{z}_{i1}}{\hat{b}_{01} + \sum\limits_{i=1}^{k} \hat{b}_{i1}\, \bar{z}_{i0}} \tag{2.30}$$

where $\hat{P}_0^t$ is a generated price for year $t = 0$ using the implicit prices of year $t = 1$. The quality change index is therefore obtained by holding implicit prices constant but allowing quality levels to vary.

Finally, the most appropriate way to estimate an index which covers a period of years is to estimate an index for each successive pair of years and then chain the resulting indices. For example, the index number, I_{03}^t, is given in this way by chaining the index numbers I_{01}^t, I_{12}^t, and I_{23}^t. In other words,

$$I_{03}^t = I_{01}^t \cdot I_{12}^t \cdot I_{23}^t.$$

(v) *Dynamic theory of input demand.* We now wish to return to our earlier discussion and analyse the demand for an input in a situation where relative prices are continually changing. It does, in fact, seem likely that in such a situation the demand for an input is always in disequilibrium, because producers never catch up with the changing pattern of prices. This point is expressed very well in the following quotation from Scitovsky,† where we have substituted "producer" for "consumer": "When relative prices change or new opportunities arise, the producer usually continues in his accustomed grooves for a while because he needs time to learn about a change, to appraise its significance and still more time to adapt his behaviour to it and face the inconveniences and hazards that changing one's behaviour involves. In other words, people's propensity to form habits and their slowness in adapting themselves to changed circumstances render their economic behaviour a function not only of current but also of past prices."

Thus we may suggest that it takes time for producers to adjust their demand for an input in response to changing relative prices and that their full response will be spread over several periods of time. This is particularly likely if they are moving to a new position on their production functions where, because of imperfect knowledge, it takes several production experiences to determine their new optimum positions. Only if a price change persists for a sufficiently long period of time will producers adjust the demand for an input to a new equilibrium level. However, because relative prices continually change, producers are continually adjusting toward a new equilibrium position in each production period, but are never actually attaining it. In other words, less than the full equilibrium adjustment of the demand for an input is made in each period in response to changing relative prices. Consequently, producers, in aggregate, are reacting during each period not only to price changes that occur in that period but also to price changes in past periods.

This partial adjustment of demand by producers to price changes seems most likely when it involves the introduction of new technology into the resource structure. Thus, whilst a change in relative prices may make the use of an innovation profitable to a farmer there may be an interval of time before it is adopted. Firstly, the farmer needs time to acquire knowledge about the innovation and become familiar with its use. Secondly, he needs time to appraise the change in relative prices

† Tibor Scitovsky, *Welfare and Competition*, Unwin, 1952, pp. 48–9.

and to decide if the use of the innovation will add to profits. Where the innovation is a higher quality brand of an existing input, this appraisal involves weighing up the advantages of the innovation against its higher market price. Alternatively, with a new input the appraisal involves weighing up the advantages of the new input against the costs involved in changing the techniques of production. Thirdly, even when a producer has reached a decision it is often operationally impossible to adopt it instantaneously. Finally, the adoption of an innovation may include a trial stage so that the innovation is only gradually introduced into production. Therefore, the change in aggregate demand to changing relative prices is likely to be spread over several production periods, where it involves the adoption of innovations.

The extent to which the aggregate demand for an input is adjusted towards its equilibrium level in each period is likely to vary between inputs. Firstly, the dissemination of knowledge concerning the profitability of adjusting input demand in response to a change in relative prices is spread at different rates for different inputs. Therefore, the learning and appraisal process which takes place between the change in relative prices and the reaction to the change is likely to be of a different average length for different inputs. Secondly, some inputs constitute a much larger proportion of the total costs of production than other inputs and it is likely that the greater the contribution made by an input to total costs the sooner will producers respond to changes in its relative price. On the other hand, if we are considering the adoption of new inputs, and there is a great deal of uncertainty surrounding their profitability, it may well be that the greater the change in production techniques involved the slower will be the adoption rate by farmers because the larger is the possible loss involved through faulty judgement.

(vi) *The partial adjustment model and a dynamic theory of resource demand.* It was suggested in the last section that we need a dynamic theory—a theory which recognizes that producers are in disequilibrium positions—to explain why the demand for an input continues to change over time. We may further suggest that a satisfactory dynamic theory of resource demand should be able to (i) state the conditions under which equilibrium is reached, (ii) analyse the speed with which equilibrium is approached and (iii) predict how demand will change over time in response to changes in relative prices. It is possible to obtain a theory which satisfies these criteria by combining our static theory of resource demand with the "partial adjustment" model of producer behaviour.† Firstly, our static theory postulates that the equilibrium (desired) demand for an input in the current production period depends upon the relative prices that exist in the same period. Secondly, the partial adjustment model states, with reference to resource demand, that between the last period and the current period actual demand for the input changes by some fraction of the difference between equilibrium demand in the current period and actual demand in the last period. Consequently, we may combine the two theories to obtain a theory of resource demand which, firstly, makes the aggregate demand for an input a function of relative prices and, secondly, recognizes that if relative prices are continually changing then producers are never in equilibrium, but are continually moving toward it.

In order to formulate this theory in algebraic terms, let us analyse the demand for a current resource, x_1, in a situation where only two resources, x_1 and x_2, have variable input flows. We shall denote the actual demand for x_1 in period t as D_{1t} and the equilibrium demand in the same period as D_{1t}^*. The equilibrium demand in period t is assumed to be a function of relative prices in the same period:

$$D_{1t}^* = f(P_{P_t}^N/P_{x_{1t}}, P_{x_{2t}}/P_{x_{1t}}, u_t) \qquad (2.31)$$

In (2.31), $P_{P_t}^N$ is the anticipated product price, $P_{x_{1t}}$ is the price of x_1, $P_{x_{2t}}$ is the price of x_2 and u_t is an error term which is included to indicate that the hypothesis is not complete but, like all statistical models, fails to completely represent the real world and therefore contains error. Reasons for including an error term in our hypotheses are given in section V of this chapter.

The partial adjustment equation may be represented as:

$$D_{1t} - D_{1t-1} = \gamma(D_{1t}^* - D_{1t-1}), \quad 0 < \gamma < 1 \qquad (2.32)$$

The adjustment equation need not be linear; for example, we might represent it as $D_{1t}/D_{1t-1} = (D_{1t}^*/D_{1t-1})^\gamma$ which gives a nonlinear adjustment path, where γ is known as the adjustment coefficient.

---

† The partial adjustment model was first suggested by Nerlove: e.g., see Marc Nerlove, *op. cit.*, p. 308.

If we transfer D_{1t-1} from the left-hand side to the right-hand side of equation (2.32) and then substitute equation (2.31) for D_{1t}^* in the resulting equation, we obtain our dynamic theory of resource demand:

$$D_{1t} = \gamma[f(P_{Pt}^N/P_{x_{1t}}, P_{x_{2t}}/P_{x_{1t}}, u_t)] + (1 - \gamma)D_{1t-1} \qquad (2.33)$$

Equation (2.33) expresses demand in period t as a function of relative prices in the same period and demand in the previous period. The greater the magnitude of the adjustment coefficient, γ, the greater is the influence of current relative prices on demand, the closer is demand to its equilibrium level, and the greater is the adjustment of demand from the previous period in response to a given change in relative prices. Equation (2.33) also expresses the notion that demand is gradually adjusted, over time, in response to a change in relative prices—that is, the effect of the price change is distributed over several periods of time. In other words, the level of demand in period t represents a response to relative prices in past periods as well as to current prices. Thus it is possible to rewrite equation (2.32) as:

$$D_{1t} = \gamma D_{1t}^* + (1 - \gamma)D_{1t-1}^* + (1 - \gamma)^2 \cdot \gamma D_{1t-2}^* + \cdots$$
$$+ (1 - \gamma)^n \gamma D_{1t-n}^*$$
$$= \sum_{i=0}^{n} (1 - \gamma)^i \gamma D_{1t-i}^* \qquad (2.34)$$

Because D_{1t-i}^* is a function of relative prices in period $t - i$, equation (2.34) expresses demand in period t as a function of relative prices in all past periods of time. However, current relative prices are assumed to have the greatest influence on current demand, whilst relative prices in the previous period have the next largest influence and so on. It is, in fact, assumed in equation (2.34) that the further back in time prices occurred the smaller is their influence on current demand and that this diminution in influence takes the form of a declining geometric progression.

If we refer back to equation (2.33), we can see that the influence of past prices on current demand is accounted for by the influence of demand in the previous period on current demand. Thus, the quantity demanded in the previous period represents the adjustment made by producers to prices of that period and of previous periods. Furthermore, the smaller is the size of the adjustment coefficient, γ, the greater is the influence that demand in the previous period has on current demand and, therefore, the greater is the implicit influence of prices of past periods on current demand. Equation (2.33) is also the equation which is used in empirical estimation of our dynamic theory of demand. However, before empirical estimation can be carried out, we have to, firstly, specify the way in which equilibrium demand is related to relative prices and, secondly, include in the equation an algebraic hypothesis of the way in which product price expectations are formed. Once the resulting equation has been estimated, current demand can be predicted on the basis of current prices and demand in the past period. This equation thus satisfies our third criterion of a satisfactory dynamic theory. The other two criteria are also satisfied by our theory. Firstly, the condition for equilibrium is given by the theory: equilibrium is only attained if relative prices remain constant for a sufficiently long period of time. Secondly, the speed of adjustment is determined by the magnitude of the adjustment coefficient. These points are brought out in more detail in the following section.

(vii) *The partial adjustment model and the estimation of short-run and long-run elasticities of demand.* It was stated in the last section that the adjustment of the demand for an input in response to a change in relative prices is spread over several periods of time. We may define the full adjustment of demand to a change in relative prices—the summation of the adjustments made in each successive period of time—as the long run response. However, we know that this full equilibrium adjustment would only occur if prices were to remain stable for a long period of time. Consequently, in a dynamic changing world, the *long run* adjustment is tantamount to the adjustment that *would* occur if producers always adjusted immediately to equilibrium. The adjustment in demand that actually *occurs* between one period and the next in response to a change in relative prices we may then define as the *short run* adjustment. We may illustrate these concepts as follows: Let us assume that the equilibrium demand for the input x_1, is linearly related to relative prices. The precise form of equation (2.31) is then:

$$D_{1t}^* = b_0 + b_1(P_{p_t}^N/P_{x_{1t}}) + b_2(P_{x_{2t}}/P_{x_{1t}}) + u_t \qquad (2.35)$$

Consequently, the precise algebraic form of equation (2.33) is:

$$D_{1t} = \gamma b_0 + \gamma b_1 \left(P^N_{p_t}/P_{x_{1t}}\right) + \gamma b_2 \left(P_{x_{2t}}/P_{x_{1t}}\right) + (1 - \gamma)D_{1t-1} + \gamma u_t$$

$$(2.36)$$

The coefficients, γb_1 and γb_2, indicate how demand changes over one period of time in response to a one unit change in each of the respective relative prices. In other words, these coefficients indicate the short run response of demand. On the other hand, the long run equilibrium (potential) response is given by the coefficients b_1 and b_2. Finally, the speed at which demand is adjusted towards equilibrium is given by the adjustment coefficient γ.

Normally, it is convenient to discuss the responsiveness of demand to a change in relative prices in terms of the elasticity of demand with respect to these prices. These elasticities may be obtained from an equation such as (2.36). Thus, it is possible by using a dynamic theory of resource demand, which is based on the partial adjustment model, to distinguish between actual short run elasticities and equilibrium long-run elasticities.

III.4. DEMAND FUNCTIONS FOR DURABLE INPUTS

If farm-firms hired the services of durable inputs from firms outside of agriculture, we would be able to analyse the demand for these services in exactly the same way as we analysed the demand for a current input. However, durable inputs are commonly owned by farm-firms and our previous analysis needs amending to allow for this fact.

A durable input, by definition, provides an input (service) flow for more than one production period. Consequently, the *stock* of the durable input, and not the quantity of the input which is purchased, provides the input flow to the production function. Thus the flow of services which is demanded by the firm leads to a demand for a particular stock of the durable input at a point in time. In order to adjust the stock of the input to the required level the firm acquires a quantity of the input during the production period. The acquisition of a durable input *over* a stated time period is called gross investment in the input. In studying the demand for a durable input we, therefore, wish to (i) analyse the factors that cause the stock of a durable input to change over time and

(ii) to derive from this demand function for the stock of the input a demand function for gross investment in the input.

(a) *Static Demand Functions for a Durable Input*

In order to make our analysis of the demand for a durable input comparable to that of the demand for a current input, let us assume that there are only two input flows which can be varied within the production period. However, whilst one input flow, x, is from a current resource, X, the other is the flow of services, s, from the stock S, of a durable resource. For the sake of convenience, we shall hereafter refer to the stock of the durable input as the *capital stock* and the service flow from the stock as *capital services*. Let us, also, assume that the only other factor of production is land area, L, which has a fixed input flow. The production function of the representative firm may, then, be described by the equation, $q = f(x, s/L)$ where q is the quantity flow of output and x, s and L are defined as above.

In order to derive a static demand function for the input we shall assume, as in our earlier treatment, that farm-firms attempt to maximize profits over the production period. The purchase of durable inputs by a producer implies that he has a planning horizon which extends beyond a single production period. Consequently, it seems likely that he will attempt to maximize the sum of discounted future profits over this horizon rather than maximizing profits in each period as it eventuates. However, it can be shown that under certain assumptions, the alternative objectives lead to the same path of capital stock adjustment over time.† Consequently, just as the equilibrium demand for a current input depends on relative prices (see equation (2.8)), so will the equilibrium demand for capital services. By strict analogy to the demand for a current input, the demand for capital services is a function of product price (P_p) relative to the price of capital services (c) and the price of x, (P_x) relative to the price of capital services. In addition, we presume in static analysis that firms provide themselves with the equilibrium level of capital services in each period. Therefore, the equilibrium

† This point is treated well on a continuous time basis in Dale Jorgenson, The theory of investment behaviour, in *Determinants of Investment Behaviour*, N.B.E.R., 1967, pp. 129–55.

(desired) level of aggregate capital services in period t, s_t^*, is a function of relative prices in that period,

$$s_t^* = f(P_{p_t}/c_t, P_{x_t}/c_t) \qquad (2.37)$$

The flow of capital services is unmeasurable and we, therefore, need to turn the demand function for capital services into a demand function for capital stock. The flow of services is related to the quantity of capital stock, which is measured at a point in time, by a factor of proportionality which represents the rate of service flow per unit of stock. This proportional factor will be constant, from one point in time to another, if (i) capital stock is utilized at the same rate at each point in time and (ii) capital stock is measured in such a way that it reflects quality change over time. If these criteria are satisfied so that the rate of service flow is always a constant proportion of capital stock then the equilibrium level of capital stock will also be a function solely of relative prices. In addition, these relative prices should refer to the same point in time as the capital stock. However, it is not necessary to postulate that capital stock is adjusted to equilibrium at every point in time. Rather, it is only necessary in our treatment to postulate that capital stock is adjusted in each period, in response to changing relative prices, to an equilibrium quantity at the end of each period. This equilibrium, end of period capital stock, which we may denote by S_t^*, is thus determined by the relative prices that occur within the period:

$$S_t^* = f(P_{p_t}/c_t, P_{x_t}/c_t) \qquad (2.38)$$

From equation (2.38), which represents a static demand function for capital stock, we now wish to derive a demand function for gross investment—that is, a function which explains the flow of purchases in the durable input over the production period. Gross investment (G_t) is conceptually the sum of two parts—replacement demand or depreciation (R_t) and net investment (N_t). If the durable input depreciates over time, then a quantity of the durable input must be bought in the production period to maintain stock at a constant level from one period to the next. This quantity represents replacement demand whilst net investment is the term given to a change in the level of capital stock between the end of the last production period and the end of the current period. Equilibrium or desired net investment (N_t^*) thus represents the augmentation or diminution of aggregate capital stock which occurs if stock is adjusted from the quantity owned at the end of the last period to the equilibrium level at the end of the current period. Equilibrium gross investment (G_t^*) thus represents the necessary flow of purchases during the production period for capital stock to be adjusted to the equilibrium quantity at the end of the period,

i.e.
$$G_t^* = N_t^* + R_t = S_t^* - S_{t-1} + R_t \qquad (2.39)$$

Therefore, because S_t^* is determined by current relative prices, equilibrium gross investment is a function of current relative prices. Gross investment is influenced (negatively) by the level of past stock and (positively) by the forces determining replacement investment. If we assume, for simplicity, that there is a constant rate of depreciation, h, then replacement demand is proportional to existing stock ($R_t = h.S_{t-1}$) and the gross investment function is:

$$G_t^* = S_t^* + (h - 1) S_{t-1} \qquad (2.40)$$

(b) *The Price of Capital Services*

Once farm-firms have purchased durable inputs the price of the capital services rendered is an imputed cost and not a direct market price. This imputed cost represents the implicit rental or opportunity cost of capital services from a unit of capital stock and is determined by three factors—the price of the durable input, the rate of interest and the rate at which the input depreciates in market value. The implicit rental is the sum of an implicit interest cost and an implicit depreciation cost. If a farm-firm invests its own capital funds in a unit of the input there is an *implicit* interest cost, because these funds could have been loaned at interest during the period. Alternatively, if the firm borrows capital funds in order to purchase the input, there is a *direct* interest cost. In either case, there is a depreciation cost equal to the loss in asset value of the input because of market depreciation.

The determination of the implicit rental of capital services may be illustrated as follows. Let us suppose that the purchase price of a unit of the durable input is $£P_g$ per unit, that the rate of interest is r per cent per period, and that the durable input depreciates at a rate of h per cent per period in the resale market. Then, firstly $£P_g.r$ is foregone by owning a unit of the input and, secondly, the fall in value of one unit of stock is equal to $£P_g.h$. It should be noted that we are making the implicit assumption that prices in the second-hand market for the input change proportionally with changes in the price of a new unit of the input.

Hence, the total opportunity cost, c, of owning one unit of the durable input for the period is equal to $£P_g(r + h)$.† Consequently, the implicit rental reflects not only the price of the durable input (the price of the investment good) but also the rate of interest and the rate of depreciation and an increase in any one of these factors leads, *ceteris paribus*, to a lower optimal level of capital stock. It must also follow that if the rate of depreciation and the rate of interest do not change over time, then changes in the implicit rental are proportional to changes in the purchase price of the input. Where this is the case, we may use the price of the durable input in place of its implicit rental in our analysis.

(c) *Anticipated Product Price and Investment in a Durable Input*

We have so far, in our analysis of the demand for a durable input, assumed that product price is known to producers. However, it will be realized from our earlier discussion that this is not the case and that producers have to formulate expectations about product price. Consequently, we need to introduce into the demand function a hypothesis concerning the way in which product price expectations are formulated. This problem may then be treated in exactly the same way as it was treated in the demand for a current input but with one proviso; this is, that expectations about the future may play a more important role in explaining the demand for a durable input. Thus the commitment of capital funds in the purchase of a durable input indicates that the purchaser has some confidence about returns in future production periods as well as in the immediate period. This is particularly the case where the input is a specialized one and is used in the production

---

† Compare H. J. Cohen and R. M. Cyert, *Theory of the Firm: Resource Allocation in a Market Economy*, Prentice-Hall, Inc., 1965, pp. 139–40. Their approach is similar to the above, but because they assume a different scheme for depreciation their formula for c is different.

of a single commodity only. The usual theoretical assumption is that past prices are the basis on which expectations about product price for several future periods are derived unless we have some other additional or more powerful indicator of the state of farmers' expectations about the future. There is in fact a need for further theoretical developments in specifying how the investment decision is related to the formation of expectations in a way which is meaningful for aggregate analysis. It would seem that this problem is more important the more immobile between alternative uses is the durable input which we are studying. We may also note that the influence of uncertainty is likely to be reflected in a disequilibrium situation in the speed with which equilibrium is approached—we might expect that the less the uncertainty about the future, the quicker the adjustment of the stock of the durable input toward equilibrium, *ceteris paribus*. At this juncture, it should be mentioned that the United Kingdom governmental price support scheme has probably helped farmers to form expectations about the future by reducing the possible volatility of product prices. Consequently, it has probably stimulated investment within agriculture.

(d) *Dynamic Demand Functions for a Durable Input*

In our discussion of the demand for a current input, we pointed out that it was unlikely that producers purchased the equilibrium quantity of an input during each production period. For similar reasons, it is unlikely that producers adjust their stock of a durable input to its equilibrium level at the end of each period. In addition, there may be higher costs involved in adjusting the level of capital stock than in adjusting the demand for a current input—particularly if producers are introducing the input into their resource structure for the first time. Also, a durable input is usually lumpy and it is difficult, therefore, for an individual producer to adjust to the equilibrium level. Finally, a change in relative prices may make it profitable for producers to increase their capital stock but, because a durable input provides services for future time periods as well as the present, they will need some evidence that the price change is likely to be "permanent" before making the adjustment.

Dynamic demand functions for durable inputs may be formulated in a similar way to dynamic demand functions for current inputs. In this way, we can obtain a dynamic demand function for capital stock by combining our theory of equilibrium capital stock with the partial adjustment model of producer behaviour. The latter suggests that the adjustment of aggregate stock between the end of the last production period and the end of the present period is some fraction of the difference between the equilibrium stock in the present period and the actual stock in the last period. A linear adjustment model is represented by:

$$S_t - S_{t-1} = \gamma(S_t{}^* - S_{t-1}), \; 0 < \gamma < 1 \qquad (2.41)$$

where γ is the adjustment coefficient.

Therefore $\qquad\qquad S_t = \gamma S_t{}^* + (1 - \gamma) S_{t-1} \qquad\qquad (2.42)$

We may then substitute equation (2.38) for $S_t{}^*$ in equation (2.42) to obtain a dynamic demand function for capital stock. This demand function leads to an investment function which implies that actual gross investment (G_t) is less than the equilibrium gross investment,

i.e. $\qquad G_t \equiv S_t - S_{t-1} + R_t = \gamma(S_t{}^* - S_{t-1}) + R_t \qquad (2.43)$

Replacement investment is related in some way to the level of past stock. Therefore, equation (2.43) indicates that gross investment is a function of current relative prices and the level of past stock. Past stock has two opposing technical influences on gross investment. Firstly, via replacement investment it has a positive influence. Secondly, via the adjustment mechanism it has a negative influence: net investment $(S_t - S_{t-1})$ is smaller the larger is past stock. This negative influence will be greater the larger the adjustment coefficient, since the larger is the adjustment coefficient the smaller is the adjustment in the present period to prices in past periods. The total influence of past stock, thus, depends on the relative strengths of these two constituent influences. This may be illustrated by assuming, as in equation (2.40), that replacement investment is proportional to the level of past stock. Then the investment function becomes:

$$G_t = \gamma S_t{}^* + (h - \gamma)S_{t-1} \qquad (2.44)$$

(e) *Demand Functions and a Time Lag in the Completion of Investment Projects*

In our discussion so far, we have assumed that the durable input may be bought "off the shelf" and any lag in the adjustment of capital stock to the equilibrium level arises because of inertia on the part of producers. However, some investment goods cannot be bought and used immediately once the decision to alter the quantity of capital stock has been taken. Thus for certain inputs, such as plant or buildings, time is required for the construction of new investment so that there is a time lag between the decision to invest and use of services from the input. If this time lag is the length of one or more periods, then it needs to be incorporated into the analysis. For example, let us assume that the average length of time between the decision to purchase the durable input and the initial use of the input is one period. If producers try to adjust immediately to price changes it will now be one period before their decisions are realized. Thus equilibrium analysis incorporating this time lag states that:

$$S_{t+1} = S_t^* = f(P_{1t}/c_t, P_{xt}/c_t) \qquad (2.45)$$

We could then combine equation (2.45) with the partial adjustment model to allow for dynamic aspects of producer decision making.

IV. Demand Functions for Inputs: A Summary

We may conveniently summarize our discussion of the derivation of demand functions for inputs by considering the situation where the input flows of many resources can be varied in production. The aggregate equilibrium demand for the ith input in period t, $D_{x_{it}}^*$, is assumed to be a function of the relative prices which exist in that period:

$$D_{x_{it}}^* = f\left(\frac{P_{pt}^N}{P_{x_{it}}}, \frac{P_{x_{1t}}}{P_{x_{it}}}, \ldots, \frac{P_{xnt}}{P_{x_{it}}}\right) \qquad (2.46)\dagger$$

† Equation (2.46) is written with prices expressed as price ratios and is therefore presumed to be homogeneous of degree zero. Often, a demand function which is to be empirically estimated is specified in the form of absolute prices. This has the implication that farmers are not necessarily as rational as is presumed by the theory which we have developed and this may, in certain circumstances, be a more reasonable assumption.

$D^*_{x_{it}}$ can represent either the equilibrium level of purchases of a current input or the equilibrium level of stock of a durable input. P^N_{pt} represents anticipated product price for the period and we substitute into the function the way in which this price depends on the price of the product in past periods. We would expect $D^*_{x_{it}}$ to be positively related to $P^N_{pt}/P_{x_{it}}$. The other prices represent input prices and for a durable input the price is the implicit rental of a unit of the input. Where the jth input is a *substitute* input to the ith input in production we cannot predict the way in which a change in the price ratio $P_{x_{jt}}/P_{x_{it}}$ will influence $D_{x_{it}}$— except to say that the influence will be positive if the substitution effect of the price change outweighs the expansion effect and negative if it does not. On the other hand, if an input is a technical *complement* to the ith input, then we would expect a fall in the ratio of the price of this input to the price of X_i to lead to an increased demand for X_i.

Often the demand function (2.46), is written with the relative prices inverted so that attention is focused on the real price of X_i relative to product price, the real price of X_i relative to the price of X_j and so on.† If this is the case then, clearly, we would expect changes in the price ratios to have opposite influences on $D^*_{x_{it}}$ to the ones just stated.

In the real world, we do not expect producers to be in equilibrium and, therefore, the equilibrium demand function needs to be converted into a dynamic one. In order to obtain a dynamic demand function, we combine the equilibrium theory with a partial adjustment model of producer decision-making. Demand in period t is then made a function, not only of relative prices in the same period, but also of demand in the previous period. In addition, actual demand may also be a function of the level of available liquid assets if farm-firms face a capital funds constraint.

Finally, we should note that our discussion presupposes that, firstly, all prices are measured on a constant quality basis and, secondly, that the measure of demand allows for quality change over time and therefore reflects the quantity of services which is incorporated in the input.

V. A Note on the Statistical Estimation of the Demand Function for an Input

The theoretical framework which has been presented in this chapter

† For example, see the demand function for tractor stock in Chapter 4.

indicates, in general terms, the variables which are thought to influence the demand for an input. As part of our empirical analysis in later chapters, we use linear regression analysis to test if these variables do influence the demand for a particular input and to measure the influence that each of the variables has on demand.

The first step, in using regression analysis to estimate a demand function, is to specify the algebraic form of the relationship between demand and the explanatory variables. This algebraic form is called the functional form of the relationship. The range of functional forms that can be theoretically considered is, however, limited by a constraint imposed by the regression procedure—the form must be linear or must be capable of being transformed into a linear relationship. Three forms which are used in later chapters are the so-called "linear", "double log" and "semilog" forms. The latter two relationships are nonlinear but may be transformed into linear relationships. These forms may be illustrated by considering demand, D, to be a function of only one variable, P. The linear form is $D = b_0 + b_1 P$; the double log is $D = b_0 P^{b_1}$ which is transformed into a linear relationship as $\log D = \log b_0 + b_1 \log P$; the semilog form is $e^D = b_0 P^{b_1}$ which is transformed into $D = \log_e b_0 + b_1 \log_e P$.† These alternative functional forms do of course constitute different hypotheses as to the way in which demand is related to the explanatory variables. If they are all equally acceptable on theoretical grounds, then we look to our estimation procedure, as described shortly, for some help in choosing between them.

The second step is to include in our demand function an error term (u). Thus we say that our theoretical function is a simplification and we do not expect a perfect relationship between demand and the explanatory variables. There are three reasons for the inclusion of the error term in estimation of a demand function. Firstly, we include in our demand function only those variables which are thought to be most important in explaining demand and we let the net effect of the excluded variables be represented in the error term. We expect these omitted factors to affect demand both positively and negatively so that the expected value of u is zero. Secondly, there is some element of randomness in human behaviour which necessitates the inclusion of a random error term. Thirdly, we can never measure demand exactly so that we include our

† e is the exponential e.

measurement error in u. Inclusion of an error term then allows us to proceed with our third step which is to estimate statistically by linear regression our demand relationship using data on demand and the explanatory variables for a number of time periods (usually years).[†] Sometimes, we may be able to specify the form of the relationship on theoretical grounds but normally several forms are experimented with and the regression procedure is used to choose between them. Thus the form normally chosen is the one which gives the best explanation of the observed variation in demand. The estimation procedure also allows us to test statistically whether or not demand for the input was associated, over the data period, with each of the proposed explanatory variables. In addition, a quantitative estimate is given of the change in demand that results from a change in each explanatory variable. In other words, the coefficients of the relationship between demand and the explanatory variables are estimated and then a test is made to see if each of these coefficients differ significantly from zero.

[†] It should be emphasized that this statistical estimation procedure involves a number of restrictive assumptions about the error term—see J. Johnston, *Econometric Methods*, McGraw-Hill, 1963.

CHAPTER 3

LABOUR

I. Introduction

The historical record reveals a massive, and still persisting, transfer of labour from the agricultural sector to the rest of the economy—a phenomenon common to all industrial economies. This chapter is primarily concerned with a quantitative description of this labour transfer together with an elaboration of those forces which generate this movement out of agriculture. The results of research on the determinants of the demand for labour by agriculture and the supply of labour to agriculture will be given and analysed. Most of the results relate to the post-war period but a limited analysis of the inter-war period is made also. A regional analysis of agricultural labour supply is made for recent years.

The other characteristic feature of the agricultural labour market, which is obviously associated with the outmigration of labour, is the persistent tendency for wages in agriculture to fall well below industrial wages. The process of wage adjustment within agriculture is examined and a quantitative analysis is attempted over the post-war period.

II. Migration from Agriculture: The Historical Record

Since the beginning of the 19th century there has been a consistent decline in the share of the national labour force employed in the agricultural sector.† At the turn of the 19th century it is likely that a third of the labour force was in agriculture and over the next fifty years this declined to about a fifth. The agricultural work force actually increased from about 1·7 millions to 2·1 millions, but its rate of growth was

† See Phyllis Deane and W. A. Cole, *British Economic Growth: 1688–1959*, 2nd ed., Cambridge, 1967.

57

considerably less than that of the total work force. During the following half-century the decline was even sharper with agriculture's share falling to 8·7 per cent and a decline in the agricultural work force of 600,000. Finally in the last half-century up to 1951 the decline moderated to 400,000, leaving British agriculture with about 5 per cent of the British work force. Subsequently this percentage has been reduced to below four.

Saville† comments on two important qualitative features of the exodus from rural to urban areas. First he observes that women were more mobile than men so that rural depopulation led to a rural–urban difference in the sex ratio. However the loss of women from rural areas was largely a decline in the secondary rural labour force, mainly domestic servants, and not a direct loss to agriculture. The other qualitative feature of migrants was their relative youth which led to significantly different age structures in rural–urban areas; and having a direct effect upon the quality of the agricultural work force. A further significant feature of the decline in the agricultural labour force was that up to 1951 it consisted almost entirely of hired workers. Census data up to 1951 give no indication of a decline in the number of farmers, indeed the number increased after 1911. There has been a decline in male relatives engaged in agriculture since 1911 but the numbers are small relative to the total outflow. Table 3.1 shows the structure of the agricultural male labour force in England and Wales at each decennial census between 1871 and 1931 and shows clearly the decline in hired workers over each ten-year period except the period 1901 to 1911 when the male hired work force increased by 34,000. Except for this period the average outflow from agriculture was nearly 10,000 workers p.a.

In the thirties the total work force in agriculture in England and Wales (excluding farmers) declined sharply, from 742,000 in 1930 to 593,000 in 1938.‡ From 1939 on through the war and early post-war periods there was a build up of the work force which peaked in 1947. The regular, whole-time, work force continued its upward path until

† John Saville, *Rural Depopulation in England and Wales 1851–1951*, London, 1957.
‡ Data available from the June Agricultural Census reports of the Ministry of Agriculture.

TABLE 3.1. STRUCTURE OF THE MALE LABOUR FORCE IN AGRICULTURE
1871–1931 (ENGLAND AND WALES)

	1871	1881	1891	1901	1911	1921	1931
Farmers	226*	203	202	203	209	245	231
Relatives	76	75	67	89	98	80	73
Workers	938	850	775	631	665	582	498
Total	1240	1128	1044	923	972	907	802
△ Total	−112	−84	−121	+49	−65	−105	

Source: G. P. Hirsch, Migration from the land in England and Wales, *Farm Economist*, vol. VI, p. 9, 1951.

We have aggregated bailiffs, shepherds and labourers into workers.

The material is taken from the population censuses for England and Wales.

* Includes retired.

1949, the decline in the total work force being largely explained by the rapid disappearance of Prisoners of War and the Women's Land Army. Since 1949 there has been a reduction in the work force of 287,000 up to 1965. Breaking down this figure we find that among regular, whole-time workers the decline in women workers has been significantly greater than that for men. There has been a substantial decline in youths in agriculture but a lot of it can be explained by the change in the school leaving age from 14 to 15 in 1949. The detailed information on the post-war agricultural labour market will be given in the next section where we set out a model of the functioning of the labour market and try to explain the declining employment level in agriculture.

Regular part-time and seasonal/temporary workers have not declined over the post-war period and have therefore assumed an increasing importance in the industry as the number of regular, full-time workers has dropped. It has been estimated, on the basis of relative earnings, that the number of man-equivalents employed in agriculture (England and Wales) has fallen by 36 per cent over the twenty-year period up to 1965. The reduction in numbers of workers has shown a constant trend over the post-war years which carries the implication that the trend in percentage terms is increasing over time, i.e. the fairly constant outflow (observed after eliminating cyclical movements) represents an increasing percentage of the declining agricultural work force, which in turn carries the implication of an accelerating rate of productivity growth if agricultural production is to be maintained.

On the qualitative side the decline in employment has been associated with a changing occupational and age structure, and a changing regional distribution. Occupationally the most significant development has been the declining proportion of general workers and the increasing proportion of tractor men, but since 1959 the number of tractor men has declined despite an increase in the stock of tractors on farms and it seems likely that more farmers have become their own tractor men as more farms are becoming purely family farms. There has been no change in the proportion of workers less than 25 years of age, but there has been a reduction in the proportion in the 25–45 age group and a build up in the 55 and over age group. Regionally the biggest reductions have been in industrial growth areas, like the London and Birmingham regions, and in Wales (South and North). In Scotland the biggest reductions have been in the more remote Highland areas.

For a more complete description of the labour input into agricultural production over the post-war period we would have to recognize the changing educational and skill characteristics of the agricultural labour force. However we have little information on these qualitative aspects of the labour force—all we can say is that we would expect the educational level of the labour force to have consistently increased over time as new entrants with more years of schooling replace older people. The stock of people with post-secondary education has also increased over time but there has been no general training scheme in operation in the industry. There is the additional question concerning the relative qualities of those who leave and those who stay in the industry. There is no direct evidence on this but we may be able to put forward some hypotheses after examining the demand and supply situation for agricultural labour over this period.

In describing the flow of services from a stock of labour we must determine hours of work as well as the qualitative characteristics of the stock and on this point we have considerable information. In 1946 a standard 48-hour week was introduced in England and Wales. In 1949 there was a reduction to 47 hours, but there then followed a period of eleven years with no further reductions in nationally negotiated hours.

In the sixties there were further 1 hour reductions in 1960, 1963 and 1966 giving a total reduction of 4 hours, less than 10 per cent, in twenty years as a result of the decisions of the Agricultural Wages Board. As opposed to hours negotiated nationally the actual hours of work for regular, whole-time male workers was 53 per week in 1945/6 and declined by 3 hours to 50 per male in 1964/5. The reduction was exactly equal to the fall in standard hours. In 1960 the 1 hour drop in standard hours led to a 0·7 hour drop in actual hours in the two following years.

The number of farmers remained relatively constant over most of the early post-war period but there is limited evidence to suggest that the number of farmers is now declining. This phenomenon is difficult to quantify as the only source of information is the population censuses (1951, 1961 and 1966) and the classification system has been changed so that the data for the different censuses is not easily compared. The general stability of farmer numbers associated with the substantial decline in the number of workers has meant that British agriculture is moving toward a family farm structure.

III. A Model of the Agricultural Labour Market

Two types of forces influencing migration out of agriculture have been distinguished: "push" and "pull". "Push" refers to the pressures generated within agriculture which tend to reduce agricultural employment—the rise of agricultural wages relative to agricultural prices and relative to the price of labour substitutes, principally tractor power. "Pull" refers to the impact of alternative, and more remunerative, employment opportunities for farm labour. Thus "push" refers to the demand for labour by the agricultural industry and "pull' represents those forces resulting in a decline in the supply of labour to the industry. The interaction of these two forces generates the flow of migrant labour from agriculture to other sectors. The simplest model of the agricultural labour would be an equilibrium one where the supply of agricultural labour at any point in time is assumed equal to the demand for labour by the agricultural industry and additionally it is assumed that wages are exogenously determined, that is they are determined by forces operating outside the agricultural industry and are not affected by changes in the level of agricultural employment. A theoretically more acceptable model would be one in which agricultural employment and agricultural wages are jointly determined, that is where they are both considered to be endogenous variables. Such a theoretical model would require us to specify a two-equation simultaneous model to be statistically examined whereas the assumption of a one-way relationship between wage and employment specifies a single-equation model for statistical analysis. We may rationalize the use of such single-equation models if we believe that the response of employment to a change in wage only takes place after a lag. This will be generally true but its significance in our analysis depends on the length of the lag. With annual data, if the lag is at least one year then we can go ahead and estimate single-equation models. The other assumption we have mentioned, about equilibrium in this market, may be untenable. Disequilibrium in the labour market is reflected on the supply side by unemployed agricultural labour and on the demand side by unfilled vacancies in agriculture. The theoretical model of dynamic price adjustment would then predict that as excess demand existed at a point in time so agricultural wages would adjust upwards, the rate of adjustment being determined by the level of excess demand. We will analyse the dynamics of such wage adjustment in agriculture after first considering models which attempt to explain the supply of and demand for agricultural labour ignoring the effects of any discrepancies between demand and supply.

Taira[†] suggests that migration from agriculture should be looked at from a different viewpoint. In order to explain the low levels of migration from agriculture in Japan when the wage differential is relatively high he puts forward the hypothesis that the wage differential is in fact determined by the level of migration in some previous period. This may be a useful hypothesis in underdeveloped economies, but in the U.K. the rate of outflow of agricultural labour is unlikely to be an important determinant of industrial wage changes. A more realistic explanation of an inverse relationship between outmigration and wage differentials might be found in the availability of employment opportunities in industry. Thus in times of industrial recession unemployment

[†] Koji Taira, Labour migration from agriculture: the case of Japan, *Journal of Farm Economics*, 1963.

increases but industrial wage levels will be relatively inflexible downwards compared with agricultural wages, partly because of union organization, but also because of the structure of industry which is likely to lead to output restrictions rather than price reductions. Thus the wage differential between agriculture and industry will widen during an industrial recession, but the employment opportunities open to agricultural migrants may have been drastically curtailed. It would seem reasonable to suggest that the potential migrant weights the going industrial wage by the probability of getting a job, so that his income expectations in industry

$$E(W_I) = W_I \left(1 - \frac{U_I}{100}\right)$$

where W_I is the industrial wage and U_I is the industrial unemployment percentage. This formulation will be both a subjective (in the case of the potential migrant) and objective (in the case of the labour market) overestimate of the employment opportunities facing the relatively unskilled, undereducated and industrially inexperienced migrant. The unemployment rate and wage earnings vary between sectors of the labour market according to the educational, training and geographical attributes of labour. Unemployment and wages probably also vary as between industries, holding the other attributes constant, and according to the degree of unionization. In all these respects farm migrant labour is liable to be worse than average.

Two different approaches have been used to analyse the labour transfer process from agriculture to industry. The first approach utilizes time-series information for England and Wales and attempts to measure these aggregate supply and demand functions for agricultural labour in the post-war and inter-war periods. The data in the inter-war period is rather inadequate so the major results will be for the post-war period. The overriding problem with such aggregate time-series analysis is the high degree of intercorrelation among the set of the variables we are using to explain supply and demand for labour resulting in very real difficulties in getting reliable estimates of the individual parameters. Partly in order to circumvent this sort of problem we have also attempted to get estimates of the determinants of migration from cross-section observations on the flow of migrants from regions within the U.K. The big problem in this context is the paucity of regional data, especially on agricultural wages.

IV. Supply and Demand for Agricultural Labour: Aggregate Time-series Analysis for England and Wales

The general form of the models to be tested will be

(1) $S_l = S_l(W_a; W_I; U_I)$

(2) $D_l = D_l(W_a; P_a; P_m; T)$

where S_l and D_l are respectively supply of, and demand for, labour by agriculture (England and Wales); W_a is an index of wages in agriculture; W_I is an index of industrial wages; U_I is the industrial unemployment rate, or alternatively industrial vacancy rates (V_I) could be used, or the difference between these rates ($V_I - U_I$) giving a measure of excess demand for industrial labour; P_m is a price index for agricultural machinery inputs or alternatively a tractor price index, P_a is an index of agricultural prices and T is a time trend used as a proxy for the level of labour productivity in agriculture. Disequilibrium, simultaneous and lagged versions of the basic, equilibrium single equation relationships will be examined.

IV.1. POST-WAR PERIOD (1946–64)

(a) *Data*

(i) *Agricultural employment.* This study is concerned exclusively with the hired labour force. No annual data is available on numbers of farmers (other than what can be deduced from data on the number of holdings) and the decennial census data problems of comparability. However the limited evidence available suggests that the number of farmers has remained pretty constant over the post-war period—at least until very recently—while the number of hired workers has declined consistently (except for the early post-war period), but at a variable rate. In determining the aggregate level of agricultural employment we are faced with a weighting problem. Different categories of workers (in *Agricultural Statistics*) are distinguished according to age and sex and these are further subdivided into full-time, part-time and seasonal. An obvious way to allow for these qualitative differences would be to weight these different groups by their relative earnings. In equilibrium this would reflect the marginal productivity differentials for these different categories of labour. Unfortunately the earnings data for these different groups is incomplete since we do not have information on the wages of less than full-time workers. Alternatively we can weight according to hours worked of which we have some estimate. This compromise will bias the employment index downwards for the later years incident to the changes in the proportional distribution within the labour force in favour of full-time, regular males. We have no information of education and training so that we cannot make an adjustment for this aspect of labour quality. Census data in 1951 gives age at leaving school for the agricultural work force but we do not have any further information. This information will be used in the regional analysis reported in the next section.

(ii) *Agricultural wages and earnings.* Since 1940 a national minimum agricultural wage has been set by the Agricultural Wages Board. The board is made up of employers and employees representatives and independents. The general pattern of behaviour which has emerged has been one of employees putting forward claims which are always partially, never completely, met—the independents appear to have steered a moderate course. In fact *real* wages were only just maintained during the first nine years of the post-war period, and there was an actual decline over the period 1949 to 1955. Total real earnings, reflecting movements in basic wage rates together with movements in overtime, piece-work and premium payments, stagnated from 1947 right through until 1953. There has been and still is no wage structure which allows for advancement with age and experience, the maximum wage being given at the age of twenty, neither is there a structure to reflect skill, training and educational differentials. These topics are under current discussion but no new structure has yet been implemented.

It is likely that adjustments in wage rates lead to movements in the same direction in wage earnings. In fact the difference between wage rates and earnings has shown a persistent and considerable tendency to increase over the post-war period such that currently weekly wages form only about two-thirds of total weekly earnings. Some of this increase is obviously due to a fall in the standard working week accompanied by a rise in the proportion of overtime hours. A later section will attempt to report on research relating to this phenomenon.

Earnings would appear to be a more relevant measure of the likely pay-off for someone deciding between agriculture and industry. On the demand side an index of labour costs per man would have to include the employer's contribution to National Insurance as well as earnings per man.

The ratio of agricultural wages to industrial wages appeared as a stable equilibrium, at about 50 per cent, for the whole period 1867 to 1938.† Thus a situation with some of the characteristics of equilibrium was produced far below the point at which wages rate were equated. Since the war another stable equilibrium seems to have persisted, this time with agricultural wages being about 70 per cent of industrial wages. Excess demand for labour over the war years could explain the upward adjustment in agricultural wages relative to industrial wages according to Reder's theory of occupational wage differentials.‡ The argument proceeds by assuming that high wage occupations will draw on lower wage occupations during periods of excess demand, but that the lowest wage occupations will be in a less flexible position so that their wages will rise relative to higher paid occupations. These diminished differentials will persist into future periods because of the downward inflexibility of most wages and the institutionalizing of wage levels. There is year-to-year variability in the 70 per cent level, but there seems to be no tendency for any definite and consistent movement from this mark to take place. The situation seems to have a close parallel in Sweden.§

(iii) *Industrial earnings.* The measure of industrial earnings considered was an All Industry earnings index published by the Ministry of Labour. A more relevant index for reflecting the income opportunities available for potential farm migrants would be one weighted by the relative importance of the occupations and industries into which these workers

† Bellerby, *Agriculture and Industry: Relative Incomes,* Basil Blackwell, Oxford.
‡ M. W. Reder, The theory of occupational wage differentials, *American Economic Review,* Vol. XIV, 5, December 1955, pp. 833–52.
§ S. Holmström, Agricultural price policy in Sweden, *J. Agricultural Economics,* Vol. X, 2, February 1953, pp. 145–57.

migrate. No published information exists on the types of work into which agricultural workers move when they leave agriculture, but it seems reasonable to assume that they will be mainly unskilled, manual occupations with a rural bias. The All Industry wage index is therefore inappropriate but it is doubtful if one would make any substantial difference to the results obtained if one were to construct a new index with weights that must be essentially arbitrary. This statement can be made since we observe a high correlation among various industry wage series over the post-war period. Following Schuh's work,[†] based on an idea by Reder,[‡] it seems that a more relevant description of the earnings opportunities open to potential migrants is a product of earnings and the probability of being employed. In times of high unemployment an objective and subjective assessment of the expected value of earnings in industry would be lower than in times of low unemployment, even holding wage earnings per man employed constant.

Thus
$$E(W_I) = W_I \left(1 - \frac{U_I}{100}\right)$$

where W_I is average industrial earnings and U_I is average industrial unemployment. For a migrant this formulation might be expected to overestimate expected earnings as we might expect higher unemployment rates and lower earnings among recent migrants.

(iv) *Unemployment and excess demand for labour in industry.* Annual average unemployment rates have been calculated for the aggregate industrial labour force for England and Wales. This variable measures the excess supply of labour but it can co-exist with a positive excess demand for labour, as measured by unfilled vacancies in industry. The explanation for this apparent inconsistency lies in the different attributes of the surplus labour and the labour required for the unfilled positions—these attributes being geographical, educational, and skill, plus the fact that unemployment includes a transitory or frictional element, that is workers moving from one job to another and being

[†] G. E. Schuh, An econometric investigation of the market for hired labour in agriculture, *J. Farm Economics*, Vol. XLIV, 2, May 1962, pp. 307–21.
[‡] *Op. cit.*

temporarily unemployed. For the potential migrant it might be assumed that some index of unfilled vacancies would be more relevant than the level of unemployment. However for the agricultural worker this is not so tenable, it being unlikely that such migrants would possess the generally desired attributes.

(v) *"Real" price of agricultural output.* The Ministry of Agriculture produce an index of average weighted prices for agricultural output. An index of "real" price is obtained by deflating by an input price index (excluding labour). The index produced shows that the "real" price of agricultural output has been declining over the post-war period. However this index takes no account of the improvements in productivity of resources used in agriculture nor does it allow for the year-to-year variability in output which may compensate for short-term price fluctuations. A planned expansion or contraction of aggregate agricultural output, and therefore a planned increase or decrease in demand for labour, will be in response to changes in expected net income (assuming profit maximizing behaviour) of which "real" output price is only one facet. Changes in the aggregate input–output ratio (assuming a constant output mix) can result from: (1) shifts in the aggregate production function (technological change), (2) improvements in the "quality" of inputs, (3) aggregate scale economics, and (4) changes in exogenous, non-economic factors (e.g. weather, pests and diseases). Alternative approaches to handling these factors might be: (1) a labour productivity index (agricultural output at constant prices ÷ agricultural employment), (2) a trend term (linear or exponential) as a proxy for technology, (3) aggregate agricultural net income. The difficulty with a productivity index is that it is really an endogenous variable determined by the level of employment (if we assume non-constant marginal productivity) the degree of substitution of capital for labour which is partly determined by relative prices as well as by the rate of technological advance, assuming disembodied technology is in fact important. A trend term, merely serving to indicate what we do not know, may be an unavoidable necessity which can result in collinearity problems. Aggregate net income may be useful but insofar as it indicates a supply of liquid assets it may be a factor determining investment in labour-saving machinery. Two alternative estimates are available, one derived from Farm Management Survey data, the other derived from estimates of aggregate input and output figures and average prices.†

(vi) *Price of farm machinery*. An index of the "price" of the flow of machinery input can be derived from price indices for fuel, oil, repairs, depreciation and interest, knowing the relative weights of these various costs of operating machines. Alternatively we might construct an index of the prices of the relevant investment goods themselves. Price series for machinery costs are available in unpublished form from the Ministry of Agriculture. A price index for new machines would require a complete synthesis from individual manufacturers' data—such an index for tractors is constructed in the next chapter, but no attempt has been made to construct a price index for all new agricultural machines. Whichever index of machinery price is used the ratio of that price to the level of agricultural wages is assumed to partly determine the rate at which machines are substituted for labour. Alternatively the number of machines could be included as a variable directly either as a broad value aggregate or as an index of "critical" machines, i.e. those which allow for a major breakthrough in reducing the agricultural labour force. Unfortunately different machines will have been critical in different regions at different times—the combine in grain-growing areas in the forties and fifties; the sugar-beet harvester in East Anglia post-war; the milking machine in essentially dairying areas in the thirties. An average machinery–labour price ratio might therefore be more effective in these circumstances and we will also experiment with the tractor price index.

(b) *Results*

(i) *Labour supply*. Some of the more interesting results are reported in Table 3.2 and the data used in regressions is included in the appendix at the end of the chapter. Equation (1), which includes money wages, in agriculture and industry, and industrial unemployment as explanatory variables, gives a good fit to the data (which is not very surprising

† Farm Management Survey data are collected from a large but non-random sample of farms, and are only available after a considerable lag. The "departmental" aggregate estimates are produced annually by the Ministry of Agriculture.

with time-series of this sort), parameter estimates of expected sign, with two of the coefficients significant (at the 95 per cent level) and with no indication of autocorrelated disturbances. Current levels of unemployment and industrial wages are found to be significant determinants of agricultural labour supply, but agricultural wages are found insignificant. This apparent lack of significance may be due to the high degree of observed collinearity between agricultural wages and industrial wages (the zero-order correlation is greater than $0 \cdot 9$). In equation (2) the same set of explanatory variables is included but this time we synthesize a variable to reflect expected earnings in industry by correcting the industrial wage variable by the probability of being unemployed. As a result the significance of the two wage coefficients is slightly improved. Equation (3) is the same as equation (1) except that now we deflate both the wage variables by a cost of living index to give real agricultural earnings and real industrial earnings. In this case the significance of the wage variables is improved and the unemployment variable becomes non-significant. The problem of interpretation is tied up with the non-independence of industrial wages and industrial unemployment—many studies of the industrial wage adjustment mechanism have shown a relationship between unemployment and the rate of wage inflation. Equation (4) is a lagged and deflated version of equation (2) and seems to give rather better determined coefficients on the two explanatory variables suggesting a lagged response by labour to wage differentials. Other experiments have shown that the formulation with the current level of unemployment used to calculate expected industrial income is to be preferred to using lagged unemployment. This suggests it is the current job situation which is important in the labour transfer mechanism but that the experience gained of past wage differences may be relevant to the current decision. This seems a reasonable hypothesis in a labour market where the flow of information about actual wages is likely to be slower than the flow of information about jobs. Equation (5) is similar to equation (4) except that now information about unemployment in agriculture is included in the agricultural wage variable. We are suggesting that an agricultural worker is more likely to switch to an industrial job if the employment prospects in agriculture are deteriorating. This suggests that the push–pull mechanism is a two-stage sequence, a shift in demand creating unemployment (push),

TABLE 3.2. REGRESSION EQUATIONS EXPLAINING LABOUR SUPPLY (S_{It}),
1946–64

Equation	(1)	(2)	(3)	(4)	(5)
Constant	837·97	855·14	1290·94	1264·92	1256·20
$W_{a(t)}$	0·276 (0·465)	0·287 (0·427)			
$\dfrac{W_{a(t)}}{P_{r(t)}}$			1·989 (2·258)		
$\dfrac{W_{a(t-1)}}{P_{r(t-1)}}$				2·089 (1·458)	
W_{It}	−1·355 (0·441)				
$\dfrac{W_{I(t)}}{P_{r(t)}}$			−8·304 (2·010)		
$\dfrac{W_{I(t-1)}}{P_{r(t-1)}}$					
U_{It}	11·255 (3·593)		6·200 (12·331)		
$W_{It}\left(1-\dfrac{U_{It}}{100}\right)$		−1·934 (0·407)			
$\dfrac{W_{I(t-1)}\left(1-\dfrac{U_{It}}{100}\right)}{P_{rt-1}}$				−8·390 (1·326)	−8·580 (1·312)
$\dfrac{W_{a(t-1)}\left(1-\dfrac{U_{at}}{100}\right)}{P_{rt-1}}$					2·375 (1·487)
$\bar{R}^2$	0·995	0·993	0·946	0·966	0·967
Von Neumann ratio	2·353	2·154	1·284	1·519	1·557

Definition of variables. S_i is agricultural employment measured as full-time man-equivalents (thousands of full-time man years); W_a is an earnings index for adult male agricultural workers; W_I is an average earnings index for industrial labour; U_I is the industrial unemployment rate (percentage of the labour force); U_a is the agricultural unemployment rate and P_r is a cost of living index.
The relevant data is presented in an appendix to this chapter.

with the worker then weighing up the job and income prospects in the two labour markets (pull). The model seems to work fairly well with the coefficient on agricultural wages being nearly twice its standard error. This is the closest agricultural wages came to being a significant variable with industrial wages being still clearly significant. Replacement of the dependent variable by unweighted numbers or by adding on agricultural unemployment to give total labour supply to the agricultural sector did not lead to a revision of any of the inferences drawn in the above discussion.

(ii) *Labour demand*. The results reported in Table 3.3 relate to a model specification with essentially three explanatory variables defined in rather different ways—price of labour, price of labour substitutes and the price of agricultural output. An independent trend term, reflecting the growth in labour productivity, is not included as it is felt this would involve double-counting if we assume that the rate of mechanization, which can be expected to cause a shift in the demand curve for labour, is itself determined by the relative price of labour and machines. The price variables throughout are expressed as ratios largely because of the contribution of this procedure to reducing the collinearity problem. The cost of doing this is the extra restriction imposed on the parameter estimates as discussed under demand theory (Chapter 2). Equation (1) includes as explanatory variables the labour–machinery price ratio and the agricultural output–machinery price ratio. The signs of the coefficients are as expected but the coefficient on the labour–machinery price ratio is non-significant, whereas the output price variable is clearly significant. Replacing the machinery price index with a composite input price index gives considerable improvement in equation (2) where both coefficients are now clearly significant. Both equations (1) and (2) are explaining current employment in terms of current price levels for output and inputs which may seem unreasonable when we remember that decisions about levels of employment are made when output prices and wage rates are still viewed with considerable uncertainty. Equation (3) therefore substitutes price variables for the previous year in the equation with the result that the overall fit is slightly improved and the importance of output price is boosted. Experiments with alternative demand variables, such as simple numbers in agricultural employment

TABLE 3.3. REGRESSION EQUATIONS EXPLAINING
LABOUR DEMAND (D_{lt}) 1946–64

Equation	(1)	(2)	(3)	(4)*
Constant	273·015	261·512	197·129	5·142
$\dfrac{W_{ca(t)}}{P_{m(t)}}$	−1·057 (1·251)			
$\dfrac{P_{a(t)}}{P_{m(t)}}$	4·696 (0·514)			
$\dfrac{W_{ca(t)}}{P_{c(t)}}$		−1·389 (0·540)		
$\dfrac{W_{ca(t-1)}}{P_{c(t-1)}}$			−1·067 (0·494)	
$\dfrac{P_{a(t)}}{P_{c(t)}}$		5·438 (0·380)		
$\dfrac{P_{a(t-1)}}{P_{c(t-1)}}$			5·590 (0·308)	
$\log\left(\dfrac{W_{a(t-1)}}{P_{T(t)}}\right)$				−0·233 (0·040)
$\log\dfrac{P_{a(t-1)}}{W_{a(t-1)}}$				0·348 (0·067)
$\bar{R}^2$	0·902	0·966	0·971	0·981
Von Neumann ratio	1·503	1·895	1·868	1·301

Definition of variables. D_l is defined in exactly the same way as S_l; W_{ca}/P_m is an index of wage costs (wage earnings plus employers national insurance contribution) as a ratio to machinery costs (derived from price indices for fuel, repairs and interest and depreciation costs); P_c is a composite input price index derived from unpublished sources based on Board of Trade price indices and weighted by relative expenditures on the different input categories as reported in the *Annual Review and Determination of Guarantees* (H.M.S.O.); P_T is an index of the price of constant quality tractors (as defined in the chapter on machinery)

* Dependent variable is $\log D_{lt}$.

or including unfilled vacancies in agriculture, gave essentially similar results. Experiments with distributed lag models were not successful due largely to the high degree of collinearity between lagged employment (D_{lt-1}) and the price variables. One result is reported in the experiments using a quality adjusted price index for tractors rather than the unadjusted machinery price index as used rather unsuccessfully in equation (1)—this is equation 4 where both the variables appear to be very significant and with coefficients of expected sign. However the Von Neumann ratio gives some indication of positive autocorrelation so that the significance tests may be inappropriate.

(iii) *Simultaneous estimates of supply and demand.* If we assume agricultural employment and agricultural wages to be jointly determined then in an equilibrium model of the agricultural labour market, where in each period we have a market-clearing mechanism such that demand is equated with supply, we will have two behavioural equations each with two endogenous variables. Then to get consistent estimates of the parameters, and assuming neither equation is underidentified, we need a simultaneous equations estimating procedure and we must abandon ordinary least squares regression. If we are not so concerned about consistency we can still go ahead and use O.L.S. procedures and probably get useful estimates. However, our main argument against the usefulness of simultaneous procedures will be that (a) agricultural wages are predetermined and not jointly determined with employment and (b) that it is lagged wages which determine demand for agricultural labour and possibly supply of agricultural labour. Under either situation (a) or (b) the variables on the R.H.S. of the demand and supply equations can be viewed as predetermined.

(iv) *Elasticities.* For purposes of comparability we are interested in converting some of the price coefficients into pure numbers—demand and supply elasticities. The elasticity of demand for agricultural labour w.r.t. its own price (agricultural wage) is

$$\frac{\partial D_l}{\partial W_a} \cdot \frac{W_a}{D_l}$$

and our regression coefficients give us an estimate of $\partial D_l / \partial W_a$. We can

TABLE 3.4. LABOUR SUPPLY AND DEMAND
ELASTICITIES

	At mean prices
Labour Supply	
(1) W.r.t. agricultural wage	0·499
(2) W.r.t. industrial wage	−1·844
Labour Demand	
(1) W.r.t. agricultural wage	−0·215
(2) W.r.t. agricultural output price	0·852

N.B. The supply elasticities are derived from the coefficients in equation (5) of Table 3.2, with the demand elasticities from equation (3) of Table 3.3.

thus calculate an infinite number of elasticities given the linear models we have estimated but we will simply calculate the elasticity at the mean level of the price in question—e.g. the demand elasticity at the mean wage will be

$$\frac{\partial D_l}{\partial W_a} \cdot \frac{W_a}{D_l}$$

Some elasticity estimates from the more successful supply and demand equations are arrayed in Table 3.4. The results show the supply and demand elasticities for agricultural labour with respect to agricultural wage (the own price elasticities) to be inelastic but the linear formulation of the model implies rising elasticities over time as agricultural employment falls and agricultural wages rise. Log-linear relations, implying constant elasticities, give elasticities very similar to those estimated at the mean wage. The supply elasticity appears to be more than twice as big as the demand elasticity in absolute value so that agricultural wage increases will tend to increase the size of the agricultural labour force in the absence of other adjustments. However, this conclusion is only tenuous since it is based on a supply elasticity based on a parameter estimate which is of doubtful significance. We have retained this interpretation because of the collinearity of W_a and W_I in the supply equation which will undoubtedly give rise to inflated standard errors. However, agricultural employment is far more sensitive to movements in expected industrial earnings and to movements in agricultural product prices relative to agricultural input prices, i.e. to agriculture's terms of trade.

IV.2. INTER-WAR PERIOD (1923–38) AND WAR PERIOD (1939–45)

The inter-war period was a period of dramatic fluctuations in the labour market which spilled over in various ways into the agricultural labour market. Total unemployment in the U.K. increased from 2·5 per cent in 1920 to 15·6 per cent in 1921, peaked at 22·1 per cent in 1932 and still ended up at 11·6 per cent in 1939. There is no time-series for agricultural unemployment but the Census of Population in 1931 revealed an agricultural unemployment rate for male agricultural employees of 11·5 per cent compared with an All Industry rate of 12·7 per cent. The rate for agriculture as a whole was much lower (5·5 per cent) because of the inclusion of farmers and family workers in the agricultural work force. Agricultural money wages declined from 33/9½ in 1921 to 28/- and then rose to 34/8 in 1938, whereas real wages rose substantially through the period except for slight falls in 1934 and 1937. From a social point of view the problem was not one of a declining standard of living for those in farm employment but one of the lack of employment at the going wage. Agricultural prices declined drastically from 1920, more drastically than the retail price index, but, perhaps surprisingly, fertilizer prices and, less surprisingly, the price of animal feed fell even faster, giving a falling real price for these inputs.

(a) *Labour Supply*

The difficulty with any attempt to estimate the supply function for agricultural labour over the inter-war period is the lack of a continuous time-series on agricultural unemployment which is bound to be an important component of labour supply over this period. We can expect a fairly close correlation between the general level of unemployment and agricultural unemployment so that where agricultural unemployment is ignored we will get a biased estimate of the impact of the general unemployment situation on the agricultural labour market. The other major data problem is the lack of data on wage earnings in agriculture and industry so that we are left with relative weekly wage rates to express the differential in earning power in the two sectors. The labour supply function reported here expresses agricultural employment S_l (total agricultural workers, not including farmers) as a function of the current real wage in agriculture (W_a/P_r), the current real wage in industry (W_I/P_r) and the industrial unemployment rate.

$$S_l = 1988 \cdot 630 + 3 \cdot 439 \frac{W_a}{P_r} - 18 \cdot 140 \frac{W_I}{P_r} + 8 \cdot 955 \ U_I$$
$$(4 \cdot 447) \quad\quad (7 \cdot 533) \quad\quad (3 \cdot 134)$$
$$\bar{R}^2 = 0 \cdot 814$$
$$d = 1 \cdot 179$$

The signs of the parameter estimates are as expected but as with the post-war results agricultural wages appear to be insignificant. The other two variables appear to be statistically significant and the explanatory power of the model is substantial but the Von Neumann ratio (d) indicates a possible autocorrelation problem. This makes any comment on significance inappropriate but it is likely that the apparently auto-correlated disturbances have arisen because of specification error in the labour supply variable which, if it were possible to rectify, would probably only serve to improve the results since U_I is unlikely to be positively correlated with U_a.

(b) *Labour Demand*

Our labour demand model expresses agricultural employment (D_l) as a function of the money wage rate in agriculture (W_a) and the aggregate price of agricultural products (P_a). The important sources of specification error in this model are first the unweighted employment variable which does not allow for any change in the structure of the labour force over time, and second the absence of any variable for the price of machines.

$$D_l = 1150 \cdot 327 - 7 \cdot 828 \ W_a + 2 \cdot 807 \ P_a \qquad \bar{R}^2 = 0 \cdot 729$$
$$ (2 \cdot 180) (0 \cdot 716) \qquad d = 0 \cdot 684$$

Both explanatory variables appear with coefficients of expected sign and apparently significant but the Von Neumann ratio indicates the likely presence of positively autocorrelated disturbances which simply points to the specification errors discussed above. It is likely that machinery prices were positively correlated with agricultural prices but the coefficient on machinery price in the demand equation would be negative so the coefficient on P_a will have a downward bias. The bias on W_a is difficult to estimate since money wages first fell and then rose to about their former level.

Data limitations put a very severe constraint on quantitative analysis of the agricultural labour market during the inter-war period. Similarly for the war period itself data is pretty scarce. The data available shows a rapid build-up of agricultural employment in England and Wales from 607,000 in 1939 to 770,000 in 1945. The result reported below shows that part of the increase in the agricultural work force may be due to the improving wages in agriculture *vis-à-vis* industry—there was a 25 per cent increase in the ratio of agricultural wages to industrial wages between 1940 and 1947—but again there are specification problems.

$$S_{lt} = 265 \cdot 240 + 5 \cdot 366 \left(\frac{W_a}{W_I} \right)_{t-1} \qquad \bar{R}^2 = 0 \cdot 389$$
$$\phantom{S_{lt} = 265 \cdot 240 + } (2 \cdot 443) \phantom{\left(\frac{W_a}{W_I} \right)_{t-1}} \qquad d = 0 \cdot 729$$

V. Agricultural Wages

Over the post-war period agricultural wages have averaged about 70 per cent of industrial wages compared with only 50 per cent prior to 1939. The persistence of a wage differential between agricultural and industrial employment can be explained by differences in the quality of labour, non-pecuniary emoluments, or an immobile rural labour force, but why should the wage differential dramatically narrow? This could be explained by a shift in the demand curve for agricultural labour, during the war period, greater than the shift in the aggregate demand curve for labour. This is very likely since there was an immense government intervention in agriculture aimed at stimulating a rapid growth in production through grants and subsidies. This narrowing of the wage differential due to differential demand adjustments would be reinforced by the greater inelasticity of agricultural labour supply relative to the industrial labour supply. Thus Reder suggests that in times of excess demand for labour higher wage occupations can recruit from lower wage occupations and thus limit the resulting wage inflation. However, for agriculture, at the bottom end of the wage scale, there is no possibility of increasing recruitment from industries or occupations lower down the scale so that the increase in wages will be relatively higher. Reder's theory will also predict that the differentials within agriculture will narrow as excess demand for labour increases—provided that there is an equal shift in the demand curves for different skills within agriculture.

V.1. DETERMINANTS OF AGRICULTURAL WAGE ADJUSTMENT†

This section reports on some attempts to explain changes in agricultural wage rates and earnings in terms of economic variables. The importance of such an analysis lies (1) in agricultural price analysis and prediction,‡ (2) in the analysis and prediction of investment in machines by agriculture and (3) in the analysis and prediction of labour migration from agriculture.

(a) *Institutional Background*

During the inter-war period a series of county wages committees together with a central wages board was set up under the Agricultural Wages (Regulation) Act 1924. In 1940 a national minimum was adopted under amending legislation and in 1942 all powers were devolved to a central board under defence regulations. A further act in 1947 made

† This section is based on an article by Cowling and Metcalf. The reader is referred to that article for a comprehensive analysis of results—only the important features of the work are considered here: An analysis of the determinants of wage inflation in agriculture, *Manchester School*, May 1965, pp. 179–204.

‡ Movements in wages and expectations of future movements enter into the bargaining involved in the Annual Price Review involving the National Farmers' Union and the Ministry of Agriculture.

the transfer of powers permanent and in 1948 the 1924 and 1947 acts were consolidated. The present Agricultural Wages Board, which stems from this legislation, consists of employers' and employees' representatives together with independents nominated by the Ministry of Agriculture. The employers' representatives are in fact nominated by the National Farmers Union with the National Union of Agricultural Workers representing the interests of the other side. The Board determines minimum wages and statutory hours of work and these decisions do not have to be endorsed by the Ministry of Agriculture.† There is no negotiated wage structure although occupational differentials do exist. The difference between the minimum negotiated wage rate and actual earnings is accounted for by premium payments, bonuses and overtime, together with some allowance for payments in kind. During the period 1948 to 1963 the average rate of growth of wage rates was 5·06 per cent and the average rate of growth of earnings 5·54 per cent giving an increasing absolute, and percentage, disparity between wages and earnings.

(b) *The Model of Wage Adjustment*

If we make the realistic assumption of an agricultural labour market in disequilibrium then the existence of excess demand (or excess supply) will set up a dynamic wage-adjustment process which can be written down as a reaction function in which the rate of change of money wages in agriculture (ΔW_a) is determined by excess demand for labour in agriculture $(D_l - S_l)$ and a set of relevant exogenous variables (Z).

$$\Delta W_a = f\left[(D_l - S_l); Z\right]$$

It is important to appreciate at this stage that the explanatory variables in the labour supply and demand equations, as discussed earlier, are components of excess demand and therefore have been taken account of in this wage adjustment equation. Any additional variables can only be justified on the basis of their influence on wage inflation independent of the forces determining labour supply and demand. Such variables

† For a description of the institutional structure of the wage bargaining process the reader is referred to an article by F. D. Mills, The National Union of Agricultural Workers, *Journal of Agricultural Economics*, Vol. 16, 2, December 1964, pp. 230–53.

considered in this analysis are the rate of change in the cost of living index (ΔP), the rate of change in the level of excess demand ($\Delta(D_l - S_l)$), the level of agricultural profits (Y_a), the level and rate of change of unionization in agriculture (UN_a and ΔUN_a) and a dummy or "zero–one" variable for national wages policy (DU). The complete model, for each alternative measure of wage change, will be a single equation one—we assume all the variables on the right-hand side are predetermined. Thus we are saying that the rate of wage inflation in agriculture will not affect the current cost of living, or excess demand for agricultural labour, or agricultural profits or unionization in agriculture. In the case of profits and excess demand, where the above implied one-way relationship may be unrealistic, we will use lagged values of the variables. We will assume there is no important feedback of agricultural wage movements on retail price movements since British agricultural products form only a small component of the retail price index. Also because of the agricultural price support mechanism there is no direct link between agricultural wages and retail prices of agricultural products. The fairly reasonable assumption of a completely elastic supply of imported agricultural products would lead to a similar conclusion.

(c) *Notes on the Variables*

(i) *Excess demand for agricultural labour.* This variable comes directly out of dynamic price analysis which postulates a positive relationship between the level of excess demand for a commodity or factor and the rate of change of the price of that commodity or factor. Most studies of wage adjustment have used unemployment as an indicator of excess demand and a few have used information on unfilled vacancies as well. This analysis will look at both measures. If unemployment is used then we would expect a non-linear relationship since unemployment will never fall to zero but within the range of the data a linear approximation may be equally acceptable. We can interpret the rate of change of unemployment variable as representing expectations of the future state of the labour market.

(ii) *Cost of living.* Changes in the cost of living are emphasized by the

N.U.A.W. as one of the bases of their case for wage increases when entering into negotiations with the wages board and therefore movements in the cost of living should explain part of the behaviour in wage rates. It is not so clear why cost of living should be considered as a determinant of movements in actual earnings, which result from bargaining at the farm level, except indirectly through movements in wage rates influencing movements in earnings.

(iii) *Aggregate agricultural profits.* It seems reasonable to hypothesize than union wage demands, and the vigour with which they are presented, will be partly explained by the unions' evaluation of the employers capacity to pay as measured by the level of profits in the previous year. Presumably it will also influence employer attitudes towards granting wage increases. Evidence from other sectors on the relationship between wages and profits is conflicting. Cowling's results suggest that, in the case of the Irish economy, profits appear relevant where the industry is highly concentrated with a highly organized labour force, but in industries, like agriculture, which are atomistic with relatively un-organized labour, profits do not appear so important in the wage adjustment process.

(iv) *Trade union activity.* Recent work on aggregate wage adjustment has suggested that the rate of change of trade union membership, intended as a proxy for union pushfulness is an important variable. The National Union of Agricultural Workers is peculiar in that it is one of the few unions in the post-war period that has increased its membership as a percentage of the labour force. It has in fact maintained its membership despite the declining level of employment in agriculture. The membership has settled at about 130,000 and the level of unionization has increased to about 18 per cent. The Transport and General Workers Union also have about 20,000 agricultural members. However, the total level of unionization remains low compared with other industries and the unions face obvious difficulties of organization with the large number of employers and the wide geographical dispersion of its membership, although there is a heavy concentration in the Eastern arable areas.

The main argument used by the union in negotiations is that of comparability with other wage earners. That their efforts in this direction have failed is evidenced by the fact that throughout the post-war period there has been no consistent move toward parity with industrial wages. The level of industrial wages is reflected in the excess demand variable (since industrial wage is one of the determinants of agricultural labour supply) and in the cost of living index since price adjustment is partly explained by industrial wage movements.

(v) *Wages policy.* The post-war period has included a number of years in which the government has actively intervened in the wage bargaining process. During the period up to 1963 two years stand out as being quite distinct—1949 and 1950 when there was a general union acceptance of a Labour government directed wage freeze. This wage freeze will be allowed for by using a dummy variable taking on a value of one for these two observations and zero in all other years.

(d) *Results*

(i) *Rate of change of wage rates.* Various formulations of the wage adjustment relationship only explain about 50 per cent of the variation in weekly wage rates. The regression equation reported below shows agricultural unemployment in the previous year ($U_{a(t-1)}$) to be a significant determinant of weekly rates with the wage freeze coefficient suggesting a reduction of nearly 3 per cent in wage inflation, given the excess demand situation in 1949–50. The coefficient on unemployment is of expected sign and indicates that a shift from an unemployment rate of 1 to 2 per cent will reduce wage rate inflation by about 2 per cent.

$$\Delta W_{at}^r = 6\cdot926 - 2\cdot062\, U_{at-1} - 2\cdot914\, DU$$
$$\phantom{\Delta W_{at}^r = 6\cdot926 -\,} (0\cdot891) \phantom{U_{at-1} -\,} (0\cdot718)$$
$$\bar{R}^2 = 0\cdot517$$
$$d\ = 1\cdot789$$

The other variables mentioned in the previous discussion do not appear to have a significant influence on weekly rates but the result for hourly rates reported below suggests that cost of living changes and the level of unionization may have an impact on the total wage rate–hours bargain.

$$\Delta W^r_{a(h)t} = -1 \cdot 886 - 3 \cdot 251\ U_{at} + 0 \cdot 280\ \Delta P_{rt-1} - 0 \cdot 002\ Y_{at-1}$$
$$\phantom{\Delta W^r_{a(h)t} = -1\cdot886}(1 \cdot 239) (0 \cdot 126) (0 \cdot 005)$$

$$+0 \cdot 591\ UN_t - 1 \cdot 861\ DU \bar{R}^2 = 0 \cdot 626$$
$$(0 \cdot 308) (0 \cdot 635) d = 2 \cdot 007$$

The coefficient on unemployment is bigger (in absolute value) than the coefficient for the weekly rate equation, as might be expected. Cost of living changes have a significant but minor effect—a 3 per cent change in prices giving less than a 1 per cent change in wage rates. The profit variable (Y_{at-1}) has a non-significant coefficient.

(ii) *Rate of change of earnings.* The economic and union variables we have discussed seem to be more relevant in the determination of changes in actual earnings than they were in determining wage rates. In the case of weekly earnings we find unemployment, price changes, level of profits, unionization changes (marginally significant) and wage freeze, all to be significant variables with expected signs.

$$\Delta W_{at} = 3 \cdot 030 - 3 \cdot 317\ U_{at} + 0 \cdot 267\ \Delta P_{rt-1} + 0 \cdot 013\ Y_{at-1}$$
$$\phantom{\Delta W_{at} = 3\cdot030}(0 \cdot 882) (0 \cdot 104) (0 \cdot 005)$$

$$+ 0 \cdot 101\ \Delta UN_{at-1} - 1 \cdot 776\ DU$$
$$(0 \cdot 058) (0 \cdot 596)$$

$$\bar{R}^2 = 0 \cdot 734$$
$$d = 2 \cdot 282$$

The coefficient on profits suggests that an increase in aggregate agricultural net income of £100 million will result in a more than 1 per cent rise in wage earnings the following year. Compared with the observed year-to-year changes in unionization the coefficient on ΔUN indicates that this variable has not had an important impact on wage earnings.

Results were very similar for hourly earnings except that the explanatory power of the model was increased to about 80 per cent.

Some experiments were made with replacements for the profits variables. First an alternative profits variable was included which was derived from the Farm Management Survey results. This did not prove as satisfactory as the aggregate estimate of profits used previously which may be due to sampling problems. Second a price series for aggregate agricultural output was used but again it did not prove as satisfactory in explaining wage movements as profits did.

(e) *Conclusions*

The results suggest that the variables considered do a pretty good job in explaining movements in actual wage earnings in agriculture but have not done so well in explaining wage rates. Our variables have included both market variables and union or institutional variables so that the results suggest either the criteria of the Wages Board for evaluating wage claims are rather arbitrary or that we have left out relevant economic and institutional variables. The structure of the Agricultural Wages Board might suggest that the first hypothesis is plausible. With disagreement between N.F.U. and N.U.A.W. representatives the majority of decisions are taken by the independents and it seems unlikely that they persistently support the one against the other. One specific conclusion coming out of the study is that the level of excess demand (represented by unemployment rate) is consistently important in determining agricultural wage movements. This is at variance with some recent evidence of aggregate and industry level wage adjustment and probably reflects the fact that agriculture approximates most closely to a perfectly competitive labour market. Results for Scotland and Ireland suggest that there also, where agricultural unemployment averages over 2 and 4 per cent respectively, excess demand is again persistently significant but this time with smaller coefficients (in absolute values). This supports the notion of a non-linear relation between wage inflation and unemployment with wages becoming progressively less sensitive as unemployment increases.

VI. Regional Labour Supply

We have already looked at the market for agricultural labour during both the post-war and inter-war periods using aggregate time series data for England and Wales. Here we will focus attention on the regional supply of agricultural labour in recent years, partly because regions are of interest in themselves and partly because regional observations give a richer source of variation in industrial unemployment rates and relative wages in agriculture and industry—factors which determine labour supply to the agricultural sector. We are looking specifically at supply (1) because of the lack of regional price information—information relevant to regional demand for agricultural labour, and (2) since migration from agriculture is ultimately a supply phenomenon with shifts in the demand curve causing variations in the ratio of employed to unemployed agricultural labour: if industrial prospects are poor migration may still be held back.

VI.1. A MODEL OF REGIONAL LABOUR SUPPLY

We only have data over a limited time series on regional wage earnings so that rather than try and estimate supply relationships for each region with very few observations we will pool the information from different regions and fit a single relationship. To do this we have to put the dependent variable into a comparable form and this we do by defining it as the rate of growth of the regional agricultural labour supply $(\dot{S}_l/S_l)$. Adapting from our aggregate model of labour supply we would then have on the right-hand side the growth rate of agricultural wages $(\dot{W}_a/W_a)$, the growth rate of industrial wages $(\dot{W}_I/W_I)$ and the growth rate of industrial unemployment $(\dot{U}_I/U_I)$. Thus we would be left with the proposition that the number of migrants leaving agriculture (i.e. the change in supply after allowing for changes in the balance between recruitment and retirement) is not affected by the level of agricultural wages relative to industrial wages and is not affected by the number of job opportunities in industry. This would lead us to expect that the migration rate would be the same whether agricultural wages were 50 per cent (the pre-war percentage) or 70 per cent (the post-war percentage) of industrial wages so long as the rate of growth of the two were the same, and also that the migration rate would be the same whether the industrial unemployment rate were 1 or 10 per cent. This is clearly untenable and one could make a good case for including the levels of these variables in the regional supply equation as well as their rates of growth. The other thing we must allow for, if we pool information over time from different regions, is the existence of different parameters on the included variables or at least differences in autonomous migration rates in different regions. One explanation for different autonomous rates of regional migration would be differences in inter-regional migration reflecting differences in labour market conditions in contiguous regions. To allow for such effects we will include regional zero–one variables (R_j). We also allow for regional differences in the age (A_{aj}) and educational structure (E_{aj}) of the agricultural labour force to influence the rate of outmigration. A lower age and higher education should allow for easier transfer to alternative occupations. The formal model for the *jth* region is then:

$$\frac{\dot{S}_{Ij}}{S_{Ij}} = f\left(W_{aj}; \frac{\dot{W}_{aj}}{W_{aj}}; W_{Ij}; \frac{\dot{W}_{Ij}}{W_{Ij}}; U_{Ij}; \frac{\dot{U}_{Ij}}{U_{Ij}}; A_{aj}; E_{aj}; R_j\right)$$

VI.2. NOTES ON THE VARIABLES

All variables are defined on a former Ministry of Labour definition of regions, these being: London and South East (r_0), Eastern and Southern (r_1), South West (r_2), Midlands (r_3), Yorkshire and Lincolnshire (r_4), North West (r_5), North (r_6), Scotland (r_7), Wales (r_8), and Northern Ireland (r_9). Labour supply in this analysis was taken to be simply full-time workers in the industry plus agricultural unemployment. It is the lack of information on regional agricultural and industrial earnings which limits this regional analysis. Regional average industrial earnings have been published since 1960, agricultural regional earnings are only just beginning to be published but the Ministry of Agriculture provided us with unpublished estimates for three years and the other two years were derived from the England and Wales average, with separate estimates for Scotland and Northern Ireland. There was in fact considerable variation in the ratio of agricultural to industrial earnings among the regions, with regions of excess labour demand giving agricultural earnings closer to parity with industrial than regions where there is a chronic excess supply of labour.

The age and education variables are derived from the 1951 Census of Population which is obviously unsatisfactory but it was found impossible to get the material out of the 1961 Census. The age variable is defined as the percentage of the occupied farm population between 15 and 34 years of age in 1951, making then between 24 and 43 in 1960 an age range which we might expect to cover the majority of migrants. The problem remaining is the problem of retirement which is picked up in our supply variable and which will be negatively associated with the age variable. The education variable is defined as the proportion of the occupied farm population who had attained a terminal education age of 16 or over in 1951. The data on age and education is given in Table 3.5.

TABLE 3.5. AGE STRUCTURE AND EDUCATIONAL
LEVELS OF HIRED AGRICULTURAL WORKERS BY REGION
(1951)

Region	Age*	Education†
London and South East	36·9	10·9
Eastern and Southern	38·2	8·7
South West	38·8	10·9
Midlands	42·3	8·7
Yorks and Lincs	42·9	7·5
North West	43·0	6·9
North	44·9	7·3
Scotland	36·2	6·0
Wales	40·5	9·3
N. Ireland	36·1	n.a.

* The age variable is defined as the percentage of occupied farm population who were between the ages of 15 and 34 in 1951.

† The education variable is defined as the proportion of occupied agricultural workers who had attained a terminal education age of 16 or over in 1951.

A measure of industrialization was also considered as a relevant variable at the regional level but the variable synthesized, which was the ratio of industrial employment to agricultural employment, proved to be non-significant. If we are trying to measure the proximity of non-farm jobs then a better measure would probably be the ratio of industrial to agricultural employment *in rural areas*.

Two other variables were brought in; the ratio of agricultural wages to agricultural product prices to reflect the different strength of the push factor in different regions and a trend term to allow for the possibility that a particular level of excess demand for labour in the economy will result in a particular *number* of migrants leaving agriculture, and not a particular ratio of the agricultural labour force. With the declining agricultural labour force a specific number of migrants represents an increasing percentage of the agricultural labour force.

VI.3. RESULTS

The equation below gives the least squares estimates of the migration relationship formulated above except that rates of growth in wages have not been included because we have very poor information on these for agriculture. The wage levels in agriculture and industry are expressed as a ratio and age and education variables are excluded as non-significant after some experimentation. Also Northern Ireland is excluded since it appears to have a unique relationship, perhaps because the G.B. labour market is more relevant than the Northern Ireland one in decisions to leave Northern Irish agriculture. The regional observations are taken annually over the period 1960 through 1964 giving us forty-five observations in total.

$$\frac{\dot{S}_{Ij}}{S_{Ij}} = \begin{array}{c} 49 \cdot 900 \\ (16 \cdot 677) \end{array} - \begin{array}{c} 1 \cdot 793 \\ (0 \cdot 896) \end{array} U_{Ij} - \begin{array}{c} 0 \cdot 019 \\ (0 \cdot 008) \end{array} \dot{U}_{Ij} - \begin{array}{c} 0 \cdot 559 \\ (0 \cdot 199) \end{array} \frac{(W_{aj})}{W_{ij}}$$

$$- \begin{array}{c} 0 \cdot 070 \\ (0 \cdot 119) \end{array} \frac{(W_{aj})}{P_{aj}} + \begin{array}{c} 1 \cdot 025 \\ (0 \cdot 733) \end{array} T$$

$$+ r_j \begin{pmatrix} \text{Regional} \\ \text{dummies} \end{pmatrix} + V_j \qquad\qquad R^2 = 0 \cdot 669$$

About two-thirds of the variation in regional migration rates from agriculture are explained by the model. All the coefficients have the expected signs except the agricultural wage-price ratio. The coefficient is, however, non-significant and this can be explained by the close collinearity with the trend variable. Without a trend term the wage-price ratio is significant and positive but the coefficient may partly reflect the trend phenomenon we were trying to allow for. The coefficients on U_j, $\dot{U}_j$ and W_{aj}/W_{ij} which are of expected sign are also significant. The regional coefficients appear to divide the regions into a High Activity and a Low Activity Group, with the High Activity

Group having small and non-significant coefficients and the Low Activity Group having large, positive and significant coefficients, suggesting that migration rates from agriculture in these regions would be bigger than the rate predicted by the variables in the model. This may mean that the underlying parameters for the two groups of regions are different. Some experimentation tended to confirm this hypothesis particularly in the case of the level of regional unemployment where the coefficient was very much bigger in High Activity regions. The model has been simplified (by omitting the wage and price variables), the time period for estimation has been extended and predictions are being made of migration rates over the period up to 1972 as part of the work of the Economic Development Committee for agriculture. We do of course have to make predictions about the course of industrial unemployment in the economy before we can get predictions of agricultural migrants but we can at least begin to follow through the likely implications of changes in government policy relating to the national economy.†

† For a more complete treatment of the original analysis of regional labour supply see Keith Cowling and David Metcalf, Labour transfer from agriculture: a regional analysis, *Manchester School*, March 1968. For some revised and updated results, together with predictions of labour outflow from agriculture through 1972 see Keith Cowling, Agricultural labour supply and the business cycle: some regional predictions, paper delivered at the Symposium on Agricultural Manpower, National Economic Development Office.

Appendix

TABLE A.1. LABOUR SUPPLY 1946–64: DATA ON THE VARIABLES

	S_{1t}	W_{at}	W_{at}/P_{rt}	W_{It}	W_{It}/P_{rt}	U_{It}
1946	700·800	100·0	100·0	100·0	100·0	2·16
1947	703·213	108·7	102·7	105·9	100·0	2·89
1948	657·781	119·9	105·5	116·0	102·0	1·50
1949	663·066	123·7	105·8	120·2	102·8	1·36
1950	650·947	127·1	105·8	125·2	104·2	1·33
1951	622·186	134·5	102·0	138·7	105·2	1·04
1952	608·260	145·9	101·7	149·6	104·2	1·84
1953	592·489	154·2	104·2	159·7	107·8	1·48

TABLE A.1 (*cont.*)

	S_{1t}	W_{at}	W_{at}/P_{rt}	W_{It}	W_{It}/P_{rt}	U_{It}
1954	572·916	165·4	109·8	170·6	113·2	1·18
1955	549·551	177·6	113·0	185·7	118·2	0·93
1956	523·395	187·8	113·9	200·0	121·3	1·06
1957	518·410	202·4	118·1	209·2	122·1	1·30
1958	502·527	213·0	120·6	215·1	121·8	1·91
1959	495·650	224·0	126·4	222·7	125·6	1·92
1960	475·037	229·5	128·1	238·7	133·2	1·39
1961	450·686	243·6	131·6	252·1	136·2	1·33
1962	431·923	252·9	131·1	258·8	134·2	1·83
1963	418·629	269·7	136·2	276·5	139·6	2·24
1964	397·993	285·4				1·60

N.B. Variables are as defined in the text.

TABLE A.2. LABOUR DEMAND 1946–64: DATA ON THE VARIABLES

	$W_{ca(t)}/P_{m(t)}$	$W_{ca(t)}/P_{c(t)}$	$P_{a(t)}/P_{m(t)}$	$P_{a(t)}/P_{c(t)}$
1946	100·0	100·0	100·0	100·0
1947	112·0	107·8	109·6	105·5
1948	111·8	112·3	101·8	102·3
1949	114·9	112·9	103·7	101·9
1950	115·4	105·3	103·5	94·4
1951	108·0	98·6	102·2	93·4
1952	105·5	95·7	94·8	86·0
1953	104·2	98·8	89·0	84·4
1954	107·3	102·3	85·8	81·8
1955	108·1	103·9	87·7	84·3
1956	110·1	106·6	83·1	80·4
1957	111·1	108·7	75·9	74·21
1958	112·4	114·8	74·7	76·3
1959	115·5	117·8	70·3	71·7
1960	112·5	118·0	63·4	66·5
1961	120·5	121·8	64·5	65·1
1962	122·5	122·9	63·1	63·5
1963	128·3	124·7	63·0	61·2

N.B. (1) The tractor price to wage earnings ratio variable $(W_{a(t-1)}/P_{T(t)})$ is as used in Chapter 4.

(2) Labour demand (D_1) is assumed equal to labour supply (S_1) and is given in Table A.1.

TABLE A.3. AGRICULTURAL WAGE ADJUSTMENT
1946–63: DATA ON THE VARIABLES

	$W^{\cdot}{}_t$	$W^r_{a(h)t}$	U_{at}	P_{rt}
1946	100	100	0·285	100
1947	112	113	0·424	101
1948	124·5	126	0·663	104
1949	128	130	0·697	109
1950	130	134	0·453	113
1951	137·5	141·5	0·535	117
1952	150	154·5	0·694	132
1953	157·5	162·5	0·671	138
1954	166·5	171	0·543	140
1955	173	178	0·602	146
1956	184	189·5	0·862	156
1957	195·5	201	1·160	162
1958	207	213	1·261	169
1959	215·5	222	0·990	172
1960	219·5	230	0·793	172
1961	231·0	243	1·063	175
1962	239·0	251·5	1·363	183
1963	251·8	265	1·066	187

TABLE A.4. REGULAR FULL-TIME AGRICULTURAL EMPLOYEES BY REGION 1960–4

Region \ Year	1960	1961	1962	1963	1964	Actual decline 1960–4	Percentage decline 1960–4
London and South East	66,145	61,952	59,071	56,830	52,608	13,537	20·5
Eastern and Southern	96,207	92,156	89,327	84,261	79,609	16,598	17·3
South West	52,236	49,427	47,268	45,696	42,550	9,686	18·5
Midland	59,977	56,219	55,121	53,905	49,963	10,014	16·7
Yorks. and Lincs.	53,306	50,073	48,781	48,132	43,701	9,605	18·0
North West	22,546	21,529	20,936	20,518	19,283	3,263	14·5
Northern	29,820	28,402	27,604	26,941	25,515	4,305	14·4
Scotland	66,988	65,634	62,200	59,600	55,685	11,303	16·9
Wales	26,262	23,875	22,399	21,823	20,244	6,018	22·9
Northern Ireland	32,695	30,091	29,700	27,200	25,580	7,115	21·8
United Kingdom	504,695	478,854	458,909	442,968	414,389	90,306	17·9

CHAPTER 4

ENGINEERING TECHNOLOGY

ONE of the most significant developments in United Kingdom agriculture in the post-war period (1947 onwards) has been the mechanization of many farming tasks. It is the primary concern of this chapter to analyse the extent of and the reasons for this mechanization process. However, to give perspective to the post-war growth in the use of farm-machinery, we first sketch out the important developments in mechanization that occurred before 1940. We then go on to look at the trends in the use of machines and power sources on farms over the period 1948 to 1965–7. Particular attention is paid to growth in the number and quality of tractors used: this being the most important single aspect of the mechanization that has occurred so far. A statistical, time series analysis of the demand for farm tractors, over the period 1948–65, forms the basis for our explanation of why this mechanization process has occurred. Here we highlight the theoretical basis of the analysis and the interpretation and implications of the results rather than the statistical methodology. On the basis of the results from the tractor study, hypotheses are put forward to explain the trends in the use of other machines. We conclude by looking at the supply conditions for agricultural machinery. The agricultural machinery industry in the United Kingdom has grown rapidly in the post-war period in order to supply not only the growing domestic market but also foreign markets and in fact, exports now account for some 60 to 70 per cent of total production. However, our main concern is with salient aspects of the domestic market—such as the degree of concentration within the industry and the system of distribution and marketing.

I. Early Developments in Mechanization†

The pioneering steps in the mechanization of agriculture occurred well over 2000 years ago with the harnessing of animal power to the cultivation of land. However, for centuries after, little progress in mechanization was made beyond minor improvements to animal-drawn ploughs and harrows. Then in the 18th and 19th centuries there were several major inventions of new farm machines which were gradually adopted by United Kingdom agriculture. The first new machine to be developed was the seed drill in the 1720's (by Jethro Tull). This was followed by the prototype of the threshing machine at the end of the 18th century; then came the all-iron plough with a chilled iron share in the 1800's (invented by Robert Ransome) and the reaping machine in the 1820's (invented by Patrick Bell). In the latter part of the 19th century the haytedder and then the reaper–binder were successfully developed. In addition, the steam engine was introduced into agriculture, initially as a stationary power source for barn machinery and threshers in the middle of the 19th century, but later as a mobile power source for ploughing.

The innovation and adoption of these new machines during the 19th century and the early part of the 20th century was no doubt a consequence of the continued commercialization of United Kingdom agriculture which was already prevalent in the 18th century. In the 17th and 18th centuries the open field system rapidly declined, as did common lands, under the enclosure movement. This led to farming for cash profit and the employment of labourers who were paid, at least partly, in cash. The root drill made possible the cultivation of a new crop—turnips and other roots—which was an integral part of rotations to maintain the fertility of the soil and keep the land "clean" from weeds. The economic effects of roots were twofold—they alleviated the need for keeping one-third to one-quarter of the land in idle fallow while at the same time they provided a new winter feed which revolutionized the keeping of livestock. The other mechanical innovations were mainly

† This section is based upon material contained in the following references: C. S. Orwin and E. H. Whetham, *History of British Agriculture 1846–1919*, Longmans, 1964. Central Office of Information, *The British Agricultural Engineering Industry*, Pamphlet R5501, 1963. C. Culpin, *Farm Machinery*, 5th ed., Crosby Lockwood & Son Ltd., 1957.

cost reducing, by lowering the demand for labour. This was particularly true of reapers and binders which allowed farmers to harvest cereals and hay using only their own staff and without recourse to seasonal gangs of labour. The adoption process was helped by the dissemination of knowledge about the new machines through the machinery demonstrations and tests held at agricultural shows.

A major development, from 1840 onwards, associated with the adoption of new machinery by farmers, was the growth of machinery manufacturing firms in the industrial centres and the decline in the role of the village blacksmith as an implement maker. By the time of the 1914–18 war these firms manufactured a wide range of equipment, mainly for use in the production of cereals and grass, with up to 75 per cent of total sales going for export. However, the next major innovation in the mechanization of United Kingdom agriculture—the provision of a mobile source of power for draught purposes—was still to come. At this time, the million and more working horses provided the main power source, supplemented by steam power which was used mainly for stationary tasks.

Although the internal combustion engined tractor was developed in the United States in the 1890's, it was not until 1917, with the invention of the "Fordson" tractor and its subsequent importation into the United Kingdom, that the tractor provided an alternative to horses as a source of draught power. However, few tractors were manufactured in the United Kingdom until 1933 when medium powered tractors were produced, in England, by the Ford Motor Company. Two major improvements of tractors occurred in the 1930's which stimulated their rapid adoption after 1939. These were: firstly, the development of satisfactory pneumatic tyres; secondly, the invention of a combined linkage and hydraulic control system by Harry Ferguson. Between 1921 and 1939 there was a gradual adoption of tractors, the number increasing, in England and Wales, from around 2000 to 55,000. Consequently, the number of working horses, in England and Wales, declined over the period from 789,000 in 1921 to 601,000 in 1939. However, the widespread adoption of the tractor and the application of machinery to all facets of farming—not just to cultivation and harvesting of cereals and hay—was really initiated during and after World War II. The rapid growth in mechanization and the develop-

ment of the agricultural engineering industry between 1939 and the
present forms the basis of the rest of the chapter.

II. Growth in Tractor Stock and Change in Quality

The most significant development in the mechanization of United
Kingdom agriculture since 1939 has been the growth of the stock of
tractors on farms, from about 56,000 in 1939 to over 450,000 by 1964.
Not only has this growth in tractor numbers been important in providing
a mobile power source, but also the adoption of the tractor has led to
the concomitant development of many other types of machinery which
are used in conjunction with the tractor.

The growth in the tractor stock led to a rapid decline in horses as a
power source so that even by 1946 horses provided only 10 per cent of
the draught power on farms.† The growth of the stock of tractors in
the United Kingdom and the decline in the number of working horses
in Great Britain is illustrated in Fig. 4.1 below; the number of tractors
referring to the September of each year, the number of horses to the
June of each year.

The elements of an S-shaped growth curve with regard to tractor
stock is clear from Fig. 4.1—a pattern which is common in the adoption
of most innovations. Numbers increased very slowly at first until 1940,
when adoption became rapid as tractors were introduced onto most
farms, followed by a slower rate of growth in the middle to late fifties
until, finally, a ceiling level was reached in the early sixties. In fact,
tractor numbers actually started to decline from 1965 onwards. The
graph also illustrates the decline in the stock of working horses from
1920 to the present-day negligible figure.

The slowing down in the growth of tractor numbers on farms and
their present-day decline can be explained partly by the improvement
in the quality of new tractors since 1948. Existing tractors have been
replaced by new, better quality, more productive tractors, with the result that the number of tractors used has declined in recent years. The
extent of quality change in new tractors has been substantial over the
post-war period: an index estimating the year to year change in the
overall quality of new tractors rising from 62·6 in 1948 to 137·8 in 1965

† Central Office of Information, *op. cit.*, pamphlet R5001.

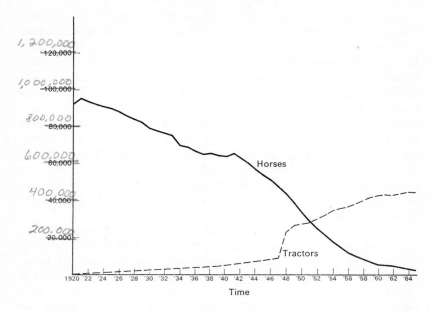

Fig. 4.1. Tractors and horses

with 1956 = 100.† Much of this quality change has been in the form of a higher horsepower and it is estimated that the average horsepower of new tractors sold rose from 24·1 h.p. in 1948 to 49·5 h.p. in 1965.‡ Consequently, the total horsepower of the stock of tractors has increased more rapidly over the post-war period than the number of tractors and is still tending to rise. It is estimated that the total horsepower of the tractor stock increased from around 4·45 million in 1947 to over 18 million in 1965 with an increase in the *average* horsepower of tractors on farms from around 22 h.p. per tractor to around 40 h.p. per tractor.§

† See A. J. Rayner, *op.cit.*, p. 291. This series is presented in the Appendix to this chapter.
‡ See A. J. Rayner, *An Econometric Analysis of the Demand for Farm Tractors*, Dept. of Agricultural Economics, University of Manchester, Bulletin 113, Appendix B, 1966.
§ *Ibid.*, p. 37

Many other significant quality improvements have also taken place. A major improvement to tractors during the war and in the immediate post-war period was the incorporation of hydraulic lift, three point linkage and power-take-off into the standard tractor.† The hydraulic linkage allowed machinery to be attached to, rather than trailed by, the tractor, whilst the power-take-off powered machinery directly from the tractor engine and thus avoided the need for a separate engine on the machine itself. Subsequent developments included considerable sophistication and improvement of the original hydraulic and power-take-off systems, improved transmission with a wide range of gears, disc brakes, power steering and differential lock. In addition, the percentage of new tractors sold with diesel engines—as compared with petrol or vaporizing oil engines—rose from 4 per cent in 1948 to the total market in 1965.‡

From the viewpoint of economic analysis, the stock of tractors should be measured in such a way that it reflects, over time, the flow of tractor services. Clearly, the input of tractor services to United Kingdom agriculture has increased far more over the post-war period than is signified by the growth in tractor numbers, because tractors have improved substantially in quality. Measuring the stock of tractors in terms of the total available horsepower which they provide is a better measure than tractor numbers but still ignores the many other quality improvements which have been incorporated into tractors over the post-war period. However, as was shown in Chapter 2, if we can obtain a constant quality price index for an input and we then deflate the value of the input by this index we obtain a measure of the input which reflects changes in the *overall* quality of the input as well as changes in the quantity of the input. Consequently, the value of tractor stock (net of depreciation) deflated by a constant quality price index for new tractors is a measure of tractor stock which should reflect changes in the flow of available tractor services. Strictly speaking, this price index should be lagged so as to reflect the average age of tractor stock. An estimate of annual tractor stock, over the period 1947–65, which is measured in

† Initially, only in tractors manufactured by Ferguson & Co., but by the early fifties the list price for all new tractors included these features.

‡ The main quality difference between a diesel engine and a petrol or t.v.o. engine is in fuel economy: diesel engines use a cheaper fuel and have a better performance at the same rated h.p.

this way is given in the Appendix to this chapter. This series indicates that the value of tractor stock in constant quality prices rose by nearly fivefold between 1947 and 1965 whereas the number of tractors on farms rose by less than two and a half times.

Since tractors depreciate over time, we may assume that a proportion of the tractor services from the stock of tractors is lost each year. Farmers maintain and adjust the flow of tractor services over time by their purchases of new tractors. Clearly, gross investment in new tractors should also be measured so that it reflects all the quality improvements which have been incorporated into new tractors. Thus, an appropriate measure of gross investment over time is the value of purchases of new tractors deflated by a constant quality price index for new tractors. A series for annual gross investment over the period 1948–65 which is measured in this way is given in the Appendix. This series indicates that the value of gross investment in constant quality prices in 1965 was between two and a half to three times that of 1948. In contrast, the number of new tractors purchased in 1948 (about 44,000) was a little higher than the number bought in 1965 (about 41,600).

III. Trends in the Use of Other Machinery

We may classify the machinery, other than tractors, used on United Kingdom farms into the following six main groups:† (i) cultivating machinery, (ii) sowing and fertilizer distributing machinery, (iii) harvesting machinery, (iv) barn and farmyard machinery, (v) vehicles (excluding tractors) and (vi) dairy machinery. An indication of the post-war changes in the stock of farm machines represented by groups (i) to (v) inclusive is given by the following estimate of the value of the stock of these machines in 1949/50 (June to May year) compared with 1966/7.‡ The estimate measures the value of stock in terms of the cost in current prices of replacing the stock of machines by new machines. This is not the "true" value of stock in current prices since we must allow for the fact that the stock is composed of machines, of different ages, which have depreciated in value. However, assuming constant rates of depreciation and no change over time in the average age of

† Following the classification used by: Board of Trade, *Business Monitor*.
‡ Data source: Author's estimate, see Appendix, Table A.2.

each machine in the stock, this estimate does indicate in terms of *current* prices how stock has changed over the period. It indicates that the value of stock, measured in this way, rose from £367·5 million to £901·8 million over the period.† Without detailed analysis, it is impossible to say how much of this increase in value of two and a half times was the result of an increase in the number and quality of machines and how much was a result of non-quality increases in the prices of new machines. Such an analysis would not only have to estimate a constant quality price index for each machine, but also would have to allow for the changing proportions over time of each machine in the total stock of machines. Price inflation in new tractors was of the order of 25 per cent over the period and price inflation in other machines was unlikely to be much different. Consequently, there has been a significant increase in the stock of machines on farms in the post-war period. Out of the global total (excluding tractors), the most rapid increases were in harvesting machinery (which was in 1966/7 the largest value category) and in sowing and distribution machinery.‡ We shall now look at the important post-1939 trends in the stocks of individual machines, particularly concentrating on those machines which were innovated in the period. Because of lack of data, we shall simply look at the changes in the *number* of these machines and hence underestimate, to a greater or lesser extent, the actual changes in stock because we shall be ignoring quality change. In addition, we shall look at the changes in stocks in England and Wales only, with the expectation that the pattern of change in Scotland and Northern Ireland is similar but with differences in timing.§

III.1. COMBINE HARVESTERS AND BINDERS

Figures 4.2 and 4.3 below illustrate the trends in the numbers of cereal harvesting machinery.

† So that the importance of tractor stock relative to other farm machinery can be compared the value of tractor stock has been measured in this way and it rises from £67 million in 1948 to £397 million in 1965. (Estimated from A. J. Rayner, *op. cit.*, Bulletin 113, 1966.)

‡ Value figures for each group comparing 1966/7 with 1949/50 are given in the Appendix.

§ Data for Scotland and Northern Ireland are excluded because of non-comparability. The data source, unless otherwise stated, is: M.A.F.F., *Century of Agricultural Statistics 1866–1966*, H.M.S.O., 1968.

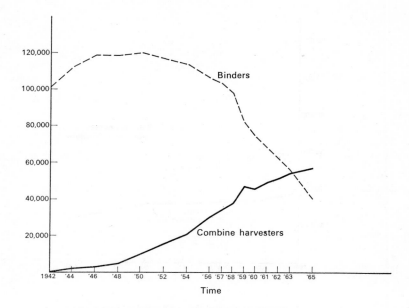

Fɪɢ. 4.2. Combine harvesters and binders

From Fig. 4.2 we can see that there was an increase in the number of binders during the war to a ceiling level of 120,000 by 1946. After 1950, the stock of binders declined rapidly so that by 1965 there were only some 45,000 on farms.

Combines were imported from the United States during the war but afterwards their production was started up in the United Kingdom. As shown, there has been a very rapid increase of about twelvefold in the number of combines, from around 5000 in 1948 to 58,000 in 1965. In addition, there have been significant quality improvements—as evidenced by the swing from tractor-drawn to self-propelled combines as shown in Fig. 4.3, by the trend towards combines with a larger cutter bar and by improvements in reliability, threshing, manœuvrability, harvesting ability (with improvements in the design of the reel and in driver control of the reel) and ease of maintenance.

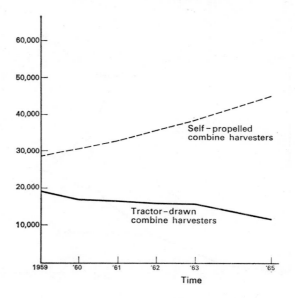

Fɪɢ. 4.3. Self-propelled combines and tractor-drawn combines

III.2. POTATO AND ROOT CROP HARVESTERS

The innovation of machines which completely harvest potatoes and root crops came after the innovation of combine harvesters for cereals. Complete sugar beet harvesters (Fig. 4.4 below) were innovated in 1946 but adoption did not really get under way until the early 1950's. Since then the number on farms has increased rapidly to the present level of nearly 15,000. In addition, there have been significant quality improvements concerned with topping, cleaning and handling beet and in general design (including the development of units which fit around a tractor rather than being drawn by it).

Complete potato harvesters were innovated a little later (about 1950) and adoption did not really proceed until the late fifties. The other machines in use—spinners and elevator/shaker diggers—require hand labour for picking and are gradually being replaced by complete harvesters. The number of spinners reached a peak in the mid 1950's

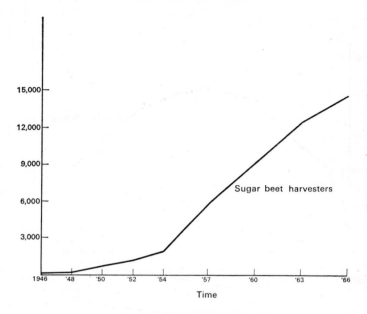

FIG. 4.4. Sugar beet harvesters

and has declined since. In contrast, the number of elevator/shaker diggers, which are more efficient than spinners, has risen steadily since they were introduced during the war. However, numbers now seem to have reached a ceiling level. These trends are illustrated in Fig. 4.5 below.

III.3. GRASS HARVESTING MACHINERY

The number of grass mowers has declined since the war (228,000 in 1946; 173,500 in 1963). There was, however, a change over during the period from horse-drawn and tractor-drawn mowers to tractor-mounted mowers. A major development in the late 1950's was the invention and adoption of the tractor-drawn forage harvester. Data are not available on the number of forage harvesters on farms, except that there were some 15,000 in use by 1962. However, purchases of forage harvesters

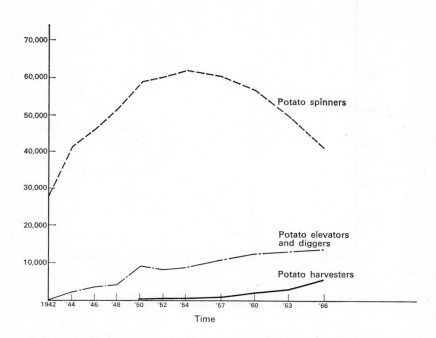

Fig. 4.5. Potato harvesters, shaker-diggers and spinners

were at their peak in 1959–60 with some 4000–4500 being bought, of which a third were imported.

III.4. PICK-UP BALERS

These tractor-drawn machines for baling hay and straw were introduced onto farms just after the war. Their number has steadily increased in a linear fashion, since 1950, to a level of 87,400 in 1965. In addition, there have been quality improvements—a change over of power source from an engine on the baler to the use of the tractor engine through the power-take-off, and an increase in work throughput.

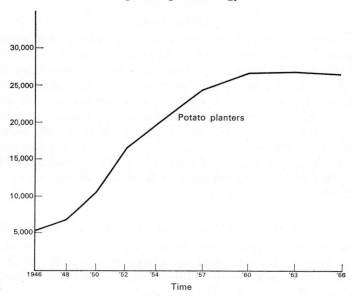

FIG. 4.6. Potato planters

III.5. CEREAL DRILLS

The increase in the stock of sowing and distribution machinery is not explained by the trend in the number of cereal drills on farms. In fact, the number of cereal drills was relatively constant from 1942 until 1956 and since then has declined. This is probably partly because new drills since the mid fifties have had a bigger capacity. In addition, there was a change from horse-drawn to tractor-drawn drills and an increase in the speed of working, with increasing horsepower per tractor, enabled drills to cover more acres per hour.

III.6. POTATO PLANTERS

The invention of the potato planter represents a significant technological development in potato production since it relieves farmers of the need to employ gangs of labour to plant potatoes. Planters were first used during the war and adoption has been rapid since, with a ceiling level being reached about 1960 (Fig. 4.6).

III.7. ROOT DRILLS

The number of traditional "root drills" has fallen by half since the war (from 82,000 in 1946 to 44,100 in 1965) with the development of more efficient techniques for growing root crops. In particular, single seed drills, which sow the seed of root crops at a uniform distance apart, were pioneered around 1952–5. These machines have the advantage over traditional root drills that they reduce the labour requirements of root crops after drilling. Sales of the single seed drills increased rapidly after 1956, reaching a peak of over 8500 in 1965 and are still at a high level. The number of these drills on farms reached 32,000 in 1961—thus tending to compensate for the decline in numbers of traditional drills.

III.8. FERTILIZER AND MANURE DISTRIBUTORS

Tractor-drawn machines for distributing fertilizer were used well before the war. However, there was a large increase in the number on farms over the post-war period, with the increased use of fertilizers, and a ceiling level of over 130,000 was reached about 1962. There has been a swing away, over the period, from broadcasting units to spinning disc machines—the latter being more efficient in terms of acres per ton-hour covered. Tractor-drawn machines for carting and spreading farm-yard manure were introduced in the early post-war period and numbers have steadily increased to 105,000 in 1965.

III.9. CORN DRIERS

Corn driers are included in the category of barn and farmyard machinery. They were innovated during the war but adoption did not proceed until the early fifties when it became very rapid such that there was a twelvefold increase between 1952 and 1964 (Fig. 4.7).

III.10. MILKING MACHINES (Fig. 4.8)

The first efficient milking machines were developed in the 1930's and adoption was rapid during and after the war until the mid fifties. In terms of the number of installations, the ceiling level was reached

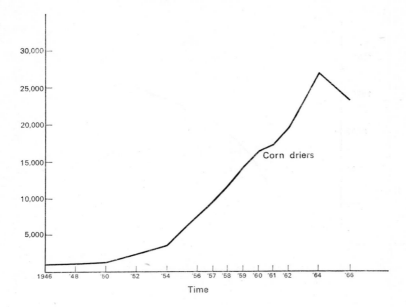

FIG. 4.7. Corn driers

around 1960; since then there has been a slight drop as milking herds have become fewer. Over the whole period, there has been continual improvement in the quality of equipment and in the design of installations.

III.11. ELECTRICITY AS A POWER SOURCE

The use of electricity as a power source on farms has steadily increased over the period as more and more farms have become connected to mains supply. Over the eleven-year period 1953/4 to 1964/5 the number of connections increased by 82 per cent (from 142,800 to 260,000). This is reflected in the increase in the value of sales from £4·37 million to £17·93 million over the period.†

† Data source: S. Robson, *Food and Agricultural Statistics*, Report 1646, Dept. of Agricultural Economics, University of Newcastle upon Tyne, 1966.

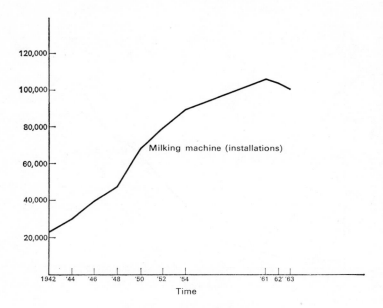

FIG. 4.8. Milking machines

Sections II and III have tried to pick out the most important post-war trends in the use of power and machinery. Our next task is to analyse these trends from an economic viewpoint and find out why they occurred.

IV. Analysis of Post-war Demand for Power and Machinery

IV.1. INTRODUCTION

We shall limit our analysis of the demand for power and machinery to the years after 1947 and thus ignore the abnormal conditions imposed on agriculture during and immediately after World War II. During the war, national food requirements dictated an increase in the U.K. arable acreage from 11·9 million acres in 1938 to 17·9 million acres by 1944. This in turn led to a technical requirement for increased mechanization, with the wartime labour shortage. However, we shall argue that post 1947 the rate of mechanization has been determined by the profit seeking behaviour of farmers and not simply by technical requirement for increased output. Our point of departure, is to look at the results of a statistical study which analyses the annual demand for tractors over the period 1948–65. We then consider the trends over the post-war period in the use of other machines. Whilst statistical analysis of these trends has not been carried out, the results of the tractor study allow us to put forward hypotheses as to the reasons for these trends.

IV.2. THE DEMAND FOR FARM TRACTORS IN THE UNITED KINGDOM, 1948–65[†]

Our analysis consists of, firstly, deriving a theoretical model (demand function) for tractors and, secondly, testing statistically for the association between the annual demand for tractors and the variables in the demand function over the years 1948–65.

(a) *Theoretical Demand Function for Tractors*

(i) *Static demand function for tractor stock.* Tractors are a durable input and therefore the flow of tractor services to the production function is provided by the stock of tractors and not by the quantity of new tractors purchased during the production period. Consequently, the demand function for gross investment in tractors is derived from the demand function for tractor stock which is itself derived from the demand function for tractor services. Recalling our discussion in Chapter 2 on the demand for a durable input, we can hypothesize that the *equilibrium* demand for tractor services in period t (s_t^*) is a function of the price of tractor services (c_t), anticipated product price (P_{pt}^N) and the prices of other input flows in period t. In addition, the demand function is assumed to be homogeneous of degree zero and therefore the demand for tractor services is expressed as a function of anticipated product price relative to the price of tractor services and of each input price relative to the price of tractor services.

[†] This section is based on: A. J. Rayner and Keith Cowling, Demand for a durable input: an analysis of the U.K. market for farm tractors, *The Review of Economics and Statistics*, vol. XLIX, Nov. 1967, pp. 590–8, and A. J. Rayner and Keith Cowling, Demand for farm tractors in the United States and the United Kingdom, *American Journal of Agricultural Economics*, vol. 50, Nov. 1968, pp. 896–912.

Next we must specify which particular input prices should enter this demand function for the period 1948–65. Therefore, we have to decide which resources provided important substitute or complementary input flows to tractor services over the period, so that changes in their prices would have induced variations in the level of tractor services.

Horses might be considered as a possible important substitute durable resource to tractors since they provide an alternative source of draught power. However, by 1948 the draught power provided by horses in United Kingdom agriculture was so small (in fact, about 10 per cent) compared to that provided by tractors *and* subsequently fell off so rapidly that this possibility may be ignored. A possible important substitute input flow from a current resource to tractor services during the period was that of labour services. This would seem to have been particularly true in terms of the substitution between the extra services provided by increased tractor quality, such as increased horsepower, and total labour hours including overtime. In addition, indirect substitution occurred in that some of the improvements incorporated into tractors allowed new machines and techniques to be adopted which were labour saving. Finally, the fact that there was a continuous drift of labour from agriculture over the period *whilst* production increased indicates that there may have been considerable substitution of tractor services for labour services. Hence, we can hypothesize that the price of labour (labour earnings), which we shall denote as P_l, should be included in the demand function for tractor services. Turning to complementary resources, fuel provides a complementary input flow to tractor services. However, since fuel costs form a very small proportion of total farm costs it was felt that changes in the price of fuel, in the range observed between 1948 and 1965, were unlikely to have had any significant effects on the level of tractor services. Consequently, we arrive at the hypothesis that variations in the equilibrium level of tractor services in the post-war period have been mainly influenced by changes in the ratio of anticipated product price to the price of tractor services and by changes in the price of labour relative to the price of tractor services. To focus attention on the "real" price of tractor services—this price relative to other prices—we may write our price relatives with the price of tractor services as the numerator rather than as the denominator and express the demand function for the equilibrium level of tractor services as:

$$s_t^* = f(c_t/P_{pt}^N, \ c_t/P_{lt}) \tag{4.1}$$

If the flow of tractor services to the productive function is always a constant proportion of tractor stock over time, then the equilibrium tractor stock, at a point in time, will be determined by just the same relative prices as the equilibrium level of services. For this factor of proportionality to be a constant it is necessary that, firstly, tractor stock is measured in such a way that it reflects changes in tractor quality and, secondly, that there is a constant rate of utilization of stock from one period to the next. With regard to this second criterion, it is likely that increasing average farm size over time could lead to a better utilization of tractor services and therefore increase the magnitude of the factor of proportionality which exists between tractor services and tractor stock. Consequently, increasing farm size would tend to depress the equilibrium tractor stock, although it would not influence the desired level of tractor services. It is also possible that increasing average farm size could influence the aggregate level of tractor *services*. Thus the amalgamation of very small farms could lead to an *increased* demand for tractor services, and therefore tractor stock, if these farms had previously been too small to use a tractor. Consequently, changes in average farm size can have opposing influences on tractor stock.

In reality, aggregate tractor stock is being continuously adjusted to meet changing conditions but we only observe this adjustment at *discrete* intervals of time. In particular, tractor stock is measured annually at the end of September. Since tractor services enter directly into crop production functions and only indirectly into livestock production functions, the end of September figures approximate fairly closely to the stock at the end of the harvest year, most crops being harvested in early autumn. We shall, hereafter, call this end of September stock, the end of the year stock. We can then regard tractor stock as being adjusted throughout the year toward an equilibrium level at the end of the year. Consequently, equilibrium tractor stock at the end of year $t(S_t^*)$ is assumed to be determined by the relative prices in year t that determine the equilibrium level of tractor services and by average farm size in period $t(F_t)$. Therefore, the demand function for equilibrium tractor stock is:

$$S_t^* = f(c_t/P_{pt}^N, c_t/P_{lt}, F_t) \qquad (4.2)$$

(ii) *Dynamic demand function for tractor stock.* As discussed in Chapter 2, it is extremely unlikely that farmers adjust the stock of a durable input to its equilibrium level at the end of each period. Instead, it is likely that they make a cautious adjustment of stock in a profit seeking direction towards this equilibrium, following changes in relative prices. We may arrive at a suitable dynamic demand function for tractor stock by combining the equilibrium demand function, which we have just developed, with the partial adjustment model. The simplest form of the adjustment model postulates that the adjustment of tractor stock from the previous year to the present year is some fraction of that necessary to bring tractor stock to its equilibrium level at the end of the current year. Thus if S_{t-1} is the actual tractor stock at the end of year $t-1$ then this hypothesis is:

$$S_t - S_{t-1} = \gamma(S_t^* - S_{t-1}), \; 0 < \gamma < 1 \qquad (4.3)$$

Therefore
$$S_t = \gamma S_t^* + (1 - \gamma)S_{t-1} \qquad (4.4)$$

An alternative way of representing this adjustment process is to postulate that the *percentage* annual change in tractor stock is a fraction of the percentage difference between equilibrium stock in year t and actual stock in year $t - 1$:

$$S_t/S_{t-1} = (S_t^*/S_{t-1})^\gamma \qquad (4.5)$$

Therefore
$$\log_e S_t = \gamma \log_e S_t^* + (1-\gamma) \log_e S_{t-1} \qquad (4.6)$$

In both models, the coefficient γ is called the adjustment coefficient. The way in which the percentage adjustment model differs from the linear adjustment model is that it assumes that the fraction of the disequilibrium which is eliminated is smaller the greater the disequilibrium. This is, perhaps, more realistic since it is likely that the closer producers are to equilibrium the less there is to learn about it and, therefore, the more inclined they are to eliminate the disequilibrium.

If we substitute equation (4.2) for S_t^* in equations (4.4) and (4.6) we then obtain two alternative dynamic demand functions for tractor stock. Both of these functions make tractor stock at the end of year *t* a function of the relevant prices in *t*, average farm size in *t* and tractor stock at the end of year *t*−1. As is described shortly, both of these functions were estimated statistically.

(iii) *Capital funds constraint on the adjustment of tractor stock.* Since farmers do not have unlimited funds they have to ration their capital between uses and the level of available capital funds may thus influence the stock of tractors on farms. One way to represent the level of available funds is to approximate it by the level of past profits (Y_{t-1}) and the interest rate charged by banks (R_t).

(iv) *Demand function for gross investment.* Gross investment in tractors in year *t* (G_t) is equal to net investment in year *t*—the change in the level of tractor stock between the end of year $t - 1$ and the end of year *t* ($S_t - S_{t-1}$)—plus replacement investment in year *t* (R_t). Net investment represents the adjustment which is made in year *t* toward the equilibrium tractor stock in that year and is therefore determined by the variables determining the equilibrium stock and by the level of stock in the previous period. Whilst the level of past stock has a negative influence on net investment, it has a positive influence on replacement investment. Consequently, the total observed influence of past stock on gross investment will depend on the relative strengths of the two influences. Finally, gross investment may be constrained by the level of available funds. Therefore, the demand function for gross investment is:

$$G_t = S_t - S_{t-1} + R_t = f(c_t/P_{pt}^N, \ c_t/P_{lt}, \ F_t, \ S_{t-1}, \ Y_{t-1}, \ R_t) \quad (4.7)$$

(b) *Measurement of the Variables*

(i) *Tractor stock* (S_t). The end of year tractor stock for each year was estimated by deflating the value of stock in current prices for each year by a constant quality price index for new tractors.† This deflation procedure attempts to remove inflationary price changes from the value of stock so that the resulting measure takes account solely of changes in

† The series for the value of stock in current prices was estimated by the perpetual inventory method in: A. J. Rayner, *op. cit.*, Bulletin 113.

the number and quality of stock and therefore reflects the services embodied in the stock of tractors.

(ii) *Gross investment* (G_t). Gross investment for each year of the period 1948–65 was also estimated so as to take account of quality change by deflating gross investment in current prices by a constant quality price index for new tractors.†

(iii) *Price of tractor services.* As shown in Chapter 2, the implicit rental of a durable input—the price for the flow of services from a unit of capital stock—depends upon the price of the input, the rate of depreciation and the interest rate. However, we have regarded the price of tractor services as being simply proportional to the price of new tractors. Consequently, the price of tractors (P_{Tt}) is substituted for the price of tractor services (c_t) in the analysis, although, as already described, the borrowing interest rate was also entered as a separate variable. The price series for new tractors was measured in index form as a constant quality price index. In other words, changes in prices paid which were attributable to changes in the quality of tractors were extracted before calculating the index. Finally, investment allowances— capital allowances for income tax relief—were given, at varying levels, during several of the years between 1948 and 1965. These effectively reduce the price of the new tractor to the farmer and strictly speaking this price reduction should be incorporated into our measure of tractor price. However, in order to measure the particular influence of investment allowances these were entered as a separate variable (I_t) in the demand function.‡

(iv) *Anticipated product price* (P_{pt}^N). It was hypothesized that anticipations made in year t about future produce prices were based on product prices received in the previous year (P_{pt-1}). In view of the dating of the tractor stock variable, the index should preferably have been on the

† The series for gross investment in current prices was compiled from data on domestic sales provided by the firms listed in the Appendix plus imports. This series and the series for gross investment in constant quality prices are presented in Rayner, *op. cit.*, Bulletin 113.

‡ The constant quality price index used in the estimation procedure is presented in Rayner, *op. cit.*, Bulletin 113.

basis of a year June$_{t-1}$ to May$_t$ (i.e. on the basis of the harvest year index number of prices of the Ministry of Agriculture, Fisheries and Food). Since this was unavailable for the whole period, then an index of the weighted average of crop prices in the past calendar year (January$_{t-1}$ to December$_{t-1}$) was used. (Data source: M.A.F.F., *Agricultural Statistics*.)

(v) *Price of labour* (P_{lt}). An index of agricultural labour earnings was used to represent the price of labour. (Data source: M.A.F.F., *Wage and Employment Enquiry*.)

(vi) *Farm size* (F_t). No satisfactory data on average farm size were available. The percentage of farms of more than 300 acres was used to represent this variable. (Data source: M.A.F.F., *Agricultural Statistics*.)

(vii) *Past profits* (Y_{t-1}). This was measured as United Kingdom net farm income. (Data source: C.S.O., *Annual Abstract of Statistics*.)

(viii) *Rate of interest* (R_t). To represent the rate of interest charged to farmers by banks, Bank Rate plus 1 per cent was used. (Data source: C.S.O., *Monthly Digest of Statistics*.)

(c) *The Algebraic Form of the Demand Functions*

(i) *Stock demand function.* To recall our earlier discussion, we have so far hypothesized that the equilibrium level of tractor stock in year t (S_t^*) is a function of three variables:

$$S_t^* = f(c_t/P_{pt}^N, c_t/P_{1t}, F_t) \qquad (4.2)$$

Further, in the discussion on measurement of the variables we said that:

(i) c_t could be represented by the variable P_{Tt}, with I_t being entered as a separate variable;
(ii) P_{pt}^N could be represented by the variable P_{pt-1}.

In addition, we should include in the demand function an error term, u_t, which represents the, hopefully, minor influence of omitted variables, measurement error of tractor stock and the randomness of producer behaviour. Therefore, we postulate:

$$S_t^* = f(P_{Tt}/P_{pt-1}, P_{Tt}/P_{lt}, I_t, F_t, u_t) \tag{4.8}$$

We now have to decide upon the algebraic form of the relationship between S_t^* and the explanatory variables. One form used in the estimation procedure was the linear form:

$$S_t^* = b_0 + b_1(P_{Tt}/P_{pt-1}) + b_2(P_{Tt}/P_{lt}) + b_3 I_t + b_4 F_t + u_t \tag{4.9}$$

Another functional form—the double log—was also employed:

$$\log_e S_t^* = \log_e b_0' + b_1' \log_e(P_{Tt}/P_{pt-1}) + b_2' \log_e(P_{Tt}/P_{lt}) + b_3' \log_e I_t$$
$$+ b_4' \log_e F_t + \log_e u_t \tag{4.10}$$

Equation (4.10) is in fact a transformation of:

$$S_t^* = b_0'.(P_{Tt}/P_{pt-1})^{b_1'}.(P_{Tt}/P_{lt})^{b_2'}.I_t^{b_3'}.F_t^{b_4'}.u_t \tag{4.11}$$

This functional form is a useful one for estimation purposes because each coefficient represents the elasticity of equilibrium demand with respect to each explanatory variable.†

We expect from our theoretical discussion that the coefficients b_1 (and b_1') and b_4 (and b_4') will be negative and the coefficient b_3 (and b_3') will be positive. Our theoretical discussion does not predict the sign of the coefficient b_2 (and b_2') except that if the substitution response to a change in (P_{Tt}/P_{lt}) is greater than the expansion effect this coefficient will be negative.

We have said that we do not expect actual and equilibrium tractor stocks to coincide. Further, we said that the adjustment of tractor stock could be described by a stock adjustment function of either a linear or a percentage (logarithmic) form. The linear adjustment function describes the level of stock in year t by:

$$S_t = \gamma S_t^* + (1 - \gamma) S_{t-1} \tag{4.4}$$

The percentage form describes the level of stock in year t by

$$\log_e S_t = \gamma \log_e S_t^* + (1 - \gamma) \log_e S_{t-1} \tag{4.5}$$

† E.g. $b_1 = \partial S_t^*/\partial(P_{Tt}/P_{pt-1})/(P_{Tt}/P_{pt-1})/S_t^*$. Therefore b_1 is the elasticity of S_t^* with respect to (P_{Tt}/P_{pt-1}).

In addition, we said that S_t might be affected positively by Y_{t-1} and negatively by R_t. Two alternative dynamic demand functions for tractor stock which were used in the estimation procedure are derived as follows. The first equation—a linear one—is obtained by substituting equation (4.9) into equation (4.4) and appropriately adding Y_{t-1} and R_t:

$$S_t = \gamma b_0 + \gamma b_1 (P_{Tt}/P_{pt-1}) + \gamma b_2 (P_{Tt}/P_{lt}) + \gamma b_3 I_t + \gamma b_4 F_t$$
$$+ (1 - \gamma) S_{t-1} + \gamma b_5 Y_{t-1} + \gamma b_6 R_t + \gamma u_t \qquad (4.12)$$

The second equation—a logarithmic one—is obtained by substituting equation (4.10) into equation (4.5) and adding Y_{t-1} and R_t in the appropriate manner:

$$\log_e S_t = \gamma \log_e b_0' + \gamma b_1' \log_e (P_{Tt}/P_{pt-1}) + \gamma b_2' \log_e (P_{Tt}/P_{lt})$$
$$+ \gamma b_3' \log_e I_t + \gamma b_4' \log_e F_t + (1 - \gamma) \log_e S_{t-1}$$
$$+ \gamma b_5' \log_e Y_{t-1} + \gamma b_6' \log_e R_t + \gamma \log_e u_t \qquad (4.13)$$

The coefficient of these two equations were then estimated by regression analysis, as is described shortly.

(ii) *Gross investment function.* From equation (4.7) and our decisions about the measurement of variables, the hypothesis explaining annual gross investment is:

$$G_t = f(P_{Tt}/P_{pt-1}, P_{Tt}/P_{lt}, I_t, F_t, S_{t-1}, Y_{t-1}, R_t, u_t) \qquad (4.14)$$

The appropriate functional form was then decided on the basis of experimentation with several possible forms.

(d) *Estimation and Results*†

Equations (4.12), (4.13) and several algebraic forms of (4.14) were estimated by multiple regression analysis. Where it was found that an explanatory variable was *not* significantly associated with stock or gross investment at an acceptable level of significance (usually 5 per cent) the equations were re-estimated with the omission of this variable. The final results are given in Table 4.1 below. We should note that $\bar{R}^2$

† This section may be omitted: an interpretation of the results is given shortly.

represents the proportion of the variation in the dependent variable (stock or gross investment) which is explained by the explanatory variables, with a correction factor for the number of variables in the equation.† The variables representing farm size (F_t) and past profits (Y_{t-1}) were eliminated as being non-significant in explaining stock or gross investment.

Equations (4a) to (4c) in Table 4.1 present results for the stock demand functions. Equation (4a) is an estimate of the linear stock demand equation—equation (4.12)—whilst equations (4b) and (4c) are estimates of the logarithmic stock demand function—equation (4.13). The variables P_{Tt}/P_{It}, I_t and S_{t-1} are seen to be significantly associated with tractor stock at the 5 per cent level in each equation and their coefficients have the expected signs. The variable P_{Tt}/P_{pt-1} is significantly associated with S_t at the 5 per cent level in equations (4b) and (4c) and its coefficient has the "correct" sign. However, it is not associated with stock in the linear equation and is therefore omitted from equation (4a). The reason why it is non-significant in equation (4a) would seem to be because of multicollinearity (a statistical problem) of the variable with P_{Tt}/P_{It}.‡ Theoretically, P_{Tt}/P_{pt-1} should be included in the stock demand function and we will therefore accept equations (4b) and (4c) as better estimates of the function than (4a). The interest rate variable is significant at the 10 per cent level in equation (4a) but not in (4b) and is therefore omitted in equation (4c). This variable was highly multicollinear with the other explanatory variables and therefore its influence on demand was difficult to pick out. We will therefore accept equation (4c) as the "best" stock demand equation. The coefficient on $\log_e S_{t-1}$ in (4c) is equal to $(1 - \gamma)$; therefore γ, the adjustment coefficient, is estimated as $0 \cdot 68$.

† Thus $R^2 = 0 \cdot 998$ indicates that 99·8 per cent of the variation in the dependent variable is explained by the included explanatory variables. Note that d in Table 4.1 is another statistical concept—the Durbin–Watson statistic. This statistic indicates if the error term is serially independent through time—this being one of the assumptions of the regression model. We may accept that this assumption is satisfied in the results (although statisticians will realize that the d statistic has little validity in the stock adjustment model).

‡ The variables P_{Tt}/P_{pt-1} and P_{Tt}/P_{It} are very highly correlated with each other and it is difficult for the estimation procedure to disentangle their separate influences. However, this problem was not so serious in the logarithmic function and the influence of both variables was picked out in these equations.

TABLE 4.1. REGRESSION EQUATIONS EXPLAINING END OF YEAR TRACTOR STOCK (S_t) AND ANNUAL GROSS INVESTMENT IN TRACTORS (G_t)

Equation no.	Dependent variable	Coefficients of					$\bar{R}^2$	d
		Constant	P_{Tt}/P_{lt}	I_t	R_t	S_{t-1}		
4a	S_t	6·33†	−0·020†	0·003†	−0·212‡	0·776†	0·992	1·89

Equation no.	Dependent variable	Coefficients of					$\bar{R}^2$	d
		$\log_e$ constant	$\log_e P_{Tt}/P_{pt-1}$	$\log_e P_{Tt}/P_{lt}$	$\log_e I_t$	$\log_e R_t$	$\log_e S_{t-1}$	
4b	$\log_e S_t$	5·734†	−0·232†	−0·657†	0·013†	0·027	0·3044†	0·997	2·29
4c	$\log_e S_t$	5·785†	−0·239†	−0·658†	0·011†		0·3211†	0·998	2·38
4d	G_t	340·2†	0·909	−55·34†	1·148†		−27·25†	0·94	1·83
4e	G_t	344·5†		−55·23†	1·163†		−27·50†	0·94	1·84

† Variable significant at 5% level
‡ Variable significant at 10% level.

S_t = Stock of tractors in £10 million (in constant quality prices).
G_t = Gross investment in £ million (in constant quality prices).
P_{Tt}/P_{pt-1} = Index of ratio of constant quality tractor prices/crop prices.
P_{Tt}/P_{lt} = Index of ratio of constant quality tractor prices/labour earnings.
I_t = per cent investment allowances.
R_t = Bank Rate + 1 per cent.

Equations (4d) and 4e) explain annual gross investment using a semilogarithmic algebraic form—this being the most acceptable one.

The theoretical form of equation (4d) is thus:

$$G_t = \log_e b_0 + b_1 \log_e (P_{Tt}/P_{pt-1}) + b_2 \log_e (P_{Tt}/P_{lt}) + b_3 \log_e I_t$$
$$+ b_4 \log_e S_{t-1} + \log_e u_t \qquad (4.15)$$

The influence of the variable P_{Tt}/P_{pt-1} was again hard to ascertain because of its collinearity with P_{Tt}/P_{lt}. It is therefore omitted in equation (4e) where all variables are significant at the 5 per cent level.

(e) *Interpretation of the Results*

(i) *The stock demand function.* The results indicate that over the period 1948–65 there existed a significant association between the variations in the annual, end of year tractor stock and annual variations in each of the following variables: the constant quality price of new tractors relative to crop price of the previous period, the constant quality price of new tractors relative to labour earnings, percentage investment allowances and the level of past stock. The results also validate the use of an adjustment model to describe how farmers adjust tractor stock in response to changing relative prices. This adjustment process is one in which adjustment is in a profit-seeking direction but is cautious. Consequently, farmers adjust tractor stock not only in response to changes in present relative prices but also in response to changes in past prices. The adjustment coefficient is estimated to be 0·68—that is, 68 per cent of the adjustment necessary to bring stock in t–1 to the equilibrium level in year t is completed within one year. In other words, tractor stock is adjusted relatively quickly to changes in economic forces.

The short run elasticities of tractor stock with respect to the explanatory variables are estimated directly by the coefficients of equation (4c). These elasticities measure the actual annual percentage response of stock to a one percentage change in each of the explanatory variables. The long run elasticities—the percentage response of equilibrium stock (the response that *would* occur if farmers adjusted stock to equilibrium each year)—is given by dividing the short run elasticities by the adjustment coefficient. These stock elasticities are:

	Short run	Long run
(i) With respect to $(P_{Tt}/P_{pt-1})^*$	$-0\cdot24$	$-0\cdot35$
(ii) With respect to $(P_{Tt}/P_{lt})^*$	$-0\cdot66$	$-0\cdot97$
(iii) With respect to I_t	$+0\cdot010$	$+0\cdot014$

* Therefore, the short-run elasticity of tractor stock with respect to (i) P_{Tt} alone is $-0\cdot90$, (ii) P_{pt-1} alone is $+0\cdot24$, (iii) P_{lt} alone is $+0\cdot66$.

It can be seen, therefore, that the dominant explanatory variable of the large post-war increase in the stock of tractors is the ratio of tractor prices (quality adjusted) to labour earnings. Thus a 1 per cent decrease in the ratio of tractor prices to labour earnings led to around a $0\cdot66$ per cent increase in tractor stock within one year, *ceteris paribus*. It is not surprising that this capital deepening process (the substitution of the services of capital goods for labour services in the production function) has been important in view of the fact that labour earnings increased by about 130 per cent between 1948 and 1965 whilst constant quality tractor prices increased by not more than 25 per cent. The results also indicate that this capital deepening process was aided by the government policy of giving investment allowances on new tractors. Investment allowances were expressed, during the data period, on a percentage basis—the percentage of the price of the new tractor which could be set against income tax—and a rise in the allowance reduced the price of the new tractor to farmers. An increase in the level of investment allowances consequently increased the level of tractor stock, *ceteris paribus*. For example, there was a change in the allowance from 20 to 30 per cent during the period (i.e. a 50 per cent increase in allowances) and the results indicate that this increase tended to raise the level of tractor stock by $0\cdot5$ per cent of its previous value within one year— after the influences of other factors on tractor stock have been accounted for. The final point indicated by the results is that tractor stock did not change very much in response to changes in the ratio of tractor prices to crop prices: a 1 per cent decrease in the price ratio tended to increase stock by $0\cdot24$ per cent over a one-year period, *ceteris paribus*. Between 1948 and 1965 the ratio was volatile from year to year but, in general, moved slightly in favour of crop prices over the whole period. Consequently, it led to some small increase in tractor stock over the whole period after we have accounted for the influence of other factors.

(ii) *The gross investment function.* Gross investment is the variable used by farmers to implement the decision to adjust capital stock. Gross investment is, therefore, seen to have been influenced by the same variables that determined tractor stock, but, being more volatile than stock, its response to changes in the explanatory variables is greater in percentage terms. The semilog equation, which was used to estimate the gross investment function, has the property that as gross investment rises the elasticities of gross investment with respect to the explanatory variables are assumed to fall. At the mean level of annual gross investment between 1948 and 1965, the estimated elasticities are:

(i) With respect to P_{Tt}/P_{lt} $\quad -2 \cdot 50$

(ii) With respect to I_t $\quad\quad +0 \cdot 05$

(iii) With respect to S_{t-1} $\quad -1 \cdot 24$

Thus, there was a marked response in annual gross investment to changes in (P_{Tt}/P_{lt}), occasioned by the desire to adjust tractor stock (as part of a capital deepening process). Even at the relatively high level of tractor sales in 1965 this response was still high—the estimated elasticity of gross investment with respect to (P_{Tt}/P_{lt}) for that year being $-1 \cdot 70$. Investment allowances also had an important influence on gross investment. Thus the increase in the allowances from 20 to 30 per cent tax relief on the price of a new tractor was associated with a rise in gross investment in the same year of £0·5 million in constant quality prices. Finally, an increase in tractor stock in one year tended to decrease gross investment in the following year. This is not surprising in view of the high adjustment coefficient which was estimated in the stock adjustment model and the fact that tractors depreciate in value at a fairly low rate—about 15 to 20 per cent per annum. Consequently, the negative influence of lagged stock on net investment was fairly high whilst the positive influence of lagged stock on replacement investment was fairly low.

As a postscript, we should note that there was no evidence to suggest that the availability of capital funds affected the level of tractor purchases. Nor did the increase in average farm size (as imprecisely measured by our variable) appear to affect the utilization of services from tractor stock.

(f) *Summary*

The foregoing analysis of the post-war demand for farm tractors indicates the following explanation of the observed trend in tractor stock. Firstly, farmers were profit seeking, adjusting tractor stock to changes in the relevant price ratios in the profit maximizing direction. Stock adjustment, while fairly rapid and continuous, tended to be cautious. It did, in fact, reflect both some inertia to change by farmers and the fact that knowledge of and reaction to price changes takes time to spread among farmers. Secondly, the dominating price ratio influencing the adjustment of tractor stock was that of constant quality tractor prices to labour earnings—as labour costs rose relatively faster, so tractor services were substituted for labour services on farms in a capital deepening process. Thirdly, but with a minor impact, changes in the tractor price/crop price ratio influenced the tractor stock: changes in this price ratio were more volatile but the overall trend over the period was slightly favourable leading to output expansion with an increase in tractor stock. Fourthly, the pattern of response was aided by government assistance in the form of investment allowances which in effect lowered the price of tractors to farmers. Finally, an important degree of technological change was incorporated in the increase in tractor stock over the period via significant quality improvement.

IV.3. POST-WAR DEMAND FOR MACHINERY

We can expect that the above explanation of the post-war increase in tractor stock applies as a general explanation of the trend in the stock of all farm machinery (excluding tractors) aggregated together. Therefore, we can hypothesize that the increase in the aggregate value of the stock of farm machines (excluding tractors) in the post-war period, as discussed in section III, has been directed toward capital deepening as a profit seeking response to labour costs rising faster than machinery costs. Also, output expansion has led to some additional increase in stock. Finally, the process has been aided by governmental assistance in the form of investment allowances. For explaining the trends in the stocks of *individual* farm machines, other than tractors, the same general explanation may be expected to hold true. However, these machines are often more specific to the production of particular crops than tractors and so additional factors may enter into the *particular* explanation of the post-war stock demand for any one of these machines. In particular, where equipment is specialized expectations about the future may be more significant than was the case with investment in tractors. This could apply both with regard to the product price and to the price of labour, if the product is one which is highly labour demanding. We will now briefly put forward hypotheses as to the trends in the use of some of these machines, emphasizing that these hypotheses have *not* been tested and are therefore open to refutation. We will deal with the specific trends discussed in section III.

(a) *Combine Harvesters*

The acreage of cereals—the crops harvested by combines—increased during the war to a peak of 7 million acres. By 1946 the acreage had fallen to about 6 million acres and declined slightly in the fifties to a low of about 5·9 million acres. By 1960 the acreage had again risen to 6 million acres and then rose rapidly to nearly 8 million acres by 1966. Hence, only latterly has there been output expansion in cereal growing. It thus seems evident that the increase in the post-war stock of combines has been toward substituting combine services for those of binders and labour in response to labour costs rising more rapidly than those of combine services. Binders have a much higher basic complementary input of labour services than combines for a given output. In addition, they necessitate extra labour for threshing at a later date. Hence their replacement by combines would seem to be the result of changes in labour costs rather than direct changes in the price ratio of combines to binders which appears to have changed little over the period. Also, with the increased use of larger combines there has been direct substitution of *combine services* for *labour services*. However, the recent increase in cereal acreage is likely to have led to an increase in the demand for combine services—and therefore an increase in combine stock—over and above the substitution of combines for binders and labour. Finally, we may infer that the adoption curve (Fig. 4.2) has its observed shape because adoption was initially in the South and on the larger farms where combines offered the most significant cost reduction. Adoption then spread to other farms as the price ratio of combine services to labour services fell further. There was also, on smaller farms, a swing away from the use of self-owned binders and towards the hire of combine services from contractors. An additional impetus to the adoption of combines was that combines proved to be more efficient than binders in avoiding loss of yield, particularly in laid crops.

(b) *Sugar Beet and Potato Equipment*

The sugar beet acreage has remained fairly constant since the war; the linear rise in the stock of sugar beet harvesters since 1954 would therefore seem to be associated with rising labour costs. On the other hand, the acreage of potatoes has approximately halved since the war and this has probably inhibited the growth in numbers of complete potato harvesters. It has been suggested that this decline in the potato acreage has been associated with the availability of new cash crops— particularly vegetables for canning and freezing—in the post-war period. Another factor which may have inhibited the adoption of complete potato harvesters could be the fact that potato acreage per farm has risen only slowly. Consequently, the potato harvesters on the market may have had too large a capacity to be used economically on many farms. From about 1958 onwards the use of potato harvesters and their substitution for spinners and diggers has been relatively rapid and would seem to be associated partly with rising labour costs and partly with the falling availability of gang labour. Also, it was only in the late fifties that technically efficient harvesters were available in a commercial form. Finally the adoption of potato planters would also seem to have been associated with the rising cost and decreasing availability of gang labour.

(c) *Fertilizer and Manure Distributors*

The growth in the stock of fertilizer distributors is associated with the growth in the use of fertilizers on farms (see Chapter 5). The swing toward spinning disc machines would seem to be associated with their lower labour requirement in terms of hours per ton-acre. Similarly, the growth in the stock of mechanical manure distributors is likely to be mainly associated with rising labour costs. It may also be associated with developments in methods of housing livestock.

(d) *Other Machines*

The innovation of the forage harvester and replacement of the mower would seem to be associated with the desire to find new methods of feeding livestock. In addition, its greater capacity would lead to economies in the use of labour. The increase in the number of pick-up balers can be associated with rising labour costs, and almost certainly with the growth in the use of the combine harvester.

(e) *Milking Machines*

Again we may surmise that the growth in the number of milking machine installations has been the result of a fall in the ratio of cost of machine services to labour earnings. In addition, the adoption of machine milking was probably given an incentive by the public health regulations regarding clean milk. The recent fall in the number of installations may be explained by the decline in farms producing milk.

(f) *Corn Driers*

We may associate the growth in the use of corn driers on farms with the increased use of combine harvesters and the increase in grain storage on farms. A guaranteed incentive to farmers to store grain on the farm has been provided by the government since 1961.

(g) *Electricity*

Electricity is used on farms to provide light, heat and especially power. Electricity is particularly suitable as a power source where automatic controls are needed in order to save labour. Electricity is also an item of household consumption on the farm, since the farm and the household are generally part of the same unit. The increase in the number of connections can be assumed to be a combination of both demands.

V. Supply Conditions for Agricultural Machinery

V.1. DOMESTIC AND EXPORT MARKETS

The production of agricultural machinery has risen rapidly over the post-war period. Thus the value of production in current prices was some £47 million in 1947, by 1952 this had risen to £106 million, by 1962 to £180 million and by 1966 had reached around £200 million. The major part of this increased production has been for export and the percentage exported, although only 21 per cent in 1947, has accounted for more than 55 per cent of annual total production since 1952. In fact, in recent years exports have accounted for some 60 to 70 per cent of total production and in 1966 the value of exports was some £132 million. Tractors have accounted for about 80 per cent of all machinery exports in recent years with the main markets being Western Europe, Australia, U.S.A., Canada and South Africa. Over the past few years the major agricultural machinery manufacturing firms have been setting up plants abroad—for complete manufacture or for assembly of parts —and this may be expected to lead to at least a slowing down, if not a diminution, in the growth of exports.

In the domestic market tractors have accounted for nearly 50 per cent of the total value of farm machinery sales per annum. For example, in 1965 tractor sales were £37 million out of a total of about £90 million. Imports account for some 10 per cent only of farm machinery sales. This may be partly explained by the tariff protection that the United Kingdom manufacturers have had over the post-war period. Since 1950 the *ad valorem* tariff on tractors has been 15 per cent; on most other farm machinery it was between 15 and 20 per cent until 1962, when it was lowered to 10 to 14 per cent. However, as a result of the Kennedy Round of Trade Negotiations the tariffs were cut in August 1968 to 12 per cent on tractors and to a range of 8 to 12 per cent on other machinery. Three further tariff cuts are scheduled in January 1970,

1971 and 1972 as a result of these negotiations, when the proposed final tariffs will be between 6 and $7\frac{1}{2}$ per cent. Lower tariffs will increase the competitive power of imports but should also benefit United Kingdom exports of farm machinery, given the good post-war performance of the British agricultural machinery industry in export markets.

V.2. CONCENTRATION IN THE INDUSTRY

The agricultural machinery industry is highly concentrated with the six largest companies supplying over three-quarters of total output. Five of these are tractor manufacturers—Ford Motor Co., British Motor Corporation,† Massey-Ferguson (U.K.), David Brown Corporation and the International Harvester Company of Great Britain—the first two producing only tractors. The other company—Ransome, Sims and Jefferies—has an agreement with Ford to manufacture machinery for use with the Ford Tractor. Concentration within the domestic tractor market is even more marked: the five major firms supply about 95 per cent of the market, whilst two—Massey Ferguson and Ford—supply more than 65 per cent of the market and in the early sixties supplied nearly 80 per cent of the market.‡ The other firms in the industry manufacture machinery other than tractors,§ and mostly specialize in a few implements. Most of these firms, however, are very small with only about 20 per cent (of some 300 firms) employing more than 25 people in 1963.¶

The high degree of concentration within the industry is probably associated with substantial economies of scale and the need for a high level of technical "knowhow" in the production of some machines—for example, tractors and combines. Additional barriers to entry for new firms are provided by brand loyalty of farmers and the product differentiation and advertising carried out by the large firms.

V.3. DISTRIBUTION, PRICING AND MARKETING

The large firms are not directly involved in retailing agricultural machinery. Instead they maintain tied distributor–dealer networks over

† Now incorporated into British Leyland Motor Corporation.

‡ There has in fact been increasing concentration within the industry over the post-war period with several manufacturers ceasing production altogether.

§ Several manufacture special conversions of standard tractor models, however.

¶ H.M.S.O., *Report on the Census of Production*, 1963.

the country. Generally, the dealers sell to farmers from stock and order from the manufacturers to restock—unless demand is unusually high. There are normally two sales peaks—in autumn and spring—and dealers are "encouraged" to maintain higher stocks over the winter period to meet these peaks. The firms also keep some stocks to meet home and export orders but these are normally not as large as the aggregate of dealers' stocks. In the home market the existence of these stocks means that even at times of high demand there is unlikely to be a lengthy lag between farmer order and dealer delivery.†

The large firms also publish list prices—recommended retail prices—which are unaffected in the "short run" by the state of demand. Retailers appear to adhere closely to these list prices in the prices they charge farmers because they have only a small margin to work on.‡ Similarly, the margin available for varying the discount given on an old tractor "traded-in" for a new tractor is small.

The nature of the pricing policies of the manufacturers has not been investigated. However, talks with people in the firms indicate that some form of a mark-up over costs may be involved. In addition, given the oligopolistic nature of the industry, the particular pricing and marketing policy of any one manufacturer is likely to be associated with the known interdependence of the firms within the market. Typical features of oligopoly which are shown are product differentiation and advertising. Product differentiation by each firm is designed to "catch" a wide range of demand requirements and stimulate replacement demand with the firm's product. Advertising expenditure in the U.K. market by the five major firms on tractors alone was estimated as some £450,000 per annum in the early 1960's: over 1 per cent of the value of total home sales.

V.4. RESEARCH AND DEVELOPMENT: TECHNOLOGICAL CHANGE

As indicated earlier, the amount of technical improvement in agricultural machinery since the war has been considerable. This development has been the result of research within the agricultural machinery

---

† At the maximum this is estimated as about one month.
‡ At the maximum this appears to be not more than 20 per cent; in addition, retailers have to finance their stocks and provide service facilities, etc.

industry. Most of the research is carried out privately by firms in the industry and it is estimated that they spend upwards of £20 million per annum in the development of their products.†

Some government supported research is provided by the National Institute of Agricultural Engineering which carries out research into and the development of new machines. In addition, it provides a testing service for the manufacturers for a wide range of equipment. Similar research and performance testing in dairy equipment is carried out by the National Institute for Research in Dairying.

† *Source:* Central Office of Information, *op. cit.*, pamphlet R5001. This is R. and D. directed at both the home and the export markets. As a percentage of total sales this works out between 5 and 10 per cent.

Appendix

TABLE A.1. QUALITY CHANGE, TRACTOR STOCK AND GROSS INVESTMENT

Year	Quality change index for new tractors (ave. 1957–60 = 100)	Value of tractor stock (£m.) in constant quality prices (ave. 1957–60 = 100)	Value of tractor gross investment (£m.) in constant quality prices (ave. 1957–60 = 100)
1948	42·5	35·77	11·16
1949	47·7	41·19	10·10
1950	49·4	44·49	10·80
1951	55·9	48·55	11·42
1952	68·1	56·82	14·73
1953	77·5	64·82	14·34
1954	83·4	74·27	19·00
1955	83·9	81·56	21·34
1956	80·7	81·85	14·77
1957	91·8	92·39	22·93
1958	99·8	103·47	28·32
1959	103·2	119·13	31·81
1960	105·5	124·08	27·86
1961	111·9	130·14	30·26
1962	114·0	130·19	28·50
1963	120·3	139·84	33·57
1964	126·3	142·51	32·35
1965	136·5	143·43	34·63

Source: Rayner, *op. cit.*, Bulletin 113.

TABLE A.2. REPLACEMENT VALUE OF STOCKS OF MACHINERY IN CURRENT
PRICES: 1949/50 COMPARED WITH 1966/7

Year	Cultivating machinery	Sowing and fertilizer distribution machinery	Harvesting machinery	Barn and farmyard machinery	Vehicles (excluding tractors)
1949/50	76·2	23·7	91·5	50·9	125·4
1966/67	141·1	109·6	383·3	121·1	146·7

Source: These figures are the author's estimates calculated for *illustrative* purposes only. Several data sources were used including: M.A.F.F., *Agricultural Statistics*, for census figures on machinery stocks; and Board of Trade, *Business Monitor*, for the calculation of the prices of new machines.

Appreciation is recorded to the following firms who provided essential data on annual tractor sales: (i) Ford Motor Co. Ltd., Basildon, Essex. (ii) International Harvester Co. of Great Britain, London. (iii) David Brown Tractor Co. Ltd., Meltham, Yorks. (iv) Perkins Engines Ltd., Peterborough. (v) Massey-Ferguson (U.K.) Ltd., Coventry. (vi) British Leyland Motor Corporation Ltd., Longbridge, Birmingham. (vii) Allis Chalmers Tractors Ltd., Essendine, Lincs.

CHAPTER 5

CHEMICAL TECHNOLOGY

1. Introduction

There are two main forms of chemical used in agriculture: first, fertilizers, which are used to improve the fertility of the soil, and so raise crop yields or allow grassland to support more livestock. The three chemical fertilizers are: nitrogen (N), phosphate (P_2O_5) and potash (K_2O). Second, pesticides and allied products, developed to eliminate plants and insects which compete for resources required in food production. Farmers spend substantially more on fertilizer than on pesticides. Currently expenditure on fertilizers is around £145 million, whereas the sales of pesticides and allied products by the major U.K. manufacturers, including exports, are around £27 million. Therefore the balance of this chapter favours an analysis and description of factors explaining fertilizer use, but aspects of pesticide use will also be examined. The plan of the chapter is as follows: In section II we describe the development of the chemical fertilizer industry and the trends in the use of fertilizers and pesticides in the post-war period. In section III the theory behind the diffusion of an innovation is investigated, with reference to chemical fertilizer. Section IV concentrates on examining factors which have influenced the demand for fertilizers in the post-war period and incorporates the results of a statistical study which tested for the influence of these variables. The chapter concludes with a section on the present structure of the chemical fertilizer industry, analysing such factors as the links between the major firms and the likely effects of the recent innovations in the production of nitrogen fertilizer.

II. Growth in the Use of Fertilizers and Pesticides

II.1. FERTILIZERS

Before describing trends in the use of chemical fertilizer, a brief description of the history of the fertilizer industry is necessary.† The ruling soil deficiency in the early 19th century was probably phosphate. Nitrogen and potash were kept at reasonable levels through growing clover (although this may not have been realized at the time), and through farmyard manure. Therefore the first inorganic fertilizer to be developed was phosphate. J. B. Lawes was the major innovator to produce phosphate from a mineral source, coprolites, the process being patented in 1842,‡ although ground bones had been used, for example for turnip crops, for a considerable time prior to this. The sector continued to grow as additional mineral sources of phosphate were developed, for example apatite imported from Norway. It was given further impetus when a process was developed for extracting calcium phosphate from basic slag and controlled experiments showed the importance of this chemical. Inorganic nitrogen had been used on farms since the early 1800's; the original source was gas liquor, a waste product of the gas industry which was diluted with water. However, this substance had the drawback of sometimes containing cyanide. Supply of inorganic nitrogen was further expanded by imports of nitrate of soda from Chile.§ The first production of synthetic sulphate of ammonia in Britain was not till the early 1920's at Billingham. The last chemical nutrient is potash. This was developed in Germany after potash deposits had been discovered whilst drilling for common salt.

The major growth in the use of chemical fertilizers has occurred in the period since World War II. During this time two important changes have taken place. First the introduction of granulated fertilizer, which made easier the application of plant nutrients in the form of compounds. (Fertilizers can be applied "straight", that is as just N or P_2O_5 or K_2O, or in compound form, which incorporates proportions of all three nutrients.) Currently over three-quarters of all nutrients are applied in compound form: the only important nutrients applied straight are nitrogen and, less importantly, phosphate in the form of basic slag.

---

† See *History of the Fertilizer Industry*, pamphlet issued at Fertilizer Manufacturers Joint Exhibit, Great Yorkshire Show, 1966.

‡ In the following year, 1843, in collaboration with J. H. Gilbert, Lawes founded the Rothampstead Research Centre.

§ We also imported substantial quantities of organic fertilizers, in the form of guano, from Peru.

Second, the concentration of the nutrients has been increased, which reduces transportation and spreading costs. This trend is likely to continue as the use of highly concentrated liquid nitrogen becomes more widespread.

Table 5.1 shows both the overall increase in the use of fertilizer in the post-war period and the changing proportion of plant nutrients used. It must be emphasized that it is not simply the tonnage applied to the soil that is being measured, but rather the plant food nutrients concentrated in this tonnage. As the concentration level of fertilizer is rising it is possible to have an increase in the tonnage consumption of plant nutrients whilst applying a stable or declining total product.

Total consumption of plant nutrients (in thousands of tons) rose from 628 in 1946/7 to 1581 in 1966/7, an increase of around 150 per cent. Over the same period the increase in the consumption of the three components was (in '000 tons) N: 164–685; P_2O_5: 357–459; K_2O: 107–437. It will be seen that the largest increase has been in the use of nitrogen, partly reflecting the increased application of fertilizer to grassland. The factors which have been responsible for the growth in the consumption of both nitrogen nutrients and total nutrients are discussed in section IV. The discussion of individual nutrients is confined to nitrogen for three reasons. First, the expansion in nitrogen use has been the greatest in the post-war period. Second, nitrogen is quantitatively more important than P_2O_5 and K_2O in the increased application to grassland. Third, following the Report of the National Board for Prices and Incomes† on fertilizer prices, prices have been restructured to favour straight application of nitrogen, in that price increases have been allowed for compounds but not for straight nitrogen where large cost economies in manufacture have either been achieved or will be attained in the near future, although this price trend may have come about independently of the N.B.P.I. Report.

The growth of nitrogen use in the immediate past can be shown from the following figures. Between 1962 and 1966 nitrogen consumption per acre on crops and grass increased by about a quarter, whilst change in phosphate consumption was small. On temporary and permanent grass nitrogen consumption increased by almost 50 per cent. The

† National Board for Prices and Incomes, *Prices of Compound Fertilizers*, Report No. 28, Cmnd. 3228, March 1967.

TABLE 5.1. FERTILIZER USE IN THE U.K.

Year	Nitrogen		Phosphates		Potash		Total	
	'000 nutrient tons	% of total	'000 nutrient tons	% of total	'000 nutrient tons	% of total	'000 nutrient tons	% of total
1946/47	164	26·1	357	56·8	107	17·0	628	100
1947/48	185	24·4	396	52·2	177	23·4	758	100
1948/49	185	23·1	419	52·4	196	24·5	800	100
1949/50	225	24·5	461	50·1	234	25·4	920	100
1950/51	215	25·0	418	48·7	226	26·3	859	100
1951/52	181	28·0	277	43·5	172	27·3	630	100
1952/53	230	27·7	369	44·4	231	27·8	830	100
1953/54	233	27·1	357	42·8	243	29·1	833	100
1954/55	242	29·4	328	39·9	253	30·7	823	100
1955/56	278	29·1	379	39·7	296	31·1	953	100
1956/57	286	29·5	374	38·5	309	31·8	969	100
1957/58	315	29·9	386	36·7	352	33·4	1053	100
1958/59	321	30·3	383	36·2	355	33·5	1059	100
1959/60	404	31·4	455	35·4	426	33·2	1285	100
1960/61	425	32·9	436	33·7	431	33·4	1292	100
1961/62	494	34·8	485	34·1	442	31·1	1421	100
1962/63	495	37·2	437	32·9	397	29·9	1329	100
1963/64	554	37·8	477	32·6	434	29·6	1465	100
1964/65	565	38·3	479	32·4	433	29·3	1477	100
1965/66	589	40·2	435	29·7	440	30·1	1464	100
1966/67	685	43·3	459	29·0	437	27·6	1581	100

Source: Ministry of Agriculture, *Statistics 27*, Annual.

TABLE 5.2 FERTILIZER CONSUMPTION PER ACRE CROPS AND GRASS
IN 1966 AND ESTIMATED CHANGES SINCE 1962
(cwt/acre × 100)

Type of farming area	1966			1962–6		
	N	P_2O_5	K_2O	N	P_2O_5	K_2O
Arable districts	62	34	38	+14	0	−4
Mixed farming and dairying	37	31	23	+5	+3	−1
Uplands and Wales	23	35	17	+8	+3	+3
England and Wales	44	33	27	+9	+2	−1

Source: Rothampstead Experimental Station, *The Survey of Fertilizer Practice 1966*, table 2.

estimated consumption per acre is given in Table 5.2 for the three major types of farming region.

Despite this large growth in the use of nitrogen the potential for further expansion is substantial. Only half of Britain's 22 million acres of grass receive any fertilizer at all and they receive only around 44 lb/acre compared, for example, with Holland's 150 lb/acre. Also investigation has suggested that the use of P_2O_5 and K_2O is near the technical optimum and thus it is to nitrogenous fertilizers that manufacturers must look for industrial growth.

Government Policy

One of the important features of the agricultural industry in the post-war period has been the impact of government intervention. This impinges on fertilizer consumption in three ways. First, indirectly through price supports for agricultural products, thereby lowering the "real" price of fertilizers, that is the price of fertilizer deflated by the price of agricultural products. Second, the government affects consumption directly, the net cost to the farmer being less than the market price through subsidies. The main purpose of the subsidy has been to speed up the diffusion and acceptance of chemical fertilizers by increasing the payoff to the innovation. During World War II and until 1951 the government gave active support to the fertilizer industry. In 1949/50, for example, the government gave the industry £14·5 million in order to stabilize prices. This represented 40 per cent of farmers' expenditure on fertilizer. These subsidies were replaced in 1951 by farmers' subsidies, which have had a chequered history. Over the period 1953–8, it appeared that the government was prepared to offset successive annual price increases by manufacturers by higher subsidies. It was suggested[†] that this led to monopolistic tendencies in the chemical fertilizer industry and in 1959 the industry was the subject of a report by the Monopolies Commission[‡] which resulted in cuts in market prices. The subsidy reached a peak of £34 million in 1961/2. Following the

[†] H. Frankel, Monopolistic tendencies in the chemical fertilizer industry, *Farm Economist*, vol. VIII, 10, 1957.

[‡] Monopolies Commission, *Report on the Supply of Chemical Fertilizers*, July 1959.

report of the Natural Resources Technical Committee,† which concluded that the subsidy encouraged "wasteful use" of fertilizer and that its removal would encourage greater efficiency, the government has reduced the real level of subsidization slightly.

The third form of intervention is through tariffs, which protect the home fertilizer industry. The tariff on compound fertilizers is £4 per ton, approximately 15 per cent of the retail price. There are also tariffs of similar magnitude on the ingredients of compound fertilizers, such as ammonium nitrate (16 per cent) and superphosphate (14 per cent). These form substantial barriers to foreign suppliers' penetration of the U.K. market and manipulation of tariff levels is a weapon which could be used to stabilize domestic fertilizer prices.

II.2. PESTICIDES

The scientific use of chemicals to protect crops is over a hundred years old. The first large scale use of an insecticide occurred in the U.S.A. in the 1860's when the application of Paris Green, an arsenic compound, was used to protect the potato crop from the Colorado beetle. Initially chemical protection measures were applied primarily to horticultural crops, vines, hops and fruit. The chemicals used were simple inorganic substances such as lime sulphur, arsenic, lead and mercury. These chemicals were superseded as newer chemical compounds were discovered which gave more efficient crop protection.

The recent growth in the sales of pesticides and allied products is detailed in Table 5.3. It will be seen that total sales in money terms have almost doubled since 1961 with an extremely large growth in the sales of herbicides. Insecticides have the beneficial effect of increased yields, improvements in quality of produce and make possible changes in the location and timing of production. Similarly, herbicides increase yields by reducing competition between crops and weeds for water, light and plant nutrients and by controlling weeds that harbour insect pests and fungus diseases. They also save inputs which would otherwise be needed

---

† Natural Resources Technical Committee, *Report of the Fertilizer Subsidy Study Group*, M.A.F.F., 1962. They did not define "wasteful". Presumably the marginal value product of a unit of input was less than the price of that unit. Alternatively, the marginal productivity of fertilizer input could have been thought to be zero.

TABLE 5.3. PESTICIDES AND ALLIED PRODUCTS SALES
BY LARGER U.K. MANUFACTURERS (£ '000)

	Total all products	Insecticides	Fungicides	Herbicides	Other
1961	14,563·1	6324·8	3117·5	4736·2	324·5
1962	15,343·1	5986·5	2986·1	6088·3	282·2
1963	18,391·0	6588·2	3610·4	7812·7	379·7
1964	20,420·5	7020·4	3689·8	9276·2	434·1
1965	22,634·5	6693·3	3574·3	12,008·6	358·2
1966	26,450·9	7609·6	3651·1	14,762·6	427·7
1967	28,097·9	7053·9	3583·2	16,875·3	585·5

Source: Board of Trade, *Business Monitor*, Production Series, Quarterly.

for mechanical weed control and the cleaning of grains and seeds. Fungicides protect crops from infection by plant pathogenic fungi.

The growth in the use of pesticides and allied products is due to the fact that the return to the farmer is large compared to the cost of the chemicals. Table 5.4 indicates the average annual acre-equivalent grain losses in cereal crops in England and Wales that would occur in the absence of specific control measures against *insects*. It shows that, for two of the three crops at least, a significant part of the output would be lost. (The output loss is presented in the table in terms of the acreage equivalent of a loss of output. Thus for wheat it is calculated that 7·7 per cent of the output would have been lost, for barley 2·1 per cent and oats 9·0 per cent.)

An increase in yields also results from the use of *herbicides*. It appears that the knowledge that the application of herbicides results in higher yields is widely diffused. A survey undertaken in 1959 found that out of 22,157 farms of 100 acres and over growing wheat as a cash crop in south east England, 83 per cent sprayed some wheat with a weedkiller. The proportion of farmers using weedkillers was larger for large farms, rising to 98 per cent on farms of over 500 acres. The effect on yields is indicated by the fact that 90 per cent of farms having yields of over 30 cwt/acre made some use of weedkiller, whilst only 44 per cent of farmers harvesting 10 to 20 cwt/acre used weedkiller.[†]

† See P. Hillebrandt, Economics of the use of selective weedkillers, *Farm Economist*, vol. IX, 5, 1949.

TABLE 5.4. POSSIBLE AVERAGE ANNUAL ACRE-EQUIVALENT GRAIN LOSSES IN
CEREAL CROPS IN ENGLAND AND WALES IN THE ABSENCE OF
SPECIFIC CONTROL MEASURES

Pest complex	Wheat	Barley	Oats
Insecta:			
Wireworms	36,000	48,000	14,000
Flea beetles	—	—	—
Leatherjackets	3000	9000	200
Wheat bulb fly	30,000	—	—
Frit fly	—	—	10,000
Other cereal stem-boring flies	2000	500	500
Aphids as virus vectors	1000	5000	1000
Aphids, feeding	—	—	—
Caterpillars	—	—	—
Nematoda:			
Cereal root eelworm	13,000	22,000	28,000
Stem and bulb eelworm	—	—	—
Mollusca:			
Slugs	41,000	—	—
Vertebrata:			
Rabbits and hares	14,000	2500	800
Total losses	140,000	87,000	54,500
Acreage grown, 1963	1,837,000	4,148,000	616,000
Total losses as a percentage of 1963 acreage grown	7·7	2·1	9·0

N.B. Dashes denote lack of information about damage which almost certainly occurs.
Source: Calculated from A. H. Strickland, *Pest Control and Productivity in British Agriculture*, Royal Society of Arts, November, 1964.

An indication of the returns to farmers from applying insecticides, fungicides and herbicides to one crop, wheat, are shown in Table 5.5. It will be seen that the return was of the order of £8 million whilst the chemicals used in these treatments are estimated to have cost growers nearly £0·9 million. The return less the cost of the chemical raw material was, therefore, of the order of £7 million per annum.

Needful treatment implies that the grower succeeds in controlling an attack that would otherwise have lowered his grain yield. This high return is of course a gross figure, for the true cost of pesticides is greater

Resource Structure of Agriculture

TABLE 5.5. ESTIMATED ANNUAL RETURNS (£ '000) FROM TREATMENTS
NEEDFULLY APPLIED TO WHEAT ACREAGE (THOUSANDS) (AVERAGE
OF YEARS 1960–64)

Potential infestation level	From pest control		From weed control		From disease control	
	Acres needfully treated	£ return	Acres needfully treated	£ return	Acres needfully treated	£ return
Severe	57	867	76	737		
Moderate	376	1490	182	1065 ⎱	1376	2477
Slight	191	259	576	1094 ⎰		
Totals:		2616		2887		2477
Cost of materials		248		497		138
Return less material cost		2368		2390		2339

Source: A. H. Strickland, *Some Problems in the Economic Integration of Crop Loss Control*, paper given at British Insecticide and Fungicide Council's Conference, 1967.

than merely the cost of the raw material. The figures indicate that the highest rate of return was obtained from disease control. To obtain details of the net return we would also need to include, for example, the costs of application, the fact that the chemicals may have been overapplied by some farmers, and the cost of harvesting the extra tonnage of output.

The Contribution of Pesticides to Yield Increases

The major increases in the use of chemicals, both fertilizer and pesticides in agriculture has been in the post-war period. It is obviously extremely difficult to estimate the contribution of pesticides to yield increases as fertilizers and pesticides are to some extent complementary. Also yield increases may be due to better seed varieties, higher quality farm machinery or other factors. Despite these difficulties, it is instructive to attempt to calculate the contributions of agricultural chemicals

TABLE 5.6. COMPONENTS OF WHEAT YIELD ESTIMATED FOR 1960–4

Factor	Estimated cwt/acre	Percentage contribution to total
Baseline yield 1940–7	19·0	61
New varieties	4·1	13
Fertilizers	5·1	17
Pest, disease and weed control	2·9	9
Total	31·1	100

Source: A. H. Strickland, *op. cit.*

to the increases in yield. This calculation has been made for wheat and the details are presented in Table 5.6.

It is only in the 1950's that pesticides were used on wheat in any substantial scale. It is therefore possible to estimate an approximate overall return from pesticides by comparing yields in the 1940's and yields in the 1960's after allowing for the non-pesticide factors introduced between the two periods. It will be seen that between 1941–7 and 1960–4 the wheat yield increased from 19·0 to 31·1 cwt/acre and about one-quarter of the increase is attributable to increased use of pesticides. Strickland points out that whilst about 45 per cent of the variable costs of wheat production went on fertilizer and 10 per cent on pesticides, the yield response to fertilizer was only about twice as big as the response to pesticides. Therefore pesticides may have been under-applied relative to the application of fertilizer.

III. The Diffusion of Innovations

The previous section described the growth in the use of inorganic fertilizers over the post-war period. It is now necessary to analyse the process of diffusion and adoption of an innovation in more detail. An innovation may be defined as "any thought, behaviour or thing that is new because it is qualitatively different from existing forms".[†] Thus chemical fertilizers were an innovation in that they differed qualitatively from the organic forms of fertilizer previously used.

† H. G. Barnett, *Innovation: The Basis of Cultural Change*, p. 7, New York, 1953.

We must distinguish between diffusion and adoption.† *Diffusion* is concerned with the spread of the new products, processes or organization. It has two elements which may, at the risk of oversimplification, be described as micro- and macro-elements. Micro diffusion is a social concept, referring to the spread of an innovation from its originating sources, in this case the input suppliers backed by agricultural scientists, among a group of potential users. The macro aspect of diffusion is geographical, describing the changing distribution of an innovation as it spreads from one or more areas where its use has become more general at an earlier time than in surrounding areas. *Adoption* is more specific, being the act of accepting an innovation. Sociologists have developed a model of the adoption process which has five stages: awareness—interest—evaluation—trial—adoption.‡ The act of adopting an innovation is therefore the last link in the chain of diffusion.

Generally, different geographical areas adopt innovations at different rates. There are *three* elements to this, which will be described in terms of chemical fertilizer. Firstly, each region will not start using the innovation in the same base year. Let us assume that the base year for each region is described when 5 per cent of the farmland acreage receives chemical fertilizer. Now it is unlikely that the base years for each region will occur simultaneously. This may be essentially a *supply* problem, in that differences in base years may be predominantly explained by differences in availability of fertilizer, where the degree of availability is a direct result of the actions by chemical fertilizer producers. These producers will enter an area according to the expected profitability, entering first those areas where profitability is likely to be highest.§ Expected profitability will be influenced by a number of factors. First, the eventual density of the market area, that is the number of areas likely to receive fertilizer and the intensity of application; second, the cost of marketing; third, the expected rate of acceptances

† G. E. Jones, The diffusion of agricultural innovations, *J. Agricultural Economics*, 1963. This article provides an excellent synthesis of the literature on the diffusion of agricultural innovations.

‡ E. M. Rogers, Categorizing the adoption of agricultural practices, *Rural Sociology*, vol. 23, 1958.

§ The differences in profitability between regions in the U.K. is not so stark as in the U.S.A. For a discussion of the factors behind the innovation of hybrid corn in the U.S.A., see Z. Griliches, Hybrid corn: an exploration in the economics of technical change, *Econometrica*, vol. 25, 4, October 1957.

of the innovation. Therefore it is more profitable to enter an area with high market density, a rapid expected rate of acceptance and low marketing costs, all of which made the arable areas more profitable than the grassland areas for the manufacturers of chemical fertilizers in the U.K.

The other two differences between regions are differences in the rate of acceptance of the innovation, and differences in the ultimate level of its use. Thus regions differ according to the speed with which they take up the innovation of chemical fertilizer and the final proportion of acres likely to use these inorganic fertilizers. These regional differences are essentially determined by factors on the demand side, because in the long run the supply of fertilizers is very elastic, and if farmers have an effective demand for fertilizer this demand will be met. These regional differences therefore depend on the profitability to the farmer of using chemical fertilizer which itself is a function of the relationship between the extra yield the farmer receives and the real price of the fertilizer, although the farmer may not be able to reach the optimal application because of, for example, a financial constraint.

If the fertilizer diffusion process were analysed for the U.K., distinguishing between arable and grassland sectors, the following would be found. First, the base year in the grassland areas occurred significantly later than that in the arable areas. Second, whilst arable areas are now approaching their ultimate level of use, given prevailing prices of fertilizer and crops products, grassland regions are still significantly below the ultimate level they will achieve. In view of these differences between different agricultural areas an understanding of the diffusion process will be enhanced by analysing in more detail the factors which have influenced the increased consumption of fertilizers over the last quarter century, and it is to this that we now turn.

IV. Demand Functions for Fertilizers†

In this section the economic variables which might be hypothesized to affect the consumption of total plant nutrients and of nitrogen

† This section is based on D. Metcalf and K. Cowling, Demand functions for fertilizer in the United Kingdom, 1948–65, *Journal of Agricultural Economics*, vol. XVIII, 3, Sept. 1967. The authors are indebted to the Agricultural Economics Society for permission to reproduce part of that article.

nutrients are analysed. We then present the results of a statistical study which tested for the influence of these variables over the period 1948–65. Lastly the results are described verbally.

IV.1. THE MODEL

The variable to be explained in this section is the consumption of fertilizer in terms of tonnage of plant nutrients by the U.K. agricultural industry over the period 1948–65; in addition, equations will be presented which attempt to explain the consumption of nitrogen. The explanatory variables used in the analysis will be mentioned briefly initially and analysed in more depth below to explain why they are considered relevant and to assess past results incorporating these explainants. The variables are:

D total nutrient consumption,

$\dfrac{P_{fe}}{P_p}$ real price of fertilizer,

Y farm income,

T time,

$\dfrac{P_{fd}}{P_{fe}}$ real price of feedingstuffs,

u error term.

The analysis takes the form of a single equation model to be estimated by least squares regression procedures:

$$D = f\left(\frac{P_{fe}}{P_p};\ Y;\ T;\ \frac{P_{fd}}{P_{fe}};\ u\right)$$

IV.2. THE VARIABLES

(a) *Dependent Variable: Plant Nutrient Consumption* (D)

The dependent variable is the simple sum of the individual nutrients in thousands of tons applied to the soil on a June–May year basis.

(b) *Explanatory Variables*

(i) *Real Price of Fertilizer*

This variable is the price of fertilizer deflated by either crop prices (P_{fe}/P_c) or by an index of all agricultural product prices (P_{fe}/P_p). The quantity of fertilizer used depends on real price (fertilizer price deflated by the agricultural product prices). Thus if fertilizers become cheaper relative to agricultural product prices, it pays the farmer to move along the production function and apply more fertilizer.†

Price either deflated or undeflated has been used in all previous studies of the demand for fertilizer, resulting in a consistently significant negative coefficient. Whilst different studies produced different estimates of the short run price elasticity of demand the series of articles by Griliches‡ provides considerable evidence that the elasticity of demand is less than unity, for the U.S.A. at least. Two possible measures of fertilizer price exist: market prices or costs to the farmer, i.e. market prices minus exchequer subsidy. From the viewpoint of affecting consumption the latter would appear more relevant.§ As the dependent variable is on a June–May year basis the price of fertilizers is taken over a similar period. The deflator is, however, crops prices in the previous calendar year. The rationale behind taking different 12-monthly periods to calculate real fertilizer price may be explained by the fact that the farmer knows the prevailing fertilizer price but can only guess at crop prices. The model explicitly assumes that crop prices prevailing in the previous year serve as his expectation. Fertilizer prices were also

---

† If the slope of the real price of fertilizers line is very flat the optimal use for the farmers may be greater than the socially optimal use. For a discussion of this in the context of pesticides see J. C. Headley and J. N. Lewis, *The Pesticide Problem: An Economic Approach to Public Policy*, p. 19, Johns Hopkins Press, 1967.

‡ See Z. Griliches, Demand for fertilizers, an economic interpretation of technical change, *J. Farm Economics*, vol. 42, 2, May 1959; Distributed lags, disaggregation and regional demand for fertilizers, *J. Farm Economics*, vol. 41, 1, February 1959; Demand for inputs in agriculture and a derived supply elasticity, *J. Farm Economics*, vol. 42, 2, May, 1959; Demand for fertilizers in 1954: an interstate study, *J. American Statistical Association*, vol. 54, 286, June 1959.

§ The problem of simultaneous determination is probably relatively unimportant. Whilst the market prices may be viewed as either maximum list price or actual (discounted) list price, the fertilizer prices are generally considered to be "administered", with disequilibrium being expressed largely in sellers' inventories. Thus in the short run price may be assumed to be predetermined.

deflated by an average of prices of all products received by farmers. This price index would appear relevant because of the use of fertilizer to produce feed for livestock. Much of the increase in the application of fertilizer, especially nitrogen, has been on grassland, increasing production of livestock and livestock products without increasing expenditure on livestock feedingstuffs to levels which would otherwise be necessary.

When analysing the demand for nitrogen individually, the price variable used is the deflated sulphate of ammonia price. Thus we are using the price of the most commonly used straight fertilizer to explain the total consumption of nitrogen nutrients (compound plus straight). The defect of using this price is that the price of nitrogen nutrients and used in compound fertilizers may have diverged from the sulphate of ammonia price.

(ii) *Farm Income* (Y)

Lagged net farm income is used to represent expected earnings and liquidity. The expected sign of the coefficient is positive: first because *a priori* reasoning indicates that an increased demand for fertilizers is associated with a higher level of income; second because higher income improves the liquidity position and the availability of funds for the purchase of fertilizer by the farmer. Under conditions of limited operating capital farmers may be unable to fertilize at optimal rates. They do not apply sufficient fertilizer to reach the point where the marginal revenue product obtained from the last unit of the input equals the price of the input. Thus assuming farmers are currently applying nutrients at a sub-optimal rate a higher level of income will help them achieve the optimum application. There is considerable evidence that nitrogen is being applied at a sub-optimal level, especially on grassland.

The bare income figures were deflated by an index of retail prices to give an estimate of real net farm income. This allows us to think of the farm household as the consuming unit. Its real income depends on the movements in both its money income and retail prices. Deflating by retail prices therefore eliminates that portion of the money income increase which is needed merely to maintain existing real expenditure levels. Two types of lags were used. First a simple lag, using the deflated income from June ($t - 1$) to May (t). Secondly a weighted average of past deflated farm incomes, giving June $(t - 1)$ to May (t) a weight of 3, June $(t - 2)$ to May $(t - 1)$ a weight of 2 and June $(t - 3)$ to May $(t - 2)$ a weight of 1. The second variable allows both expectations and ability to pay to depend on three past years' income and not solely on very recent income.

(iii) *Time* (T)

The time variable is included as a relevant economic variable. The economic justification behind the inclusion of time in its own right is the expectation of an upward shift in the demand function through time because of the greater technological knowledge of farmers, resulting from their own findings, education, sales programmes and extension services. The time variable running from 1 in 1948 to 18 in 1965 therefore represents the diffusion of knowledge and acceptance of chemical fertilizers. Whilst the diffusion process was fully worked out in arable areas some time ago the process is at present continuing on grassland. We may therefore regard the process as continuous with the grassland diffusion being superimposed on the arable diffusion.

(iv) *Prices of Other Inputs*

A positive relationship is hypothesized between consumption of nutrients and the real price of feedingstuffs (ratio of feed to fertilizer price (P_{fd}/P_{fe})) for two reasons. Firstly, one of the features of fertilizer usage has been the increasing application to grassland. Fertilizer may thus be considered a substitute for purchased feed; if the price of feedingstuffs rises relative to the price of fertilizer this will induce farmers to apply more fertilizer to grassland thereby increasing the productivity of the grassland and reducing the amount of bought feedingstuffs necessary for livestock. It is anticipated that this will hold especially for nitrogen which is the most important fertilizer nutrient applied to grassland. Secondly, if the price of feedingstuffs rises this may induce farmers to increase fertilizer application to those crops used for animal feed, inducing higher yield and enabling farmers to either sell these feed-grains at the higher price or to use them on their own farms.

Fertilizer consumption is assumed to be unaffected by the prices of other inputs.

(v) *Dynamic Considerations*

The analysis assumes that the desired level of use of fertilizers depends on their real price and on other variables which cause a shift in the price/ quantity relation. However, the actual level of use is not assumed equal to the desired level except in the long run, in that the real price change may not be considered permanent and adjustment to the change is not costless; also the adjustment takes time. Therefore a distributed lag model is used which allows adjustment to changes in the various independent variables to be spread over more than just one year.

IV.3. THE RESULTS†

The results for regression equations explaining total consumption of plant nutrients are shown in Table 5.7. Equations (1)–(4) are linear and (5) is log-linear. The latter equation gives direct elasticity estimates but also assumes a constant elasticity throughout the time period under consideration—possibly an unrealistic assumption. The discussion of the results concentrates on the implications of different elasticity estimates. A comparison of equations (1) and (2) where the complete model is presented in linear form, emphasizes two main points. First (P_{fe}/P_p) has a larger, more significant coefficient than $(P_{fe}/P_p)_t$.‡ Second, equation (2) where (P_{fe}/P_p) is the price variable has a better fit, with 95 per cent of the variance in fertilizer consumption explained, as against 91 per cent in equation (1). These two facts hold throughout the analysis: the coefficient of (P_{fe}/P_p) is consistently larger than that of $(P_{fe}/P_p)_t$. Similarly, equations including (P_{fe}/P_p) have a higher R^2 value than those in which $(P_{fe}/P_p)_t$ is the price variable. Equations substituting lagged for current price for both price formulations were also estimated, resulting in similar coefficients but lower R^2 values.

When translating the price coefficients to elasticity estimates we find

---

† This section may be omitted, The results are described verbally shortly.

‡ A variable is taken to be significant if its coefficient is at least twice the size of its standard error. This roughly corresponds to the 5 per cent level.

…$_{-1}$	$\left(\dfrac{P_{fd}}{P_{fe}}\right)_t$	D_{t-1}	R^2	$\bar{R}^2$	d^+_+
74 75)	$-2 \cdot 074$ $(2 \cdot 120)$		$0 \cdot 913$	$0 \cdot 886$	$2 \cdot 49$
10 52)	$-1 \cdot 211$ $(1 \cdot 680)$		$0 \cdot 945$	$0 \cdot 928$	$2 \cdot 21$
			$0 \cdot 928$	$0 \cdot 919$	$1 \cdot 45$
		$0 \cdot 334$ $(0 \cdot 159)$	$0 \cdot 945$	$0 \cdot 934$	$2 \cdot 76$
32 79)	$-0 \cdot 341$ $(0 \cdot 366)$		$0 \cdot 908$	$0 \cdot 880$	$2 \cdot 11$

…ients.

…y of the equations presented.

…er year June $(t-1)$ to May (t). U.K. total.

…o May (t)) deflated by an index of crop prices received by
…J.K. prices.

…o December $(t-1)$ to May (t)) deflated by an index of all
…$t-1)$ to December $(t-1))$, 1948 = 100. U.K. prices.

…index to give real net farm income. The resulting index is

…)) $\times 2 +$ (June $(t-3)$ to May $(t-2)$) $\times 1$

…$ to May (t)) deflated by an index of price of fertilizer paid
…ures.

TABLE 5.7. REGRESSION EQUATIONS EXPLAINING TOTAL CONS

Equation	Constant	$\left(\dfrac{P_{fe}}{P_c}\right)_t$	$\left(\dfrac{P_{fe}}{P_p}\right)_t$	T_t	Y
(1) Linear	389·204	−4·584 (3·050)†		47·660 (7·977)	2· (1·
(2) Linear	1016·151		−9·000 (2·670)	43·061 (6·249)	1· (0·
(3) Linear	1789·841		−10·889 (2·574)	39·309 (3·398)	
(4) Linear	1519·630		−10·181 (2·348)	25·328 (7·563)	
(5) Log-linear	12·388		−1·738 (0·318)	0·261 (0·064)	0 (0

† The figures in parentheses are the standard errors of the associated coef
‡ d is the Von Neumann ratio. There is no evidence of autocorrelation in

Definition of the variables

D_t — Sum of individual nutrients in thousands of tons. Fertili

$\left(\dfrac{P_{fe}}{P_c}\right)_t$ — Index of price of fertilizers paid by farmers (June $(t-1)$) farmers (January $(t-1)$ to December $(t-1)$), 1948–100.

$\left(\dfrac{P_{fe}}{P_p}\right)_t$ — Index of price of fertilizers paid by farmers (June $(t-1)$) agricultural product prices received by farmers (January

T_t — Time trend running from 1 in 1948 to 18 in 1965.

Y_{t-1} — Aggregate U.K. net farm income deflated by retail price then weighted, viz:

$$\frac{(\text{June }(t-1) \text{ to May }(t)) \times 3 + (\text{June }(t-2) \text{ to May }(t-}{6}$$

$\left(\dfrac{P_{fd}}{P_{fe}}\right)_t$ — Index of price of feedingstuffs paid by farmers (June $(t-$ by farmers (June $(t-1)$ to May (t)), 1948 = 100. U.K. f

D_{t-1} — D_t lagged one year.

that the elasticity of demand declined sharply through time, having halved in magnitude between 1948 and 1965.† The demand elasticity with respect to (P_{fe}/P_p) was $1\cdot2$ in 1948 and had fallen to $0\cdot6$ by 1965. At the mean values of (P_{fe}/P_p) and D_t the estimated elasticity is unity indicating that a 10 per cent increase in the real price of fertilizers (i.e. a 10 per cent rise in fertilizer price or 10 per cent fall in agricultural product prices) is associated with a similar reduction in fertilizer consumption. The elasticity at the mean using $(P_{fe}/P_p)_t$ as the price variable is a little over half that of (P_{fe}/P_c). This implies that a reduction in crop prices by 10 per cent will cause only half the reduction in fertilizer consumption that a reduction in all agricultural product prices by 10 per cent would cause. The better fit of equation (2) compared with equation (1) and the higher price coefficient indicates that fertilizer consumption depends on the overall level of agricultural product price rather than solely on the prices of arable products.

Of the remaining variables in equation (2) the dominant explainant of fertilizer consumption is time. The significant coefficient indicates that, other things being equal, consumption will increase by some 43,000 nutrient tons per annum. The coefficient of the income variable, which is just about significant at the level chosen, indicates that a rise in income of £10 million will increase fertilizer consumption by 19,000 nutrient tons. The income variable incorporated in equation (2) is the weighted variable. This variable proved superior to the simple lagged real net farm income and does tend to confirm that the sustained prosperity of agriculture is important in explaining fertilizer consumption in that the farmers' liquidity position is influenced by past income as well as current income. The coefficient of the feed price variable is non-significant. The coefficient is significant and positive when this variable alone is added to price, which supports *a priori* belief in a substitute relationship between fertilizers and feedingstuffs, but the variable is dominated by the time variable in equation (2).

In equation (5) the complete model is presented in log form. This has a lower explanatory power than the corresponding linear equation

† Whilst equations estimated in log form assume constant elasticity through time, elasticity is assumed to vary in linear models. To estimate the elasticity of demand at different points in time, if b is the price coefficient and P the price ratio the price elasticity of demand at year t is given by $b(P/D)_t$.

($R^2 = 0 \cdot 91$, as against $0 \cdot 95$ in equation (2)). However, it confirms the importance of the price and time variables, which have coefficients significant at the 1 per cent level, compared with income and feed price variables which have non-significant coefficients.

Because the income and feed price variables appear relatively unimportant, they are dropped in equation (3). It will be seen that the remaining coefficients are similar compared with equation (2) and the R^2 only worsens by $0 \cdot 02$ with their omission. It is interesting to note, however, that the implied price elasticity of demand is now estimated to be higher, being $1 \cdot 2$ at the mean. Further results (not reported here) spanning the more recent period 1955–65 give an estimated price elasticity of $0 \cdot 5$. This gives some support for the linear models which imply a declining price elasticity through time. The importance of the weather as an additional explainant of fertilizer consumption is seen when examining the residuals from the regressions. A large unexplained negative residual in 1962–3 probably indicates the extreme weather conditions prevailing in the winter and spring of that year. The fit of the 1955–65 equation improves by 20 per cent when the fertilizer year 1962–3 is omitted.

The results for the distributed lag model appear as equation (4). The coefficient of D_{t-1} in an equation excluding T was $0 \cdot 67$, which implies that only 33 per cent of the adjustment to price is carried out in a given year. The true short-run adjustment towards equilibrium is probably much greater than this. In equation (4) when the time variable is included, the coefficient of D_{t-1} is reduced to $0 \cdot 33$, which suggests that two-thirds of the equilibrium adjustment to price is undertaken in the current year. This indicates that the long-run elasticity of demand is one and a half times the short-run demand elasticity.

The results for equations explaining nitrogen consumption are presented in Table 5.8, equation (6) being linear and (7) and (8) log-linear. The complete model is presented in linear form in equation (6) and in log form in equation (7). The price variable having all agricultural product prices as the deflator is again superior to the variable where crop prices are the deflator in terms of significant and explanatory power so only equations incorporating the former are reported. It will be noted that a similar pattern to that in Table 5.1 emerges. The linear formulation has a better fit (R^2 of $0 \cdot 97$ as against $0 \cdot 90$ in the log relationship).

TABLE 5.8. REGRESSION EQUATIONS EXPLAINING CONSUMPTION OF NITROGEN (D_t^N)

Coefficient / Equation	Constant	$\left(\dfrac{P_{fe}^N}{P_p}\right)_t$	T_t	Y_{t-1}	$\left(\dfrac{P_{ra}}{P_{fe}^N}\right)_t$	D_{t-1}^N	R^2	$\bar{R}^2$	
(6) Linear	−244·620	−0·932 (0·739)	25·085 (2·600)	1·597 (0·352)	−1·245 (0·649)		0·965	0·954	2·26
(7) Log-linear	2·027	−1·143 (0·342)	0·438 (0·109)	1·917 (0·713)	−0·674 (0·590)		0·901	0·870	1·71
(8) Log-linear	4·455	−0·679 (0·211)	0·086 (0·046)			0·742 (0·110)	0·963	0·955	2·86

The coefficient of the price variable is non-significant in the linear formulation (possibly because it is correlated with T) but significant in the log equation; the time and income coefficients are significant in both equations (6) and (7), but the feedingstuffs variable, whilst having a significant positive coefficient in an equation where it is added by itself to the price variable, is again dominated by the time variable, resulting in a non-significant coefficient. The coefficient of the (weighted average) lagged income variable in equation (7) indicates an income elasticity of demand of almost 2, a 10 per cent rise in net farm income being associated with a 20 per cent increase in the consumption of nitrogenous nutrients.

Equation (8), which takes account of the dynamic aspects of demand, indicates a short run elasticity of demand of around $0 \cdot 7$. Thus a rise in the price of fertilizer or drop in prices received by farmers by 10 per cent is associated with a fall in nitrogen nutrient consumption of 7 per cent. A slow adjustment towards equilibrium in any given year is indicated, with an adjustment coefficient of $0 \cdot 26$. This implies that the long-run elasticity of demand is about four times as large as the short-run demand elasticity, that is about $2 \cdot 8$ indicating a very substantial response to a decline in real price—but only after a substantial period of adjustment.

IV.4. INTERPRETATION

Our results indicate that a statistically significant relationship exists between fertilizer consumption and its "real" price. The derived elasticity estimates indicate that a 10 per cent increase in "real" price will mean a fall in consumption of about 6 per cent at the present time. This could arise because of an upward adjustment in prices, a downward adjustment in fertilizer subsidies following the trend in the 1960's or a downward adjustment in agricultural prices due to subsidy policy or market conditions. However, while the price response has been demonstrated it has also been shown that a strong upward trend exists associated with the post-war diffusion of this technology through U.K. agriculture. Adjustments to price are made around this upward trend causing year-to-year variations in consumption. It is likely that the propelling force behind the trend has undergone some structural change in the period. During the earlier period it represented the diffusion of fertilizer technology among cash-crop producers and then more recently, as crop producers have attained optimal usage, this has been superseded by the diffusion among livestock producers for use on grassland. Because of the high correlation between the ratio of feed to fertilizer prices and the linear trend variable (T) it is likely also that the trend coefficient reflects also the declining price of fertilizer relative to feed. Thus the strong trend is in itself partly a price adjustment mechanism. Also the measure of farm income used is correlated with trend so that here again trend is partly reflecting an improved liquidity position. Income does appear especially important in explaining nitrogen consumption.

For total fertilizer consumption the analysis indicates that two-thirds of the adjustment in use towards equilibrium application is made within one year. Thus the long-run demand elasticity is not too different from the short run, currently being around unity. This may well mean that in the longer term the revenue of the manufacturers may not increase as much as anticipated when they raise fertilizer prices, which they argue is a necessary step for expansion of the home fertilizer manufacturing industry. Again it appears that with the current wave of investment in the new ammonia processes, there will exist excess capacity in the near future, and this will be a force operating to reduce fertilizer prices in the longer run.

V. Supply Conditions

V.1. THE MAJOR FIRMS

The industry is currently dominated by three firms, Imperial Chemical Industries, Fisons and Shellstar. I.C.I. dominates the nitrogen sector, but Shellstar has recently set up its own large-scale new ammonia plant and I.C.I. is building a similar plant for Fisons. Fisons is basically a phosphoric acid producer, but through bought nitrogen and imported potash it has the majority of the compound fertilizer market. Shellstar is the jointly owned subsidiary of Shell and Armour,† the dominant fertilizer manufacturer in the U.S.A. (Shell itself has had a small ammonia plant for some time with a contract to supply Fisons.) To gain access to the U.K. market, Shellstar initially imported its requirements at a loss from Holland, but is now producing its own chemical

† This was written prior to Armour withdrawing from Shellstar, which is now 100 per cent owned by Shell.

requirements. The current market for compound fertilizers is probably split in the ratio Fisons 40 per cent, I.C.I. 25 per cent, Shellstar 10 per cent.

Relations between the major producers are complex. Fisons has traditionally not produced ammonia and for a long time relied on I.C.I. for its requirements. Dissatisfaction with these arrangements led to a contract with Shell to buy its output from a small new plant (80,000 tons p.a.) at Shellhaven. The situation was, however, radically altered in 1962 with the development, by I.C.I., of a new ammonia process which reduced costs substantially. I.C.I. recently established a large scale (200,000 tons p.a.) ammonia plant for Fisons at Immingham. The new Shell–Armour link up is very natural, with Shell providing the basis for cheap ammonia production from oil and Armour controlling large sources of phosphate rock and potash, together with great experience in fertilizer production and marketing.

Location is an important element in determining efficiency where the product, as with fertilizers, is bulky and has a spatially very diffuse demand. I.C.I.'s production capacity is mainly concentrated in the North-East. It recently established three 1000 tons a day ammonia plants costing £40 million at Billingham. In addition one of its new plants is being built at Severnside. Fisons operations are centred in the South-East together with new nitric acid plants at Immingham and Avonmouth. The new Shellstar plant is at Ellesmere Port on Mersey-side. Currently fertilizers are used more intensively in the arable areas of the South and East, but fertilizer usage in these areas is approaching its technical optimum and is unlikely to expand much further. As indicated in section II the main future expansion is likely to be on grassland, which is found predominantly in the North and West. Thus Shell and I.C.I. are well placed for low cost distribution in these "growth areas", whereas Fisons is not well located.

V.2. TECHNOLOGICAL INNOVATIONS

Recently a number of important technological innovations have been developed within the industry. The most important of these has been the introduction of a new low cost method for producing ammonia by I.C.I. This is the steam reforming process using naphtha feedstock (oil derivative), which has reduced labour input in producing one ton of ammonia from 11·6 man-hours to 0·3 man-hour. I.C.I. have now three large scale plants at Billingham, one at Severnside and one at Immingham. These, together with Shellstar's new Ellesmere Port ammonia plant (capacity 750,000 tons p.a.) imply a tremendous increase in the capacity for producing fertilizer nitrogen. In 1965 production of fertilizer nitrogen was around 600,000 tons, equivalent of 730,000 tons of ammonia. Given a realistic assessment of home demand through to 1970 of around one million tons per annum, this implies an excess above home capacity requirements of approaching one million tons.

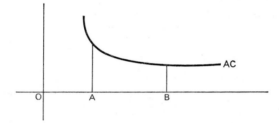

FIG. 5.1

Despite the fact that I.C.I. is using one of its new ammonia plants at Billingham for the production of urea, a highly concentrated fertilizer intended purely for the export market, it is unlikely that all the extra capacity will be used for export production. (1965 exports were only 120,000 tons, and I.C.I. is setting up overseas plants.) If excess capacity does exist this can have two potential results. First, a rise in the firm's unit costs—that is (Fig. 5.1), the firm will be forced back along its average cost curve to a point (*A*) to the left of the output at which it attains minimum unit average cost (*B*), the technically optimum plant having a minimum ammonia output of around 300,000 tons p.a. The extent of the increase in unit costs depends on the steepness of the *AC* curve to the left of output *OB*. Second, the firm may attempt to maintain an output which achieves minimum unit cost by reducing fertilizer prices in order to stimulate demand. The three major firms are attempting to counteract this profits squeeze via an agreement to pool technical information and to establish a joint promotional effort to increase the demand for fertilizers on grassland.

Fisons too have developed certain improved processes. They have developed a more efficient compounding process which uses liquid ammonia nitrate instead of water as the matrix and is useful in the production of ultra-high nitrogen compounds. Fisons have also developed a new cost-reducing process for producing phosphoric acid. This innovation is especially welcome because the fact that Fisons is a phosphoric acid producer has left the firm vulnerable to the present world shortage of sulphur (sulphuric acid is reacted with phosphate rock to give phosphoric acid), which doubled the world price of sulphur between 1965 and 1967.

V.3. A NATIONAL PRICE

A fundamental problem in resource allocation exists when transport costs form a relatively large proportion of total costs and consumers are spatially diffuse. This revolves round the choice of pricing policy. Broadly the choice is between a *national* price where manufacturers quote a price which does not discriminate according to the remoteness of the consumer and *ex-works* pricing which does discriminate, the final price being production costs plus transport costs for each individual consumer. The fertilizer industry has traditionally operated the former system. A national price distorts the price system in that it fails to reflect differences in transportation costs to different consumers. In fact, the national price inverts locational advantage. Those farmers located near to the producer pay the same price as those located more distantly, the degree of distortion depending on the importance of transport costs in total costs. The use of a national price could lead to the adoption of wrong location policies by manufacturers. If transport costs are important they will be minimized by a wide distribution of fertilizer plants, whilst the present plants are highly concentrated spatially. Similarly, the absence of transport differentials would mean that the large manufacturer can compete effectively with the local manufacturer in a remote area, whilst it may be in the national interest for the large producer to operate in a more spatially restricted market, thereby cutting costs and prices. It is interesting to note that a move toward ex-works pricing would make Fisons less competitive in the likely growth areas of the North and West.†

---

† In June 1968 Fisons switched to a version of ex-works pricing. The farm delivered (national) prices were replaced by ex-depot prices, 12s. 6d. per ton below the delivered prices. Therefore, those farmers located near Fisons' 38 depots are likely to pay, per ton, less than previously. Those further away will pay more. It should be noted that this pricing system only charges farmers the haulage costs from the local depot to the farm and not from the factory to the farm.

CHAPTER 6

LAND AND BUILDINGS

I. Introduction

The agricultural industry is by far the largest land user in Great Britain accounting for somewhat over three-quarters of the total land area, in contrast to urban development which utilizes somewhat less than one tenth of the land area. In section II the alienation of agricultural land to urban use is analysed, and it is indicated that the proportion of land entering urban use should not be overemphasized. In section III we analyse the movements in the price of agricultural land, dwelling especially on attempting to afford an explanation of the extremely large price rises in the last ten years. This section also details the changing structure of land tenure, which is intimately tied to movements in the price of land; during this century the proportion of farms under owner occupation has risen from one-tenth to around a half. The factor market for land is inherently linked with such factors of production as farm buildings and drainage. The land area itself is fixed but capital investment is a variable. Therefore the chapter concludes with an analysis of fixed equipment in British farming.

Before going on to analyse the land market it is necessary to point out that the economic importance of agricultural land as a factor of production has declined through time,† because of the physical increase in the intensity of land use, that is by adding more non-land inputs to the fixed stock of land.

It is to some extent a matter of semantics to decide what constitutes "land", that is which factors of production receive the reward of rent (including imputed rent for owner occupied farms). As agricultural land

† See O. T. W. Price, The economic significance of land as a factor of production, with particular reference to agricultural land, *The Farm Economist*, vol. VII, 6, 1953, and T. W. Schultz, The declining importance of agricultural land, *Economic Journal*, vol. LXI, 244, Dec. 1951.

typically incorporates fixed capital such as farm buildings and roads some of the rent must be viewed as interest on this capital. Having stated this qualification we may now look briefly at trends in agricultural rents. The gross income from ownership of agricultural land in the U.K., as a proportion of national income at factor cost, fell from 4 per cent in 1895 to 1 per cent in 1938, thus agricultural rents declined in importance as national income rose. It is interesting to note, however, that the relative importance of agricultural rents increased in the agricultural depressions of the early 1920's and 1930's, reflecting the fact that rent payments are far more rigid than movements in national income, largely owing to institutional factors such as arbitration, and rent control legislation.

The relative importance of land can also be estimated by calculating rent (including implicit rent) as a proportion of total farm expenditure. Price indicates that rents declined in importance between 1932 and 1953, largely because farm rents were stable during the war years whilst other factor prices rose, the declining importance being more marked in arable areas than on grassland farms. More recent data† hint that rent and interest as a proportion of farm expenses have been rising slightly, standing presently at 10·7 per cent. This is partly due to the relaxation of rent control, but also to the higher interest payments on the increased stock of capital equipment in agriculture, encouraged during the post-war period by investment allowance and cash grants.

II. Major Trends in Land Use

The pattern of land use in Great Britain in this century is detailed in Table 6.1.

The two major features indicated by this table are the continuous decline in the total agricultural acreage and the rapid expansion of the land area covered by urban development, doubling in England and Wales from 5·4 per cent in 1900 to 10·8 per cent in 1960. The early land use statistics, especially for Scotland, were somewhat inaccurate; this is primarily borne out in the column headed unaccounted for. Improvements in the agricultural statistics have enabled the proportion unaccounted for to diminish through time; it is for this reason that the

† Ministry of Agriculture, *Annual Review and Determination of Guarantees*, 1968.

Resource Structure of Agriculture

TABLE 6.1. CHANGES IN THE MAJOR LAND USES OF GREAT BRITAIN BETWEEN
1900 AND 1950

	Agriculture	Woodland	Urban development	Unaccounted for*	Total land area
	'000 acres	'000 acres	'000 acres	'000 acres	'000 acres
England and Wales					
1900	31,050	1900	2000	2180	37,130
1925	30,780	1880	2300	2170	37,130
1935	30,380	2120	2800	1830	37,130
1939	30,180	2290	3200	1460	37,130
1950	29,920	2370	3600	1240	37,130
1960	29,440	2540	4000	1150	37,130
Scotland					
1900	14,290	870	170	3740	19,070
1925	14,350	1070	—	—	19,070
1935	14,980	1090	360	2640	19,070
1939	15,020	1120	—	—	19,070
1950	15,320	1330	470	1950	19,070
Great Britain					
1900	45,340	2770	2170	5920	56,200
1925	45,130	2950	—	—	56,200
1935	45,360	3210	3160	4470	56,200
1939	45,200	3410	—	—	56,200
1950	45,240	3700	4070	3190	56,200
England and Wales					
1900	83·6	5·1	5·4	5·9	100·0
1925	82·9	5·1	6·2	5·8	100·0
1935	81·8	5·7	7·6	4·9	100·0
1939	81·3	6·2	8·6	3·9	100·0
1950	80·6	6·4	9·7	3·3	100·0
1960	79·3	6·8	10·8	3·1	100·0
Scotland					
1900	74·9	4·6	0·9	19·6	100·0
1925	75·2	5·6	—	—	100·0
1935	78·6	5·7	1·9	13·8	100·0
1939	78·8	5·9	—	—	100·0
1950	80·3	7·0	2·5	10·2	100·0
Great Britain					
1900	80·7	4·9	3·9	10·5	100·0
1925	80·3	5·2	—	—	100·0
1935	80·7	5·7	5·6	8·0	100·0
1939	80·4	6·1	—	—	100·0
1950	80·5	6·6	7·2	5·7	100·0

*Includes part of the special uses, ungrazed deer forest and other totally unutilized rural land, and land that has escaped enumeration under the other major land-use categories.

Source: R. H. Best, and J. T. Coppock, *The Changing Use of Land in Britain*, pp. 229, Faber & Faber, London, 1962.

statistical percentage decline in the agricultural has not been as large as the percentage increase in the urban and woodland acreage. At the present time unaccounted for figures include, for example, military airfields and open-cast mining. Also for Scotland it is largely composed of ungrazed deer forest.

The aggregate 1960 national figure of nearly 11 per cent of total England and Wales land area in urban uses conceals important regional differences, with London and the South-East and the North-West having 36 per cent and 29 per cent of land respectively so covered, whilst the total area of the North, South-West and Wales in urban use is only around 5 per cent. It is also important to emphasize that whilst the urban land area has expanded rapidly in percentage terms, the absolute displacement of agricultural land by urban use must not be exaggerated. At the present rate of urban growth it would take more than a thousand years for the agricultural land in Britain to disappear.†

Details of the transfer of agricultural land to alternative uses are presented in Table 6.2.

The statistics indicate the annual average transfer of agricultural land to other uses. The major feature shown by the table is that the rate of urban growth was faster in the mid and late 1930's, than in any previous or subsequent period of similar length, reaching an all time peak of 60,000 acres. There are a number of interlinked reasons for this. First, the new lower density standards for housing initially adopted in the 1920's were now accepted as the norm. Second, and more important, was the fact that whilst industrial incomes began to rise in the mid and late 1930's, following the 1929–33 depression, agriculture remained relatively depressed. Because planning control in the form it has operated in the post-war period hardly existed, land for urban uses such as building and recreation facilities was relatively cheap. Third, the growth of both public and private transport (especially the motor car) made this agricultural land more accessible.

The period 1939–45 and immediately following was naturally atypical, with marginal land such as sports grounds being brought into agricultural use to cut down on food import requirements, and simultaneously the agricultural sector transferring over 100,000 acres per

† R. Best, The transfer of agricultural land to urban use, paper given to Town Planning Institute Conference, 1967.

TABLE 6.2. ANNUAL AVERAGE TRANSFERS OF AGRICULTURAL LAND TO URBAN
AND OTHER USES

Transfers / Year to:	Building and general constrnl. develmt.	Sports grounds	Total urban area	Service depts. and miscs.	Woodlands and forestry develmt.†
	acres	acres	acres	acres	acres
England and Wales					
1927/28–1933/34	37,800	9000	46,800	1300	n.a.
1934/35–1938/39	50,000	10,000	60,600	15,000	n.a.
1939/40–1944/45	15,200	4500‡	19,700	101,500	17,900
1945/46–1964/65	33,900	4600	38,500	12,500‡	19,600
1960/61–1964/65	35,100	3100	38,200	2400‡	16,200
Scotland					
1951/52–1958/59	3300	500	3800	1200	n.a.
1960/61–1964/65	5500	600	6100	900	44,200
Great Britain					
1960/61–1964/65	40,600	3700	44,300	1500‡	60,400

† Including allotments in England and Wales.
‡ Plus figures indicate net gains to the agricultural area.
Source: R. Best, *op. cit.,* table 1.

annum to use by the armed forces. In the early post-war period much
of this land was returned to farming and there was an upsurge in the
demand for urban use. However, this immediate post-war (1945–58)
increase in the demand for urban and recreational facilities was not
sustained and the annual average post-war transfer has been about
38,500 acres in England and Wales, which is less than two-thirds the
loss in much of the 1930's. An interesting feature of the post-war period
is that fluctuations around this annual average figure of 38,500 (mainly
between 30,000 to 45,000) are positively correlated with the level of
economic activity.†

Post-1960, urban displacement of agricultural land has been at a rate

† R. Best, *op. cit.,* para 8. This would seem to be entirely consistent with the fact
that 70 per cent of private house building is still "speculative" and these constructors
will be seriously affected by economic policy instruments such as the credit squeeze.

of about 38,000 acres per annum, and in Scotland 6000 acres, giving a total Great Britain figure of 44,000. It will be noted from the table, however, that this is some 16,000 acres *less* than that transferred annually to forestry. Thus the switch to urban use is significantly behind the transfer to woodland—an alternative rural use.

Just as the static description of the aggregate proportion of land area in urban use in any one year conceals significant differences between regions, so to does the national figure of the dynamic element of the switching of land uses. Details of the regional pattern of land switching are almost non-existent, but one study has calculated these regional transfer differences over the years 1955–60 in England and Wales.† The rate of transfer to urban use was relatively small (less than 0·5 per cent of total county area) in eastern, northern, western and south western areas of England and Wales. In six contiguous eastern counties there was even a net gain of land to agriculture. The primary area of urban growth was in the industrial belt stretching from the S.E. Lancs. conurbation diagonally south-east through the Midlands to the London–South Coast area, with transfer rate greater than 1 per cent of total land area (in contrast to a national transfer of 1·0 per cent for the *ten* years 1950–60). The greatest shift in use was on the northern fringe of the London conurbation (for example, Beds. 1·5 per cent, Herts. 1·3 per cent).

II.1. FUTURE URBAN GROWTH

Both the rising population and higher per capita incomes are likely to increase the annual needs of the urban sector through year 2000, the latter via a demand for more liberal housing densities and more land for recreational use. It is estimated that the total urban area of Great Britain will extend by 1·8–1·9 million acres between 1960 and 2000.‡ This involves an average transfer of between 45,000 to 47,500 acres per annum, somewhat greater than the present figure. The bulk of this movement will be in England and Wales where between 1·6 and 1·7 million

† R. Best, Recent changes and future prospects of land use in England and Wales, *Geographical Journal*, vol. 131, March 1965.
‡ See R. Best, The transfer of agricultural land to urban use, paper given to Town Planning Institute Conference, 1967.

acres will be added to the 1960 figure of 4 millions. However, even by the end of this century the urban area is unlikely to exceed 16 per cent of total land area (that is, around three times the figure for 1900). These calculations assume that the extent of the transfer of agricultural land to urban uses depends entirely on urban forces. However, if farmers were willing to pay more for land than urban users, because the returns to land in agricultural use were greater than the returns to alternative uses, then the predictions of the amount of land transferred from agriculture to urban use would have to be modified. Similarly, these calculations do not take account of the fact that the demand for land for urban use is not totally price inelastic: the rise in the price of agricultural land may reduce the quantity demanded.

III. The Price of Farmland

In this section we describe the changes in the sale prices of farms in England and Wales during the last century. We then isolate a number of the determinants of sale price over the whole period, but emphasize especially the factors responsible for the very sharp rise in the sale value of farm land in the more recent post-World War II years. The changing structure of land tenure is also described in this section as the changing relative proportion of farms in the two groups of owner occupation and tenanted is related to movements in land price and other factors, especially rents.

It is necessary to distinguish between the aggregate stock of land and the the flow of land entering the land market in any time period. The total land stock in the U.K. does not change at all in response to price changes. However, we may hypothesize that that part of the total stock which enters the market in any time period does depend on land price. Broadly the agricultural land market may be split into two sectors: land with and land without planning permission. The former is likely to be more highly priced than the latter. However, we make no such distinction here: rather we examine the determinants of average agricultural land price.

The factors which influence the price of agricultural land may be seen with the help of a simple model:

$$S_L = s(P_L; X) \tag{1}$$

$$D_L = d(P_L; Y) \tag{2}$$

Equation (1) states that the supply of agricultural land (S_L) entering the land market is a function of the price of that land (P_L) and a number of exogenous variables (X). We would expect that S_L is positively related to P_L. An example of an exogenous variable which might influence the supply of land is fiscal legislation. If death duties rise or a wealth tax is instituted, this is likely to shift the supply function rightwards.

Equation (2) states that the demand for agricultural land (D_L) is a function of the price of that land (P_L) and a range of exogenous variables (Y). Two examples of relevant exogenous variables influencing the demand for land are the following. First, the level of agricultural prices and incomes: we would expect a positive relationship between these and demand for agricultural land. Second, the cost and availability of funds to both potential agricultural and urban users: we would expect an inverse relationship between the demand for land and the rate of interest.

It will be noted that the exogenous variables are "shifters" of the relationship between the supply (demand) of agricultural land and its price: they cause more or less supply (demand) to be forthcoming at a given price.

In this section we are interested in the factors which influence the price of agricultural land. We therefore assume that the land market is in equilibrium $(S_L = D_L)$. This enables us to let the price of agricultural land depend on the exogenous factors:

$$P_L = p(X; Y)$$

The equilibrium assumption is possibly unrealistic. It would conceptually be possible to set up a model so that: $\dot{P}_L = f([S - D]; Z)$. This reaction function explains the *rate of change* of agricultural land price by the excess demand for land, whether positive or negative, and a portmanteau of relevant exogenous variables (Z). However, on variable is readily available as a proxy for excess demand for land (cf. Chapter 3 where unemployment is a proxy for excess demand for labour). We therefore retain the equilibrium assumption.

We now consider some of the factors which have influenced the land price over the last 100 years. A description of the changing pattern of tenure arrangements is included because it appears to have had a significant influence on land price.

The detailed method of calculation of farm sale prices is described by D. K. Britton.† Briefly the method is as follows. The sources of information were, up to 1945, *Estates Exchange Year Book*, and post-war, *The Estates Gazette*. Thus the results are based on prices paid for farms sold at auction. This imposes a number of qualifications on the aggregate figures presented in Tables 6.3 and 6.4. For example, the following are unknown:

(a) The proportion of land sold by auction compared with the proportion sold by private treaty.
(b) Whether auction sale prices are roughly representative of all land sale prices.
(c) The quality of the land sold (either by auction or privately), i.e. maybe poor quality land enters the land market more frequently than better quality land.
(d) Regional price variations.

To obtain the average price per acre the total sum realized in each year for the farms in the sample is first divided by their total acreage. This figure is then corrected for the *average* size of farms sold in the given year. This latter correction is necessary because the average price per acre is higher for farms of smaller size than for those comprising a larger number of acres.

III.1. 1860–1939

Details of trends in farm sale prices up to 1939 are given in Table 6.3. It is unnecessary during this period to distinguish between farms sold with or without vacant possession, the vast majority of farm sales being without possession (although it should be noted that the proportion of owner occupiers rose from one tenth in 1914 to one-third by 1930). The years 1860–1939 may be divided into six separate periods according to the prevailing trend in farm sale land prices:

† D. K. Britton, The sale value of farm land between the wars, *The Farm Economist*, vol. VI, 1959, pp. 126–8.

1864–75	rising prices
1876–95	secular, severe fall in prices
1896–1906	stable prices
1907–20	improving prices, especially the latter four years
1921–30	falling prices
1931–9	gradual strengthening of prices.

TABLE 6.3. FARM SALE PRICES IN ENGLAND AND WALES, 1860–1939

Years	All farms price per acre	Years	All farms price per acre	Years	All farms price per acre	Years	All farms price per acre
	£		£		£		£
1857–61	39	1877–81	45	1897–01	20	1917–21	28
1858–62	40	1878–82	43	1898–02	20	1918–22	28
1859–63	39	1879–83	38	1899–03	20	1919–23	29
1861–65	38	1881–85	35	1901–05	20	1921–25	28
1862–66	37	1882–86	33	1902–06	20	1922–26	28
1863–67	38	1883–87	31	1903–07	21	1923–27	28
1864–68	39	1884–88	31	1904–08	20	1924–28	27
1865–69	41	1885–89	27	1905–09	21	1925–29	25
1866–70	41	1886–90	26	1906–10	21	1926–30	24
1867–71	44	1887–91	27	1907–11	22	1927–31	23
1868–72	44	1888–92	25	1908–12	22	1928–32	21
1869–73	48	1889–93	24	1909–13	24	1929–33	20
1870–74	49	1890–94	21	1910–14	24	1930–34	22
1871–75	52	1891–95	20	1911–15	23	1931–35	22
1872–76	53	1892–96	19	1912–16	23	1932–36	23
1873–77	54	1893–97	19	1913–17	23	1933–37	24
1874–78	52	1894–98	19	1914–18	24	1934–38	25
1875–79	51	1895–99	20	1915–19	25	1935–39	24
1876–80	49	1896–00	20	1916–20	27	1936–40	25

Source: J. T. Ward, Farm sale prices over a hundred years, *The Estates Gazette*, 3 May 1958.

The period to 1875 was part of the "golden age" of British agriculture. The industrial population was expanding rapidly; technological developments lowered unit costs, coupled with the expansion of the railway transportation network, this encouraged specialization. Farm sale prices increased by over a third, from £40 an acre in 1860 to £54 in 1875. The next twenty years were a period of depression. The fall in home agricultural product prices was due mainly to the expansion of international trade in agricultural products, resulting in a substantial increase in cheap food imports. But the enormous drop in land sale price per acre, the 1896 price of £19 being marginally greater than one third of the 1875 price, reflected also the general depression conditions. Prices stabilized at around £20 per acre for ten years, then improved gradually. The wartime blockade led the government, in 1916, to encourage increased home food supplies through legislation and favourable guaranteed prices for wheat and oats, and land prices rose to £29 an acre in 1920. In 1921 prices on world agricultural markets declined severely, causing the government to repeal the price support measures and the resulting fall in agricultural product prices and farm incomes caused the land price to fall through the 1920's, gradually at first then more rapidly. During the 1930's agricultural prices rose via the stabilization policies of the newly established Marketing Boards, wheat subsidies and controls on imported food. The rise in land prices, to £25 per acre at the outbreak of war, was also caused by the large transfers of agricultural land to urban uses, reaching an all time peak in the mid 1930's.

Whilst we are not primarily concerned with tenure arrangements in this section, it is necessary to indicate that fundamental changes took place in the land tenure structure in part of this period. In the early years of this century, nine-tenths of the farms in England and Wales were tenanted and only 10 per cent owner occupied. By 1927 the proportion of owner occupation had risen to 36 per cent, from which figure it fell marginally by the outbreak of World War II. The upsurge in owner occupation in the ten years after World War I, when about a quarter of farms were bought by tenants, was due primarily to the fact that during the first two decades of the century the price of agricultural land (sale value) had increased, but rents had lagged behind, thus encouraging landowners to sell land, typically to the existing tenant. Tenants were provided with a good reason for buying. Although they had more freedom in making their own farming decisions and were more likely to get compensation for improvements, their tenure position was not as secure as at present. An alternative purchaser could acquire possession within one year of the date of purchase.

During the agricultural depression years up to 1939 few tenants were prepared to take on the responsibilities of owner occupation, and the proportion of farms in this group declined marginally probably because a number of owner occupiers were unable to keep up the interest charges on their mortgaged property.

III.2. 1939–65†

It is now necessary to distinguish between farms sold with and without vacant possession for security of tenure provisions have resulted in substantially different prices for the two groups. The details of the sale value of farmland for these two classes of property are given in Table 6.4. The last column of the table is the "vacant possession premium", the difference in price per acre a vacant possession farm and that paid for an occupied farm, expressed as a percentage of the price of the latter. The extremely large growth in the premium in the first half of this period was because the two types of land yielded different returns. Up to 1941 a landowner could obtain possession within a year of purchasing an occupied farm, but wartime security of tenure provisions (introduced primarily to stop capital gains resulting from land speculation), which were retained after the war by the 1948 Agricultural Holdings Act, coupled with elements of rent control, made it extremely difficult to get possession of occupied land. Thus whilst the buyer of a vacant possession farm could farm the land himself, or let it out at a market rent, the purchaser of a without possession farm received a rent which was low in relation to farm income, that is, below the prevailing market level. The fall in the vacant possession premium post 1958 was largely due to the easing of rent control provisions; since then the play of market forces has resulted in a consistent upward movement in rents. We thus see that the stream of annual returns (rents) are an important determinant of the value of the stock of land, the rent control pre 1958 resulting in an artificially low price in the investment market for without possession land.

Let us now turn to the other variables which are important in explaining land price. The sale value of farmland has, as in previous periods,

---

† For a more detailed exposition see J. T. Ward, Changes in the sale value of farm real estate in England and Wales, 1937–9 to 1951, *The Farm Economist*, vol. VII, 4, 1959 and G. H. Peters, Recent trends in farm real estate values in England and Wales, *The Farm Economist*, vol. XI, 2, 1966.

TABLE 6.4. SALE VALUE OF FARM LAND, ENGLAND AND WALES, 1937–9 TO 1965

| | Vacant possession | | | | Without possession | | |
| | All farms | | Farms less than 300 acres | | Farms less than 300 acres | | Premium % for farms less than 300 acres |
	£ per acre	Index	£ per acre	Index	£ per acre	Index	
1937–39	25	100	31	100	23	100	35
1940–42	35	140	41	132	28	123	46
1943–45	46	184	54	174	32	139	66
1946–48	69	276	82	264	42	183	93
1949–51	82	328	95	306	46	197	108
1952	76	304	95	306	44	190	116
1953	73	292	83	267	41	177	102
1954	75	300	85	274	44	188	95
1955	80	320	90	290	49	212	84
1956	78	312	87	290	48	209	80
1957	73	292	84	270	40	174	110
1958	85	340	94	302	53	229	77
1959	101	404	110	354	68	296	61
1960	123	492	132	425	67	290	97
1961	124	496	132	426	81	348	65
1962	134	536	139	448	77	333	81
1963	168	672	168	540	98	424	71
1964	214	856	224	721	125	543	79
1965	235	940	238	766	150	652	58

Source: G. H. Peters, Recent trends in farm real estate values, *Farm Economist*, vol. XI, 2, 1966.

changed in similar proportion to the prosperity of the industry, here indicated by the change in farm incomes. Both vacant possession land values and net farm income increased approximately eightfold between 1937/8 and 1965/6. It has been shown, however, that this Ricardian explanation of land values is an oversimplification.† The funds invested in agricultural land do have an opportunity cost. We find that in 1937/8 the interest charge of $4\frac{1}{4}$ per cent on the prevailing vacant possession land value of £31 per acre (= £1·32 per acre) compares closely with the average rent of £1·25 per acre existing at that time. In 1966, in contrast,

† G. H. Peters, *op. cit.*, p. 50.

the interest charge of $7\frac{3}{4}$ per cent on the land price of £238 an acre equals £18 which is substantially greater than the rent or income per acre. Thus the correlation between the movements in land price and agricultural incomes are to some extent spurious in that the present price of agricultural land is in excess of its basic agricultural value. Therefore, we now examine additional explanatory variables which explain land price, concentrating on explaining the sale price of vacant possession land of farms in this size group 5–300 acres.

There are three distinct phases in the price trends. In the ten years to 1948 prices were rising. The largest rise came in the latter years, largely owing to the improvements in absolute and relative agricultural income (based primarily on the shortage of foreign exchange and our need to grow more food at home). Between 1949 and 1957 prices were approximately stable at around £90 per acre; the minor fluctuations around £90 were related to interest rate changes, reflecting changes in the availability of funds for land purchase, rather than being important in its own right as a price of funds.

The position with respect to changing land tenure during World War II and after is similar to that described above in the corresponding wartime period. Land values were increasing because of the improving agricultural income position, rent rises again lagging behind. Paradoxically it was the much enhanced tenure security which stimulated a growth in owner occupation. At first glance it would be hypothesized that the security of tenure provisions introduced in wartime and maintained after the war, coupled with rent control, would decrease the impetus to owner occupation. However, we noted above that the security of tenure legislation resulted in a price differential between the two types of with and without vacant possession property. The price of the occupied property was suppressed to an artificially low level. If a holding in this property group was sold, the sitting tenant was the only person able to gain possession. He was thus encouraged to buy his freehold at the artificially low price, for he then experienced an overnight capital gain (of up to 100 per cent in some years). If he resold the land he would receive the higher vacant possession price. In the same way, when a tenant died or retired, landlords frequently sold off land at the higher price rather than reletting it, thus again adding to the proportion of owner occupiers.

We need to dwell much longer on the third period, spanning the years 1958–65, when vacant possession values rose by two hundred and fifty per cent to £238 per acre in 1965/6. It is virtually impossible to provide a complete explanation of this enormous rise in prices, but here we present a number of *potential* causes of which four may be eliminated after detailed analysis. Three important explanatory factors are: first, the effect on prices of land going to urban development; second an increase in the rate of amalgamations, and third land is bought as a hedge against inflation.

Urban development alienates some 40,000 acres of agricultural land per year. This causes land price rises for two reasons. It is likely that a proportion of the initial sellers re-enter the land market quickly, backed by their large stock of funds. Second, land price is bid up due to investment in land by speculators in the hope of their land being required for urban use. This speculative motive was accentuated in 1959 since when compensation for compulsory purchase has been paid according to the value of the land in its use (i.e. urban) rather than at its basic agricultural value.

The second cause of rising land price has been an increase in the rate of amalgamations. There is considerable evidence that amalgamation substantially increases net profits per acre, especially in dairying, so enhancing the land value. Reference to Table 6.5 shows the rate of reduction of holdings, and therefore increase in the average size of farms, was far greater in the years after than before 1958. (Transfer of land to urban use also results in a reduction in holdings). Since 1965 the government has actively encouraged amalgamations through grants towards the cost of amalgamating and grants and pensions to those farmers made redundant.

The last important cause of the rising land price has been the use of land as a hedge against inflation, purchasers being prepared to accept a lower yield on their investment in land than they could obtain by investing in alternatives, for example gilt edge stock, providing the capital value keeps pace with or exceeds the general rate of inflation.

A number of additional reasons have been advanced to account for the increase in the price but these may be dismissed. First, the level of interest rates, which were, in fact, higher at the end of the period than those prevailing in 1958. There does, however, seem to be a limited

TABLE 6.5. AGRICULTURAL HOLDINGS IN ENGLAND AND WALES

Year	(1) Total holdings	(2) Holdings less than 5 acres	(3) (1) − (2) Total holdings over 5 acres	(4) Rate of change of col. (3)
1945	362,504	67,988	294,516	
1946	361,448	67,961	293,487	−0·3
1947	360,805	67,555	293,250	−0·1
1948	362,972	68,810	294,162	0·3
1949	367,242	72,039	295,203	0·4
1950	372,774	77,022	295,752	0·2
1951	377,198	80,866	296,332	0·2
1952	380,031	83,973	296,058	−0·1
1953	380,015	84,839	295,176	−0·3
1954	375,432	82,688	292,744	−0·8
1955	369,565	79,618	289,947	−1·0
1956	365,025	78,112	286,913	−1·0
1957	361,736	76,984	284,752	−0·7
1958	356,283	74,264	282,019	−1·0
1959	351,378	73,183	278,195	−1·4
1960	344,936	71,801	273,135	−1·8
1961	338,295	70,061	268,234	−1·8
1962	334,449	69,383	265,066	−1·2
1963	330,307	68,934	261,373	−1·4
1964	323,067	67,104	255,963	−2·1
1965	317,792	65,931	251,861	−1·6

Source: Ministry of Agriculture, *Agricultural Statistics,* Annual.

correlation between changes in interest rates and changes in the degree of inflation of land price, changes in rates probably therefore acting as a proxy for the availability of funds. Second, there have been no substantial gross additions to the capital value of land in the form of additions to fixed equipment, nor have building costs risen significantly. It has been estimated† that the increase in the acreage value of land due to additions in factors such as drainage, roads and fences is only £12, which contributes only marginally towards explaining the 250 per cent spiralling of land price.

Two further hypothetical causes of the price rises, namely investment

† A. H. Maunder, Fixed equipment in agriculture, *The Farm Economist*, vol. X, 2, 1962.

in land to attain the greater death duty relief than is afforded by (say) holding equities, and the increase in utility due to the prestige of being a landowner, are unlikely to be important in explaining the post 1958 price increases as they were also present before 1958. They therefore exercised a continuous influence on price, rather than solely affected price in the last few years.

Other possible influences on land price include the effects of government legislation. First, the relaxation of rent control in 1958. This had a marked effect on realized without possession land values as rents could now more nearly mirror the actual land values. It is not possible to assess how far this resulted in a spillover to the vacant possession market. If anything it would be surmised that any side effects on the vacant possession market would have led to a fall rather than a rise in prices, and it is unlikely that this legislative change incorporated in the 1958 Agriculture Act) is a prime reason for the rise in land price. However, more sophisticated knowledge of the demand and supply schedules for the two classes of property would be needed to draw a firm conclusion on this point.

Second, the agricultural legislation of 1957 might have had a favourable influence on farmers' expectations. The 1957 Agriculture Act gave home farmers certain long term assurances regarding the guaranteed prices of their output. The guaranteed price for any product would not be allowed to decline by more than 4 per cent per year. In addition, the guaranteed price for livestock products could not decline by more than 9 per cent in three years. Overall, the total value of production grants and deficiency payments, after allowing for cost changes, could not decline by greater than $2\frac{1}{2}$ per cent a year.

These long-term price guarantees gave farmers an assurance that the prices they received for their products would not decline suddenly. This may have favourably influenced farmers' expectations regarding the future income they were likely to get from agriculture (although, of course, income depends on quantity produced as well as price). This, in turn, might have encouraged farmers to enlarge their holdings and bid against each other and against urban interests for available farm land, thereby accentuating the upward pressure on agricultural land prices post 1957.

IV. Investment in Farm Buildings

Economic growth is associated with an increase in the capital/labour ratio. This has been observed in agriculture where the number of durable inputs has increased greatly whilst the labour input has declined. Details of gross fixed capital formation in agriculture are given in Table 6.6. Expenditure on new buildings and works rose, in current value figures, from £21 million in 1948 to £72 million in 1967. In constant value terms the rise between 1950 and 1967 was 73 per cent. The proportion of total fixed asset investment accounted for by new buildings and works has risen substantially, being 39 per cent in 1967 as against 24 per cent in 1948.

A model of the demand for durable inputs was developed in Chapter 2. The theory developed there allows a prediction of the variables likely to influence the demand for new farm buildings. We indicate first of all why the existing stock of buildings influences the level of investment. Second, we indicate those variables which determine the desired stock of capital equipment. Finally we indicate three factors which influence the speed of adjustment towards equilibrium. Statistical problems would prevent all these variables being included in a demand function to be estimated by least squares regression techniques, but some combination of the variables discussed below would comprise a reasonable model of the influences on the annual demand for farm building investment.

IV.1. EXISTING STOCKS

The demand for gross annual investment in farm buildings comes from two sources. First, the need to replace existing buildings because of capital consumption (depreciation). The greater the stock of farm buildings the greater the absolute amount of depreciation and the higher is the replacement demand. Second, the desire to increase the stock of buildings to the level indicated by the values of the decision variables. Greater stocks of farm buildings decrease the marginal product of the flow of services accruing from the stock. The existing stock of buildings thus has a dampening influence on the investment. Therefore, the two sources from which the investment demand is derived pull in opposite

TABLE 6.6. GROSS FIXED CAPITAL FORMATION IN NEW BUILDINGS AND WORKS
IN AGRICULTURE, 1948–67

Year	Gross fixed capital formation £m.	(1) as an index 1950 = 100	Index of gross fixed capital formation in constant value†	Gross fixed capital formation in new buildings and works as a percentage of total agricultural gross fixed capital formation
	(1)	(2)	(3)	(4)
1948	21	95	100	24
1949	23	104	107	26
1950	22	100	100	25
1951	22	100	92	24
1952	20	91	76	21
1953	23	104	85	26
1954	24	109	87	25
1955	26	118	90	25
1956	27	123	90	28
1957	25	114	80	24
1958	29	132	90	23
1959	38	173	118	27
1960	45	204	137	31
1961	53	241	156	34
1962	58	264	165	38
1963	62	282	171	37
1964	64	291	172	38
1965	66	300	169	39
1966	63	286	155	37
1967	72	327	173	39

† Column (3) is col. (2) deflated by an index of retail prices, 1950=100.
Source: Calculated from C.S.O., *National Income and Expenditure*, H.M.S.O., Annual.

directions. We are here concerned with the latter problem: namely to indicate the variables which influence the farmers' desire to increase or decrease the stock of farm buildings, and these are indicated below.

IV. 2. PRICES

The price of an input relative both to the prices of other inputs and to the price of the output is likely to influence the demand for the input. The importance of the ratio of farm building prices to the prices of other inputs, whether substitutes or complements, stems from marginal theory. As the relative input prices change this induces a change in the input mix. The ratio of farm building prices to the product prices received by farmers is a relevant variable in the investment function because the product prices received by farmers are likely to have an important influence on their expectations as to the future product prices. These, in turn, influence expected farm incomes. A programme of guaranteed farm product prices, coupled with long term guarantees as to their level, is likely to have a favourable influence on expectations as to future product prices, and therefore incomes and investment.

IV.3. MONETARY VARIABLES

Classically the rate of interest was thought to be the main determinant of investment. Theoretically, the farmer should invest in a durable input if the rate of return on that investment is greater than the rate of interest. However, studies both of aggregate investment and investment in agriculture cast doubt on the importance of the rate of interest as a determinant of investment.†

This may be because the rate of return on capital in agriculture varies widely because of exogenous factors such as weather. Therefore, ability to pay considerations may be more important than the rate of return on capital.

Nevertheless, the interest rate is likely to be important in explaining investment if it acts as a proxy variable (that is, if it represents) the availability of funds. Evidence does suggest that an inverse correlation exists between these two financial variables. An increase in the supply of funds to potential borrowers is associated with a decrease in the rate of interest. Therefore, when the interest rate falls, investment is likely to rise both because it becomes cheaper to borrow funds and because the supply of these funds increases.

† J. Meyer and E. Kuh, *The Investment Decision*, p. 8, Harvard University Press, Cambridge, Mass., 1957; W. Cromarty, The farm demand for tractors, machinery and trucks, *J. Farm Econ.*, vol. 41, 3, 1959. See also Chapter 4.

IV.4. FISCAL VARIABLES

The government does much to encourage capital formation. The estimated cost of support to U.K. agriculture in recent years with respect to agricultural buildings and works is given in Table 6.7. It will be noted that the two major costs have been subsidies towards farm improvements and field drainage. These subsidies do not normally cover the whole cost of the investment in the capital equipment, and must be viewed partially as catalysts which encourage investment. For example, between 1960 and 1964 total capital investment in projects covered by the Farm Improvement Scheme was £83·9 million, the cost of the subsidy being £37·5 million. Similarly, fixed capital formation in drainage was valued at £20·1 million of which £8·3 million was met by the exchequer.

Gross fixed capital formation in agriculture, as in the rest of the economy, has been encouraged during the post-war period by investment allowances, which enabled firms to offset a certain percentage of the cost of a new machine or building against profits for taxation purposes. This system was replaced in 1967 by a system of cash grants which cover a certain proportion of the cost of the investment. In agriculture the government provides a grant of one-tenth of the cost of all fixed equipment.† The cost to the exchequer of these investment incentives will be around £10 million in 1968/9.

IV.5. THE ACCELERATOR

The accelerator relates investment to the change in output. It assumes a prescribed capital/output ratio. If farmers increase their output the accelerator principle assumes that they then invest to increase their capital stock to maintain the capital/output ratio. In fact it is very difficult to isolate the causal relationship. The value of output may increase because of investment in the capital inputs. Or, farmers may invest in the durable inputs to maintain the capital/output ratio. If it is thought that investment in farm buildings does depend on output, then the investment function should include a variable to represent output. One possibility would be to deflate the index of gross farm income by an index of product prices received by farmers, giving, in some sense, a measure of aggregate farm output.

† Increased temporarily during 1967 and 1968 to 12½ per cent.

TABLE 6.7. COST OF EXCHEQUER SUPPORT ON SELECTED CAPITAL ITEMS (£ million)

Year ending Item	1960	1961	1962	1963	1964	1965	1966	1967	1968	1969
Field drainage	2·6	2·7	2·7	3·0	2·6	3·1	3·1	3·2	4·0	4·5
Water supply	0·7	0·8	0·8	0·8	0·7	0·7	0·6	0·5	0·5	0·5
Farm improvements	6·6	7·8	9·2	10·3	10·2	11·5	11·6	11·1	12·3	13·2
Investment grants	—	—	—	—	—	—	—	—	7·0	9·5
Silos	1·4	0·9	0·8	0·6	0·3	0·3	0·2	0·2	0·1	—

Source: Cmnd. 2558, *Annual Review and Determination of Guarantee 1968*, H.M.S.O.

IV.6. FARM SIZE AND OTHER TECHNICAL FACTORS

Average farm size is increasing through time through amalgamation and consolidation of holdings. This can have either a favourable or dampening effect on investment in farm buildings. The structural adjustment might cause an increase in the demand for new buildings through a desire to make the enlarged farm technically up to date. Alternatively, it could result in a discouragement of new investment as the existing building capacity could be more fully utilized.

Another technical factor which might influence the demand for farm buildings is a shift in the relative proportions of agricultural products produced. For example, a rise in the relative price of beef and milk might encourage farmers to switch out of cash crops and into livestock production. This would result in an increase in the demand for farm building investment because of the greater shelter and feedlot needs of livestock and the enhanced requirements for storing feedingstuffs. (Incidentally, it would result in a simultaneous decrease in the demand for farm tractor services.) This output ratio could be specified in the investment function as the ratio of livestock income to total farm income. The higher this ratio, the higher the likely demand for farm buildings.

IV.7. NET FARM INCOME

Net farm income, like the two remaining variables considered, is perhaps more important in explaining the speed of adjustment to the desired level of equipment than the level itself. Net farm income (gross receipts less production expenses) is similar to profits. The level of income is likely to affect investment for two reasons. Theoretically a durable asset should be purchased if the present value of the discounted stream of future earnings from the asset is greater than the price of the asset.† Past levels of net farm income are likely to figure largely in

† This assumes that the objective of the firm is to maximize profits. Whilst it is recognized that this may well be an unreasonable assumption of the objectives of firms comprising some industries, who may be concerned with some other objective such as sales maximization, it remains a reasonable assumption of the objective function of firms in agriculture. The market structure of the agricultural sector approximates to perfect competition. Under this structure firms must maximize profits (minimize costs) or accept a rate of return below that gained by the profit maximizers and ultimately probably leave the industry.

farmers' expectations about future income and therefore in their expectations of the future stream of earnings resulting from the asset. Second, the decision to invest in a durable asset will be influenced by the farmer's ability to pay for it. If past farm incomes have been high a farmer is more likely to be able to purchase it, or at least pay the minimum required deposit. Also his assessment of his ability to meet future mortgage commitments will depend on his expectations as to net farm income. These are likely to be based, partly at least, on past levels. Similarly, if he wishes to borrow to purchase the asset, the financial institution lending the money will probably be more interested in his ability to repay the loan than in the rate of return on the asset. The rate of return might be highly variable. This would affect the farmer's ability to repay the loan in regular instalments. Therefore past levels of net farm income affect both internal (the farmer's) and external (the institution's) expectations about his ability to repay the loan.

Both ability to pay and expectations are influenced by past levels of net farm income. Therefore, in specifying the investment function, a weighted average of net farm income should be included as the relevant variable. For example, where $Y =$ net farm income and $t =$ years, the weights might be

$$\frac{3Y_{t-1} + 2Y_{t-2} + 1Y_{t-3}}{6}.$$

IV.8. IMPROVED QUALITY AND IMPROVED KNOWLEDGE

Durable agricultural inputs have been subject to substantial quality changes through time. This quality improvement increases the marginal physical productivity of the input which will lead to an increase in the demand for the input. Similarly, the demand function will also be shifted outwards through time because of the greater technical knowledge of farmers. This results from their own findings, education and sales programmes and extension services. These improvements in quality and knowledge can be represented in the investment function by a time trend.

IV.9. PRESTIGE

The farmer may increase his satisfaction, though not necessarily his profits, by buying a new building, or replacing an old one, earlier than the date indicated by economic criteria. He may therefore view the building as a consumer good rather than as a capital good. This prestige motive for investment may be accentuated by the fact that the possession of the new building may enhance utility by increasing the farmer's leisure time. These factors are all likely to lead to a level of building investment greater than the economic optimum.†

† For a fuller discussion of the theory concerning investment in farm buildings see E. Heady and L. Tweeten, *Resource Demand and the Structure of the Agricultural Industry*, Iowa State U.P., Ames, 1963, Chs. 10 and 12.

CHAPTER 7

RESEARCH AND DEVELOPMENT, EXTENSION AND EDUCATION

I. Introduction

After taking account of the inputs from the household sector (labour), from the engineering sector (power and machines), from the chemical industries, from the building industry and allowing for a change in the availability of land to the agricultural sector we will still be left with unexplained increases in agricultural production over time due to the fact that these inputs are being transformed into output by a changing mechanism over time. Improved crop and animal varieties and methods of production are being produced as a result of public and private research and they are being developed, tested and adapted for commercial use, the actual rate of diffusion of these innovations being affected by the technical awareness of the decision-maker, the farmer and by the flow of information to him. We must, therefore, recognize important additional inputs of intellectual investment in research and development (R. & D.), education and extension which have not been taken account of in the estimates of inputs of labour, machines, chemicals and land.† Of course we have in fact valued the output of a vast amount of R. & D. directed towards the agricultural sector since, in deriving our estimates of the flow of services from the stock of tractors available we have put a market value on the innovations that have been made in tractor technology. For labour and chemicals we have not

† Conceptually we could have redefined our labour input variable to include the growth in the educational stock in the industry and to include labour used in the ancillary services. Empirically this would have been impossible since we do not have complete time-series on these qualitative features of the labour force. Also it seems important to isolate these scientific and intellectual inputs so that we can examine more closely the progress of technology.

183

allowed for any quality change in the man-hours available or the nutrients absorbed. In this chapter we will array the limited data available on educational investment in the agricultural labour force and we will pick up in the R. & D. figures research aimed at fertilizer improvements such as concentration and granulation. As far as land is concerned improvements in quality will be picked up in the estimates of fixed capital investment in land improvements and buildings, but in the R. & D. and extension figures we will pick up the work of the Agricultural Land Service. The other important input category, animal feed, is omitted from separate analysis but research and extension related to nutrition will be picked up in our estimates of expenditure in these areas.

Much of the investment in research, extension and education is public investment and this poses peculiar problems in analysing the demand for these resources because of the supply conditions. In these areas of public investment there is no market mechanism whereby excess demand is eliminated by price or supply adjustments. Any figures that we obtain on expenditures reflect essentially the supply of R. & D., extension and educational services. If, as Griliches[†] observed for the U.S., there is a pronounced disequilibrium in both fertilizer input and research and extension input into agriculture, then although we can observe farmers adjusting pretty rapidly in fertilizer consumption there is no way in which they can directly effect an increase in research expenditures in the public sector. What we can observe is the rate of adjustment to any new supply situation, e.g. the rate of diffusion of a new crop or animal variety, or of a new technique, through the farming population. We can also observe the changing rate of utilization of an extension service, if excess demand does not already exist. As far as private R. & D., extension or education is concerned this can be viewed in the same way as any other input. In fact the output of public R. & D. is funnelled through the private sector for commercial application and as such can also be viewed as any other input in agriculture. The missing link in the chain of adjustment is the public decision, but wherever excess demand exists private investment can move in. However, the underlying reason for public intervention is usually that the social

† Zvi Griliches, Research expenditure, education and the aggregate production function, *American Economic Review*, December 1964, pp. 961–74.

payoff is larger than the private and this would lead to the prediction of lower levels of investment in the absence of the public sector.

Faced with these non-market institutions and the difficulties they pose, we will examine (1) the fragmentary evidence on intellectual investment in agriculture to detect any trends which may be apparent and (2) the institutional framework. We will look at some evidence on farmers' decision criteria for evaluating new varieties of a crop under conditions of uncertainty about their performance relative to other varieties. We will also examine the possibility of cost–benefit analyses of intellectual investment. Such an analysis would provide guidelines for public investment and may also indicate the future supply of intellectual investment given that government attempts in various ways to check on the costs and benefits of its actions.

The next three sections will separately examine R. & D., extension and education drawing together recent estimates of expenditures, manpower involved and the structure of the institutions. These sections will be followed by a section looking at intellectual investment as a whole together with comparisons with previous periods, other countries and the rest of industry.

II. Research and Development

Both the public and private sectors are involved in agricultural research and development but we have very little information on the size of private expenditure in this area. Some information was collected by a sample survey of commercial firms engaged in research activities by Lord and Rodgers† and they estimated a total U.K. expenditure for the private sector of £10 million in 1965/6 compared with their total U.K. public expenditure figure of £15·9 million. They also quote a figure for private expenditure on R. & D., and extension in 1955/6 and if we apply the 1965/6 ratio of expenditure on R. & D. to extension expenditures then private R. & D. expenditure in 1955/6 was about £4 million compared with public expenditure of nearly £5 million. Whilst acknowledging various inaccuracies in making the estimates,

† R. F. Lord and S. J. Rodgers, *The Current Organization of Research Education and Extension in British Agriculture*, Agricultural Adjustment Unit, The University, Newcastle upon Tyne, 1967.

the main problem being allocating expenditure on manpower between research and other activities related to extension and promotion of commercial products, it appears that the private sector is one of substantial and continuing importance and in the ensuing discussion which is necessarily centred on the public sector we must recognize that we are only examining between a half and two-thirds of the resources flowing into agricultural R. & D.

II.1. PUBLIC RESEARCH AND DEVELOPMENT

The public sector itself is dominated by one organization, the Agricultural Research Council, which administers and controls something like 85 per cent of public expenditure in agricultural R. & D. Other organizations involved in R. & D. are the departments of agriculture (England and Wales, Scotland and Northern Ireland), the University Grants Commission (responsible for Faculties of Agriculture and Veterinary Colleges) and Marketing Boards. The Ministry of Agriculture's expenditure on R. & D. is funnelled through the (1) National Agricultural Advisory Service, which runs experimental husbandry farms and specialist provincial centres, (2) Research Stations (e.g. Veterinary, Pathology and A.I. laboratories), (3) Economic and Management research (i.e. the Provincial Agricultural Economics Service, whose academic activities are now run by the University Grants Commission, and the Economics Division of the Ministry) and (4) the National Institute of Agricultural Botany which is responsible for testing and multiplying new crop varieties developed in research by A.R.C. units together with private and foreign plant breeders. The departments for Scotland and Northern Ireland, in addition to the activities mentioned above, have also got a direct interest in agricultural education and the associated research activities.

(a) *The Agricultural Research Council*

The Agricultural Research Council is financed by, and can be directed by, the Department of Education and Science although it generally acts autonomously. Being by far the largest dispenser of public funds in agricultural research the A.R.C. must obviously play a major role in the development and direction of agricultural research in the U.K. A section in its publication, *The Agricultural Research Service* (1963), indicates that the council is not so much concerned with the tactics of research but is concerned that the overall strategy should be problem orientated: "No central direction of research is attempted. To those who demonstrate that they have outstanding capacity for original research, the Council gives a large degree of freedom to pursue lines of their own choice. On the other hand, the Council must . . . be able to encourage staffs of the institutes in general to work along lines that are likely to contribute to the solution of problems of practical importance." There seems to be an explicit attempt to make some sort of informal analysis of the likely economic benefits.

Table 7.1 below gives A.R.C. expenditure figures over the period 1955/6 to 1968/9. Column 1 refers to expenditures measured at current prices (i.e. in money terms) and is not likely to be a very good indicator of changes in real resources going into agricultural research. There is no price index available which is directly relevant to agricultural research but if we assume that a high proportion of expenditure in research institutes represents wages and salaries† then it seems reasonable to assume a 5 per cent annual rate of inflation in research costs.‡ This is likely to understate the rate of inflation in some years and overstate it in others, but the general trend will not be far out. Column 2 shows these deflated expenditures and we see that although public research expenditures have apparently quadrupled over the period the actual commitment of public resources to agricultural research in real terms has only doubled. Nevertheless this represents a very significant increase over a thirteen-year period. The average growth rate in real terms turns out to be 6·25 per cent p.a.

† For non-A.R.C. research the Ministry of Agriculture have estimated that the proportion of total expenditure spent on salaries was 70 per cent in 1966/7, 72 per cent in 1967/8 and 57 per cent in 1968/9. Thus salaries appear as a very major element of costs although unstable. Adding on wages we cover a very large proportion of total costs. The 1968/9 figure is indicative of the current tendency to spend a larger proportion on plant and equipment as research becomes more sophisticated.

‡ There is actually very little data on salaries in the U.K. but wages have grown at an average rate of about 5½ per cent p.a. in the post-war period and salaries are likely to have grown at least as fast. Prices of materials and capital equipment have grown typically at 3 per cent p.a. Our assumption of 5 per cent is a rough weighted average of these cost elements.

TABLE 7.1. AGRICULTURAL RESEARCH COUNCIL
EXPENDITURE

	(1) Expenditure at current prices (£ million)	(2) Expenditure at 1956/7 prices (£ million)
1955/56	3·58	3·76
1956/57	3·63	3·54
1957/58	3·86	3·68
1958/59	4·20	3·81
1959/60	4·82	4·16
1960/61	5·66	4·62
1961/62	6·08	4·76
1962/63	6·51	4·86
1963/64	7·39	5·25
1964/65	8·15	5·52
1965/66	9·3	6·00
1966/67	10·31	6·33
1967/68	11·97	7·00
1968/69	13·17 (esti- mate)	7·33

Source: Reports of the Agricultural Research Council.
N.B. Expenditure is approved parliamentary grant in
aid now administered by the Department of Education
and Science.

We can also measure the growth in research activity of the A.R.C.
by looking at the growth in employment of scientific personnel. In
this way we could have integrated R. & D. into the labour input into
agriculture with the appropriate weights to reflect the changing quality
in that labour input over time. Conceptually there is no reason why we
should not treat R. & D., education and extension as we treat any other
input, but in reality the institutional background is different and it
seems useful to analyse them separately. Table 7.2 gives information on
the numbers of scientific personnel in each of three years. Scientific
officers are always graduates, experimental officers are at a lower salary
level but many are graduates and scientific assistants are typically not
graduates. In addition to these people industrial, administrative and
clerical workers are also employed.

TABLE 7.2. AGRICULTURAL RESEARCH COUNCIL: SCIENTIFIC PERSONNEL

	1955/6	1965/6	1967/8
Scientific Officers	631	1057	1059
Experimental Officers	515	954	999
Scientific Assistants	658	1244	1251
Total	1804	3255	3309

Source: Reports of the Agricultural Research Council.

The average growth rate for scientific staff turns out to be 5·2 per cent, which is rather less than the estimated growth rate for total expenditure in real terms, suggesting that the growth rate for equipment has been even more rapid. However, we also note that the average growth rate for staff between 1955/6 and 1965/6 was 6·08 per cent p.a. whereas between 1965/66 and 1967/68 there has been very little growth, actually averaging 0·8 per cent p.a. despite a continuing growth in real expenditure. This suggests that the contemporary growth in research is related to the "sophistication factor" described in the 1967/8 report—that is a move towards more capital intensive research methods.

We have already mentioned that the A.R.C. is interested in stimulating practical problem-solving research and in a later section of the chapter we will examine some estimates made of the payoffs from specific research. At this point we need to simply observe that the mechanism for determining priorities in research recognizes the importance of practical commercial benefits but there is no formal framework for assessing these. The three departments of agriculture in the U.K. can and do inform the A.R.C. of the industry's research requirements and the departments themselves are guided by Advisory Councils whose job is rather loosely interpreted as defining the long-term research needs of the industry.

(b) *N.A.A.S. Research*

In addition to its main activity of extension the National Agricultural Advisory Service (N.A.A.S.) is also the second most important public research agency currently spending about £1·5 million p.a. in this area. The N.A.A.S. operates a series of experimental farms, the aim being to (1) generalize experimental results under a variety of environments; (2) to help solve regional problems, and (3) to exploit the economies arising from the joint development of research and extension.† Thus N.A.A.S. activity is essentially seen as a contribution to the development phase in R. & D. The scientific manpower involved doubled over the ten-year period 1955/6 to 1965/6 from 45 professional officers to 92 professional officers (with a complement of 115).‡ The growth rate is rather higher than for the A.R.C. but the scientific manpower is small in comparison.

(c) *Total Public Expenditure on R. & D.*

Table 7.3 gives some figures on total R. & D. expenditures by public agencies in England and Wales. The average growth rate is 5·6 per cent in real terms and thus is rather less than that for the A.R.C. by itself indicating that it is taking an increasing share of public funds. Public R. & D. expenditures in Scotland were £2·67 million in 1967/8 and £2·22 million in 1968/9 and in Northern Ireland they were £0·74 million and £0·94 million in the same two years.

If we are thinking in terms of the influence of R. & D. on agricultural production then the cumulated series of expenditures is the relevant time-series for it is this series which would reflect the stock of knowledge, the state of the arts, assuming we could ignore depreciation.

The figures quoted in Table 7.3 ignore research in Universities not financed by the A.R.C. or the Ministry of Agriculture. This expenditure was estimated at about £1·6 million in terms of current expenditure financed by the University Grants Commission. Assuming overheads at 20 per cent this would give us an extra R. & D. expenditure at current prices of about £2 million.

III. Extension

In the last section we have described the resources moving into agricultural research and development, but further resources are needed

---

† See P. J. Macfarlan, The organisation of agricultural experimentation, *Journal of Agricultural Economics*, May 1961, pp. 322–7.

‡ Lord and Rodgers, *op. cit.*, p. 19.

TABLE 7.3. PUBLIC R. & D. EXPENDITURE
(ENGLAND AND WALES)

	(1) Expenditure at current prices (£ million)	(2) Expenditure at 1956/7 prices (£ million)
1956/57	4·46	4·46
1961/62	8·29	6·50
1966/67	12·30	7·55
1967/68	14·27	8·34
1968/69	15·37	8·56

Source: Data supplied by Ministry of Agriculture.
N.B. All the figures refer to estimates and not actual expenditure but the figures are very similar. The expenditures quoted are also net of product sales by the research agencies.

before the discoveries made as a result of R. & D. expenditure can be utilized in production. In most cases the new technology will be embodied in physical capital inputs of various types and these resources will generally be picked up as engineering or chemical technology input. In addition we have new varieties of crops and animals where resources have to be used in building up a stock of seed or breeding animals. These inputs are not covered in this book as they are considered as internal transactions within the agricultural sector. We still have left the problem of estimating the resources used to promote the actual innovation and diffusion of the new technologies. Before any real benefits can accrue to R. & D. expenditure, farmers have got to make decisions to change their methods of production and a prerequisite for action is information about the new production opportunities. Information about new technology can come from commercial advertising and farm journals and from public and private extension agencies.

III.1. PRIVATE EXTENSION

Private extension falls in two groups: (1) that offered by specialist extension services, most importantly by management consultants, and

(2) that offered by firms in ancillary industries to agriculture, either on the input side (e.g. information and advice on fertilizer use) or on the product side (e.g. information and advice on varietal selection by fieldmen of the British Sugar Corporation).

The specialist extension agencies are an interesting phenomena since they co-exist with public and private extension services which are available free to the farmer. This may be explained on three grounds: (1) they may give higher quality service on the same sort of subjects, (2) they may be filling in gaps in existing free services, or (3) there may be some sort of Veblen effect working where farmers are distrustful of the information they receive gratis. The second phenomenon has probably been widely observed in the lack of a complete farm planning service in the National Agricultural Advisory Service. For a long time the N.A.A.S. seemed technically orientated and did not analyse the farm as an integrated business and social unit. An adjustment is now being made and farm management specialists have been appointed and farm management training is being given. Little information is available about the size of the effort in private extension. A basic difficulty is separating the sales from the extension function when one man in many cases performs both. Lord and Rodgers† have made an estimate for 1965/6 of £4·2 million compared with R. & D. expenditure of £10·2 million.

III.2. PUBLIC EXTENSION

The main agency for agricultural extension in England and Wales is the National Agricultural Advisory Service. Specialist extension activities in England and Wales are also provided by the Agricultural Land Service, the Veterinary Service and the National Institute of Agricultural Botany which deals mainly with crop varietal selection. Producer marketing boards generally have specialist advisory staff also. Scotland and Northern Ireland operate independently of this system, extension services being provided by the regional agricultural colleges in Scotland and by the Ministry of Agriculture in Belfast for Northern Ireland.

The National Agricultural Advisory Service (N.A.A.S.) is organized with a hierarchy of control with the headquarters located in London

† *Op. cit.*

and with regional, county and district strata below it. The regional headquarters provides laboratory services and some specialist advisory services (e.g. the relatively new Farm Management specialists are located here), the county headquarters provide most of the production specialists (i.e. livestock, crop, horticultural, and machinery specialists) and at the district level there is a general extension man, the District Officer, who acts as G.P. for about 500 to 600 farms. This hierarchy of direct extension activity is supplemented by the work of the Experimental Farms which as well as performing R. & D. work have a major role in extension with public open-days and demonstrations.

Data quoted by Lord and Rodgers† show extension expenditures by the Ministry of Agriculture totalling £8·79 million for England and Wales in 1965/6. They do not give separate figures for extension in 1955/6 but they do give a figure for expenditure on R. & D., Education and Extension. We therefore take the observed proportion of total expenditure used in extension in 1965/6 and use this proportion to estimate extension expenditure in 1955/6. We estimate the figure to be £4·34 million in 1955/6 so in money terms expenditure on extension has risen by 105 per cent in the ten-year period. In real terms this represents perhaps a rise of 25 per cent giving an average growth rate of real resources in extension of 2·26 per cent p.a. This growth rate seems to be more than double the increase in professional staff over the same period: there was a professional staff of 2120 in 1956 and 2350 in 1966,‡ giving an increase of nearly 11 per cent over the period and an average growth rate of 1·05 per cent p.a. This could be due to a general upgrading, an increase in ancillary workers per professional worker or an increase in the non-manpower component in extension.

More recent data supplied by the Ministry of Agriculture indicate a falling off in real expenditure on extension (Table 7.4).

III.3. INNOVATION AND DIFFUSION OF NEW TECHNOLOGY

An extension service is aimed at providing information and advice on new technologies produced as a result of R. & D. activity. We have already discussed the supply side, from research through to extension,

† *Op. cit.*, table 5, p. 21.
‡ Lord and Rodgers, *op. cit.*, table 9, p. 34.

TABLE 7.4. PUBLIC EXTENSION EXPENDITURES
(ENGLAND AND WALES)

	(1) Expenditure at current prices (£ million)	(2) Expenditure at 1956/7 prices (£ million)
1955/56	4·34	4·56
1965/66	8·79	5·67
1966/67	8·2	5·03
1967/68	7·7	4·50
1968/69†	8·2	4·57

† Forecast.
Sources: (1) Lord and Rodgers, *op. cit.*; (2) Ministry
of Agriculture, private communication.

now we must consider the demand side to understand what determines
the rate at which new ideas are implemented and the information that
is sought by farmers. In previous chapters we have examined the uptake
of new technologies which are embodied in machine and chemical
inputs using a model based essentially on profit maximizing behaviour,
but allowing for a gradual adjustment to equilibrium over time. Here
we will focus attention on the selection of new varieties of animals and
crops which constantly arise from the work of animal and plant
breeders. The problem of optimal selection of variety can be structured
in the same way as the optimum brand analysis in Chapter 2.

The first thing to note about the innovation and diffusion of new
varieties is that the process is slow. Dadd and Osborne† reported some
observations on the changing market share of three cereal varieties
all with a clear superiority over their rivals. The market share of Cappelle Desprez was still expanding seven years after introduction—in
1960/1 its market share in the U.K. was 80 per cent.

The rate of diffusion is probably related to the relative profitability
of the specific new variety,‡ but the fact remains that a lot of time can

† C. V. Dadd and L. W. Osborne, Factors influencing the choice of cereal varieties,
Outlook in Agriculture, vol. II, No. 1, Spring 1958.

‡ See Zvi Griliches, Hybrid corn: an exploration in the economics of technological
change, *Econometrica*, vol. 25, 4, October 1957.

TABLE 7.5. DIFFUSION OF NEW CEREAL VARIETIES

	Year first marketed	Percentage of acreage		
		1955	1956	1957
Cappelle Desprez	1950	31	51	71
Procter	1953	34	59	75
Koga II	1955	2	30	64

Source: from a survey of 1000 farms in Cambridgeshire 1955/7.

elapse before equilibrium is reached. Extension seeks to speed up this process by providing more information and an experiment reported by Dadd and Osborne showed that there was a bigger response to Cappelle for those receiving a leaflet explaining its merits compared with the standard variety grown at that time, Hybrid 46. In a situation where the rankings of different varieties are invariant to changing weather conditions the process of making recommendations is straightforward (especially if the price of seed is constant). Difficulties arise however when this condition does not hold and where weather conditions cannot be predicted at the time of planting. Then in order to make the extension effort effective we have to find out the behaviour of producers under conditions of uncertainty. The section below reports on a study of the selection of sugar-beet varieties.

Selection of Crop Varieties: A Case Study†

Here we take as an example the problem of the selection of sugar-beet varieties and in order to suggest some hypotheses about farmer behaviour we generate solutions to several probabilistic and game theoretic models and compare these solutions with actual selections made by farmers. Six alternative decision criteria were tested out, Laplace and Markowitz being derived from alternative probabilistic

† A detailed account of the analysis is given in a paper by Keith Cowling and R. J. Perkins, Producer behaviour in the choice of sugar-beet varieties: comparisons of game theoretic solutions with actual selections, *Bulletin of the Oxford Institute of Statistics*, vol. 25, No. 2, 1963, pp. 109–18.

models and Wald (maximin), maximax, Hurwicz and Savage representing alternative game theoretic models. The Laplace criterion is a particular case of the more general Bayes criterion where events are assumed to be equiprobable. Thus different types of weather are assumed equally likely in the future so that farmers simply go ahead and choose the variety with the highest average yield experienced over a series of past years if the Laplace criterion is relevant. In contrast the Bayes criterion would require us to get information on the probability distribution for the elements of weather which are important in sugar production and this proved impossible to accomplish. Algebraically the Laplace criterion says that the variety is chosen which maximizes $E_i = (a_{i1} + a_{i2} + \ldots + a_{in})/n$ for varieties, $i = 1, 2, \ldots, m$, over years, $j = 1, 2, \ldots, n$, whereas the Bayes criterion says we should choose Max $E_i = (p_1 a_{i1} + p_2 a_{i2} + \ldots + p_n a_{in})/n$, where $p_j (j = 1, 2, \ldots, n)$ is the probability of occurrence of nature's jth type of weather.

The Markowitz criterion considers the variance of the payoff distribution to be important as well as the mean. The Laplace solution will be accepted if the yield variance is no higher than for any alternative variety but if not, then we must consider some tradeoff between yield variance and mean yield.

Of the game theoretic criteria the Wald criterion dictates the most conservative course of action since it requires the farmer to select that variety which does best (relatively) with the worst weather. This may be relevant if the farmer is cautiously pessimistic or if financial contingencies make it imperative to "play safe". At the polar extreme from the Wald criterion is the maximax criterion, the gambler's strategy, which focuses entirely on the largest possible payoff.† The Hurwicz criterion is a compromise between maximax and minimax extremes and requires the decision-maker to weight the best and worst outcomes for each variety using some index of optimism. Lastly the Savage or minimax regret criterion involves computing the opportunity cost of a particular course of action and then selecting a variety so as to minimize this.‡

We can see from the above discussion that the probabilistic models can be viewed as profit maximization models extended into a situation

---

† Wald or maximin involves maximizing $E_i = \text{Min}_j a_{ij}$ whereas maximax involves maximizing $E_i = \text{Max}_j a_{ij}$.

‡ Maximize $E_i = \text{Min}_i r_{ij}$ where $r_{ij} = a_{ij} - \text{Max}_k a_{kj}$ ($i = 1, 2, \ldots, k, \ldots, m$).

of uncertainty whereas the game theoretic models represent a departure from profit maximization where we are no longer necessarily interested in the highest expected payoff. However, of the criteria examined the Laplace criterion was found to correspond most closely with farmers' revealed preferences—the well-known Wald or maximin criterion was *not* found to reflect farmer behaviour. The payoff matrix in this example consisted of sugar yield per acre for each variety for each of the previous five years.

The results suggest that growers are neither unduly optimistic nor pessimistic in their expectations. The results also perhaps raise the possibility that the decision process reflects that of the adviser rather than that of the farmer. The adviser can be expected to ignore the maximin strategy because he personally does not stand to lose anything, and similarly not to gamble since he does not get the payoff. Nevertheless, the results do suggest that varieties bred to do well in adverse years but which are on average inferior to existing varieties will not achieve large market shares. However, we would expect more concern about performance under adverse conditions where specialization is more intense and thus where income could be highly volatile. Such considerations must always be implicit when making recommendations about new varieties.

We can say that our results here give further justification to our previous theoretical underpinning of profit maximizing behaviour, given a particular assumption about the probability distribution for weather. Profit from any particular course of action is now assumed to follow a probability distribution and farmers select that course of action giving the highest mean profit.

IV. Education

The level of education in the agricultural labour force is likely to be an important determinant of the rate of innovation and diffusion of new technology. Extension services are likely to be more effective in a literate and scientifically aware community. However, it is impossible to measure the changing stock of education within the industry. All we can hope to do is to describe the present system and give some fragmentary quantitative evidence when it is available.

IV.1. UNIVERSITIES

In 1961/2 there were 1700 undergraduates and 350 postgraduates studying agriculture in universities in the U.K.† At that time this represented 2 per cent of the university student body but since that time there has been little change in agriculture students while total student numbers have risen quite fast. In 1965/6 580 students graduated with degrees in agriculture and 264 got degrees in veterinary science.‡ In the U.K. as a whole there are 13 departments of agriculture, 6 departments of veterinary science and 3 separate departments of agricultural economics. In recent years the University Grants Commission has exerted some pressure to close down smaller departments and to curtail general degrees and stimulate applied science and social science degrees. Expenditure on universities in 1955/6 and 1965/6 is given in Table 7.6. In real terms spending rose by 40 per cent over the period giving an average increase of 3·42 per cent p.a. in real resources going into education at the university level. The split between research and teaching was estimated to be nearly 2 : 1 in favour of teaching in 1965/6.

IV.2. FURTHER EDUCATION

This covers college and institute full-time courses, and block and day release courses run at farm institutes and technical colleges. In 1965/6 there was an output from the college system of 436 National Diplomas in Agriculture and from the institute system there was 1779 National Certificates in Agriculture.‡ Between 1957/8 and 1962/3 the number of students at farm institutes was growing at 4·75 per cent per annum but the area of rapid growth was in the number of part-time students at technical colleges. There was an increase of more than 100 per cent in students taking agriculture, forestry or fishing at grant-aided institutions between 1957/8 and 1962/3, giving an average growth rate of nearly 19 per cent p.a.§

In Table 7.6 we see that expenditure in non-university areas of

† See H. Frankel, Economic changes in British agriculture 1959–1964, *Agricultural Economics Research Institute*, Oxford, 1964.

‡ Lord and Rodgers, *op. cit.*, p. 30.

§ Frankel, *op. cit.*

further education has risen rather more rapidly than expenditure on universities. There was an average increase in real resources in the non-university sector of 5·75 per cent p.a. but compared with the rapid increase in student numbers this growth rate does not appear large, especially compared with the university situation with relatively stagnant student numbers. Expenditure on teaching in the non-university sector was about 50 per cent higher than for university teaching but we can see that no research activity was allowed for.

V. Aggregate Intellectual Investment

The different components of intellectual investment in agriculture

TABLE 7.6. RESEARCH AND EDUCATION EXPENDITURE AND ALLOCATIONS BY UNIVERSITIES, COLLEGES AND INSTITUTES IN ENGLAND AND WALES, 1965/6 AND 1955/6 AT CURRENT PRICES (IN £ '000)

	1965/6			1955/6
	Research	Education	Total	Total
(a) *University Grants Committee**				
Schools of Agriculture,				
Horticulture and Forestry	901	1620	2521	1265
Veterinary Colleges	653	1183	1836	646
Total	1554	2803	4357	1911
(b) *Allocation of the Department of Education and Science and Local Education Authorities*				
Farm Institutes	—	2918	2918	1419†
Agricultural Colleges‡	—	157	517	81†
Institutes and Colleges				
Capital allocation	—	1196	1196	—
Total	—	4271	4271	1500

* Excludes university overhead costs.
† Funds administered by the Ministry of Agriculture (capital expenditure included).
‡ Excluding the Royal Agricultural College, which receives no maintenance grant.
Source: Lord and Rodgers, *op. cit.*, p. 26.

are highly interdependent in their impact on agricultural production. Without a system of extension, R. & D. will show no benefits to the industry as a whole, and extension itself will be made ineffective if the audience does not have a sufficient background education to absorb technical material. Similarly increased extension expenditures will rapidly lose impact if there is not an associated growth in new technology. Education will give only a minimal payoff in a technologically stagnant industry—with static technology experience can rapidly take the place of education. We can extend this analysis of interdependence in production and therefore demand outside intellectual investment and look at the linkages between this sector and other sectors. The expansion of the use of nitrogen on cereals would have been rapidly cut off without the associated plant breeding work giving stiff-strawed varieties which would not lodge with high fertilizer use. Similarly developments in combine-harvesting technology were made simpler with the advent of short strawed varieties. These interdependencies must be remembered when we attempt to apply cost–benefit techniques to public investment in any particular area of public intellectual investment. Here we will simply describe total expenditure on R. & D., Extension and Education, and then describe a simple cost-benefit analysis for illustration. Lord and Rodgers† estimate total intellectual investment in agriculture in the U.K. at £51·7 million, public investment accounting for £37·3 million and private investment being £14·4 million. This contrasts with their estimate for 1955/6 which was £20·5 million, £15 million public and £5·5 million private. This represents an increase of 54 per cent *in real terms* over the period, implying an average growth rate of 4·41 per cent p.a. in real resources. The average growth rate for the public sector was slightly lower (4·3 per cent p.a.) than that for the private sector (4·85 per cent p.a.). As a percentage of Gross Agricultural Product public intellectual investment rose from 1·1 per cent in 1955/6 to 1·8 per cent in 1960/1 and 1·9 per cent in 1963/4.‡ A comparison among O.E.E.C. countries showed the U.K. ratio of intellectual investment to G.A.P. to be about average in 1955/6. Belgium, Canada, Netherlands and Sweden had higher ratios, while

† *Op. cit.*, table 1, p. 4.
‡ A. J. Davies, Research, education and extension, in *Agriculture 1967*, Agricultural Adjustment Unit, The University, Newcastle upon Tyne, 1968.

Greece and Turkey had very low ratios.† Comparing the distribution of public funds among R. & D., Extension and Education it was apparent, from the same report, that the U.K. along with the U.S. and Canada had a larger than average share devoted to research (although U.K. university education was not included), while Italy and Greece devoted a large share to education and only a small part to extension.

Comparing the intellectual investment/output ratio between U.K. agriculture and the U.K. economy as a whole we see that agriculture appears pretty low. In 1955/6 R. & D. *alone* constituted 1·8 per cent of G.N.P. whereas in 1964/5 it had grown to 2·6 per cent of G.N.P.‡

VI. Cost–Benefit Analysis of Intellectual Investment

Three levels of cost–benefit analysis could be envisaged if we were seeking guidelines for public intellectual investment policy or if we were seeking to assess likely developments in the supply of and demand for new technology assuming some equilibrating mechanism. The first level of analysis would be concerned with the social rate of return of *aggregate* intellectual investment in agriculture, the second level would be concerned with comparing the rates of return in the three major sectors, R. & D., Extension and Education and the third level would relate to specific innovations or areas of research or extension projects. Because of the many interdependencies a realistic appraisal of micro projects would be very difficult.

Some evidence on the rate of return at the aggregate level is available for the U.S. The estimate of returns to R. & D. and Extension expenditures was obtained by fitting a Cobb–Douglas production function to cross-section state data.§ Along with conventional inputs, Griliches included state annual budgets for R. & D. and extension in $t − 1$ and $t − 6$ as well as weighting labour input by an educational variable. The average elasticity of production with respect to R. & D. and Extension inputs was estimated to be 0·05, and the marginal product was 13 dollars p.a. per dollar spent on R. & D. and Extension, a gross rate of

† *Intellectual Investment in Agriculture*, Report No. 60, O.E.E.C.
‡ *Report on Science Policy*, Cmnd. 3007, H.M.S.O.
§ Zvi Griliches, Research expenditure, education and the aggregate agricultural production function, *American Economic Review*, December 1964, pp. 961–94.

return of 1300 per cent. After allowing for reasonable estimates of private investment in these areas and allowing for a lower social marginal product the rate of return still appeared very big. An analysis along these lines would be very difficult for the U.K. A cross-section analysis would be impossible since we do not have well-defined regions with different institutions and a time-series analysis is impossible because of the lack of data. A cross-sectional European analysis may be considered as a thing for the future.

At the second level—comparing rates of return to R. & D., Extension and Education, Griliches' results for the U.S. did suggest a higher rate for R. & D. and extension as a whole compared with education. At the third level, looking at specific projects, a study has been made of the benefits accruing from public investment in the development of a potato harvester.† The National Institute of Agricultural Engineering developed a new potato harvester in 1954 and the patents were passed to the National Research and Development Corporation. They financed a prototype and modifications and as from 1959 the model was successfully marketed. Grossfield and Heath calculated the public benefits as the difference in costs using the N.I.A.E. machine or alternative methods then available times the acreage involved. They cut off the flow of benefits after 1965 since further sales were assumed to be due to manufacturers, post-invention developments. All R. & D. costs and the benefits as defined were carried forward to 1967. Total cumulative benefits were estimated at £662,000 with cumulative costs at £250,000 (including interest charges). The limitations of this analysis are that it ignores the impact on the potato market of the innovation, it does not attempt to allocate the benefits and it does not attempt to see if there is a real gain from the labour released or if part-time secondary workers simply drop out of the labour force. Griliches in his study of hybrid corn tries to assess the impact on the market and gets a rate of return greater than 700 per cent.‡

The problem with such estimates is that they are derived from ex-post analyses of successes and for every success in research there is

† K. Grossfield and J. B. Heath, The benefit and cost of government support for R. & D.: a case study, *Economic Journal*, 1966, pp. 537–49.

‡ Zvi Griliches, Research costs and social returns: hybrid corn and related innovations, *J. Political Economy*, 1958, pp. 419–31.

a number of complete failures from a commercial viewpoint. Therefore the problem becomes one of allocating costs to the particular success. Thus if we examine the benefits accruing to the introduction of Procter barley then on the cost side we would have to allocate a proportion of expenses incurred at the Plant Breeding Institute not related to the Procter project. Since the benefits will also be affected by the rate of diffusion of the new variety, expenditures connected with the promotion of the variety should properly be included also. The expected payoff will also be affected by the receptiveness of farmers to new and superior varieties which will be conditioned by their education. Thus the analysis will involve R. & D., Extension and Education costs and we will be analysing the payoff to this intellectual mix.

We must therefore conclude that micro-level cost–benefit may very easily result in overestimates of the benefit-cost ratio since they are likely to focus on successful innovations and ignore the numerous failures. The important problem then becomes that of estimating the probability of success in different lines of research. Aggregate estimates of the benefits arising from R. & D. investment may give the most accurate indication of the relative merits of R. & D., *vis-à-vis* investment in physical or human capital, but they of course tell us nothing about allocation of funds between different R. & D. projects. No aggregate cost–benefit analysis of intellectual investment has been made for U.K. agriculture and this will be exceedingly difficult to accomplish using aggregate time series because of the close correlation over time between capital stock, human capital, R. & D. and extension expenditures. Perhaps some estimates could be obtained from a European cross-section, or series of cross-sections, where we are likely to observe more independent variation in intellectual investment.

CHAPTER 8

DEMAND FOR RESOURCES AND THE SUPPLY OF AGRICULTURAL PRODUCTS

IN THIS chapter, we collate the results of the analyses, contained in the previous chapters, of the demand for individual resources. Firstly, we give an overall picture of how the resource structure of United Kingdom agriculture has changed in the post-war period. We go on to consider the way in which the demands for different resources have been interrelated in determining this changing resource structure. The interaction of input flows also determines the supply of output via the production function. Consequently, it is possible to estimate the responsiveness of planned supply to price changes from the analysis of the demand for inputs. This is a useful procedure because the adjustment of output to changing relative prices cannot necessarily be described by a simple adjustment model when inputs are adjusted at different rates in the resource structure. Therefore, in section III, we show theoretically how the own price elasticity of aggregate supply can be obtained from a knowledge of the demand functions for inputs. Using this theoretical analysis, we derive, for United Kingdom agriculture, some estimates of this elasticity. Finally, in section IV, we consider how the resource structure of agriculture is likely to change in the future.

I. The Changing Resource Structure of United Kingdom Agriculture in the Post-war Period

Some of the major changes in the resource structure of United Kingdom agriculture between 1954 and 1966 are illustrated in Table 8.1 opposite.

TABLE 8.1. THE RESOURCE STRUCTURE OF UNITED KINGDOM AGRICULTURE 1954/5 TO 1966/7 (ALL FIGURES IN £m IN CONSTANT PRICES (Ave. 1954/5 TO 1956/7 = 100))

Resources*	Selected years (end May)						
	1954/5	1956/7	1958/9	1960/1	1962/3	1964/5	1966/7
1. Value of stock of machinery (replacement value)	860·2	897·8	946·6	947·0	971·6	1113·0	1185·9
2. Value of livestock (at June)	677·6	681·6	703·4	733·6	759·5	751·7	751·8
3. Expenditure on hired labour	286·1	276·6	264·0	228·3	211·4	186·4	165·8
4. Expenditure on fertilizer	55·8	65·4	70·8	86·0	86·6	100·6	108·6
5. Expenditure on feeding-stuffs (includes interfarm sales)	379·1	374·4	437·7	445·0	489·7	494·5	496·3
6. Expenditure on seed	30·7	30·0	32·7	33·1	34·9	31·6	32·7
7. Sundry expenses	133·5	136·0	144·3	153·8	163·1	174·4	175·5

* Items 1 and 2 are the author's estimates based primarily on the census figures for machinery and livestock. Also utilized in calculating a price index for machinery was the author's constant quality tractor price index (*op. cit.*, *J.A.E.*, 1968). The helpful advice of Mr. J. Stewart and Mr. K. Yates was utilized in preparing the livestock figures. Items 3–7 are calculated or given directly from relevant series in the *Annual Abstract of Statistics*.

Whilst some of the figures in the table contain a "guess" element (particularly for items 1 and 2), the major trends in the resource structure of agriculture are identified. We can observe that since 1954/5 there has been a fairly substantial increase in the stock of machinery, whilst the demand for hired labour (including family workers, except for the operator and his wife) has declined considerably. Current capital inputs have also increased over the period—particularly the input of fertilizer, which has nearly doubled, and sundry expenses, such as herbicides and pesticides. There has been an increase over the period in the output of livestock products, and this is reflected in the increase in livestock on farms and the increase in purchased feeding-stuffs. Finally, the trend in the stock of farm buildings, which is not detailed in the table, should be mentioned. Estimates of the stock figure are not available; however, it was pointed out in Chapter 6 that investment in buildings has doubled since 1954, and this indicates a fairly substantial rise in the stock of farm buildings. Therefore, there has been a substantial and continuous substitution of durable capital services for labour over the period. In addition, there has been a fairly considerable increase in other capital inputs, particularly those produced by the non-farm sector.

So far, in this section, we have looked at the absolute changes in resource demands that have occurred between 1954 and 1966. We may also illustrate the changing resource structure by analysing changes in the proportional contribution that each input flow makes toward total costs. If costs are measured as opportunity costs and we assume zero economic profits then this analysis also shows how factor shares have changed over time. An analysis of the percentage contribution of different inputs to total costs comparing 1956/7 with 1965/6 is given below in Table 8.2. Inputs to agriculture were classified into ten groups for this analysis and an estimate of the opportunity cost of the service flow from each input group was made. These cost estimates for each year were arrived at as follows:

(i) *Hired labour.* Annual expenditure on labour (includes family labour, except that of the farmer and his wife).

(ii) *Fertilizer.* Annual expenditure on fertilizer minus the fertilizer subsidy.

(iii) *Feedingstuffs.* Annual expenditure on feedingstuffs minus an estimate of the value of grains produced in the United Kingdom which were sold for feed purposes. This is therefore an estimate of the value of imported feedingstuff, plus the value added to home grown feed. Interfarm transfers, which are not an input to agriculture in the aggregate, are excluded by this method.

(iv) *Seed.* Expenditure on imported seed plus merchants' margins on home-grown seed.

(v) *Sundry expenses.* Annual expenditure on sundries.

(vi) *Machinery.* The opportunity cost of the flow of services from machinery consists of a depreciation cost and an imputed interest charge. Costs associated with machinery, such as fuel and repairs, were also included in the machinery input costs category. Published figures for depreciation and associated costs are available. The imputed interest cost was estimated by multiplying an estimate of the current value of the stock of machinery (the value of machinery at replacement cost, reduced to allow for the average age of machinery) by bank rate.

(vii) *Livestock.* It was assumed that an imputed interest charge represented the opportunity cost of livestock on farms. The current value of livestock on farms at June of each year was estimated, with allowance made for seasonality, and multiplied by bank rate to give the interest cost.

(viii) and (ix) *Land and buildings.* No estimates are available of the division of landlord's capital between land and buildings. It was arbitrarily decided that one quarter of the value of landlord's capital should be allocated to the value of the stock of buildings in each year. Two estimates of the opportunity cost of landlord's capital were made, leading to estimates A and B in Table 8.2. Estimate A is an estimate of the annual rental of United Kingdom farms, including an imputed rent for owner-occupied farms. However, it was felt that the rental figure may underestimate the opportunity cost of the land input to agriculture, particularly as the majority of farms are owner-occupied. Consequently estimate B was arrived at by multiplying the estimated current value of landlord's capital in agriculture by bank rate.

(x) *Labour of the farmer.* An estimate of the cost of the input flow provided by farmers can be approached in two ways. Either we can take this cost as the residual given by subtracting the total of all the other cost estimates from gross output (and assuming zero "profits"), or

TABLE 8.2. OPPORTUNITY COST OF INDIVIDUAL RESOURCE FLOWS AS PERCENTAGE OF
TOTAL COSTS IN U.K. AGRICULTURE: 1956/7 COMPARED WITH 1965/6

	Estimate A		Estimate B	
	1956/7	1965/6	1956/7	1965/6
Hired labour	24·1	20·4	22·8	18·9
Fertilizer	5·0	5·9	4·8	5·5
Feedingstuffs	20·5	20·2	19·4	18·7
Seed	2·3	1·8	2·2	1·7
Sundry expenses	6·4	8·0	6·1	7·4
Machinery	18·3	18·2	17·4	16·9
Livestock	3·3	3·6	3·2	3·4
Land	4·0	5·9	7·7	10·9
Buildings	1·4	2·0	2·6	3·6
Labour of farmer	14·6	14·0	13·9	13·0

N.B. Estimate A differs from estimate B in the valuation of the input flow of landlord's capital.

we may assume that farmers earn the same wage as hired labour. Both estimates were made and were found to be fairly close to each other so that a final estimate was arrived at as a compromise figure between the two separate estimates.†

The proportional contribution of each input flow to total costs is given in Table 8.2 above.

Several trends stand out in Table 8.2. Firstly, there has been a marked decline, over the ten-year period, in the share of hired labour in total costs. Secondly, although the service flow from machinery has increased over the period, it has not increased in relation to the increase in total costs. Thirdly, the share of current capital inputs, as represented by fertilizer and sundry expenses, has increased over the period. Finally,

† Sources utilized in estimating the cost of input flows were as follows: for hired labour, fertilizer, feed, seed, sundry expenses, depreciation and associated machinery costs, the rental value of landlord's capital and the residual estimate of the cost of farmers' labour: M.A.F.F., *Annual Review and Determination of Guarantees*. For preparing the feed cost estimate a further source was utilized: Commonwealth Economic Committee, *Grain Crops Agreement*. The imputed interest charge on machinery, livestock and landlord's capital are the author's estimate based on various published sources. In addition, an article by Bosanquet was utilized in preparing the landlord's capital estimate: Bosanquet, Investment in agriculture, *Journal of Agricultural Economics*, vol. XIX, 1968.

the inflation in land values is represented by the increased share of the land input in 1965/6 compared with 1956/7.

II. Interactions between Demands for Different Resources

The previous section indicates that there has been a considerable and continuous change in the resource structure of United Kingdom agriculture in the post-war period. This picture of the changing resource structure links together the changes that have occurred in the demands for individual resources and it suggests that these demands are in fact related to each other. Interaction between the usage of different inputs is, of course, implied by the concept of the production function. This assumes that resource flows can be substituted for each other, albeit at a diminishing marginal rate, to produce a given quantity of output. Consequently, when economic factors stimulate a change in the resource structure of agriculture the extent of the change partly depends upon the ease with which resource flows can be substituted for each other.

Some of the important substitution possibilities in agriculture have been detailed in earlier chapters. For example, we described the possibility of substitution occurring between machinery services and labour, between the services of different machines, and between fertilizer, as an input to farm-grown forage, and purchased feed. However, the most important substitution possibility, as far as economic growth is concerned, is that between capital services, in aggregate, and labour. Some work by Tyler† indicates that capital services and labour could be substituted quite easily for each other in production in the post-war period. Tyler analysed the production function relationship between net output (value added) of U.K. agriculture and the service flow of capital stock (a value aggregate of machinery and equipment, buildings, breeding livestock and land) and labour. He estimated that the elasticity of substitution between capital services and labour was of a magnitude greater than unity and probably close to two.‡ Consequently, it was

† G. J. Tyler, Factors affecting the growth of productivity in United Kingdom agriculture 1948–65, paper delivered at the Symposium on Agricultural Manpower, December 1968, National Economic Development Office.

‡ The elasticity of substitution between two inputs is defined as the proportionate

fairly easy to substitute capital services for labour and thus there was scope for substantial changes in the capital/labour ratio.

Whilst the production function shows the technical possibilities of resource interaction, economic factors stimulate the actual resource substitutions that occur. The changing resource structure therefore illustrates the interaction of the economic factors and the technical possibilities. Our analysis in earlier chapters suggests that similar economic factors determine the demands for individual resources and therefore the changing resource structure. Thus the results indicate that farmers, in the post-war period, have adjusted the use of inputs to changes in the relevant price ratios in a profit-seeking direction. Consequently, changes in the demand for one input could not have occurred without simultaneous changes in the demands for other inputs, particularly those which were close substitutes. For example, the separate studies on the demand for labour and the demand for machinery indicated that both the drift of labour from the land and the increased mechanization of agriculture were partly a result of a falling machinery price/labour price ratio. Thus the increase in the machinery/labour ratio in the resource structure over the period was partly a consequence of changes in this price ratio. It seems likely that this change in the resource structure created pressure for the amalgamation of farms so that machinery could be more effectively utilized. Hence, the machinery/land ratio on the average farm did not increase as rapidly as it did at the aggregate level.

The demands for individual resources were also connected via changes in the product price: a *ceteris paribus* increase in this price tended to increase, to a greater or lesser extent, the use of each individual resource. There was also an interrelationship between the adoption of new technologies, in the sense that the introduction of one innovation was often aided by the adoption of another. For example, the trend toward tractors which incorporated a power-take-off was increased by the introduction of new machines which were specifically designed to be

---

change in the ratio of factor inputs caused by a proportionate change in the marginal rate of substitution between the inputs. For a two-input production function, the elasticity of substitution describes the degree of curvature of the isoquants. The greater the elasticity of substitution the flatter are the isoquants and the easier it is to substitute one input for the other.

powered by the power-take-off. Similarly, new developments for feeding livestock were aided by the adoption of new machinery for harvesting forage. Therefore, we should view the changing resource structure of agriculture as a description of the interrelationships of the demands for various resources over time.

The market mechanism stimulus for the changing resource structure has generally been provided from outside agriculture. Firstly, the suppliers of inputs to agriculture, such as the machinery and chemical firms, have developed new and improved inputs and have lowered the real price of their products. Secondly, government assistance to agriculture through production subsidies, such as the fertilizer subsidy and investment allowances, has lowered the real price of some inputs to farmers. Thirdly, governmental sponsored research has developed new and improved inputs. In addition, the extension services have helped to spread the knowledge amongst farmers of new technology and of the profitable adjustment of resource structure in response to changing prices. Farmers in their turn have responded relatively quickly to economic factors (as evidenced by the adjustment coefficients put forward in the earlier chapters) and have brought about substantial changes in the resource structure of agriculture.

III. Resource Demand and a Derived Supply Elasticity

It has been shown in previous chapters that resource demand in agriculture changes with changes in relative prices. Consequently, the planned supply of aggregate output must respond to price changes since output is related to resource flows via the production function. We show in section III.1 the way in which it is theoretically possible to derive an estimate of the elasticity of output with respect to "real" product price from a knowledge of the demand elasticities for inputs with respect to product price. We go on to argue that this indirect estimation procedure may be preferable to direct estimation of the elasticity. Finally, in section III.2 we give some estimates of the elasticity for United Kingdom agriculture for the two years 1956/7 and 1965/6.

III.1. THEORETICAL CONSIDERATIONS†

We have suggested in earlier chapters that although farm-firms adjust their resource structure toward equilibrium in each period, they do not actually attain an equilibrium position. We therefore made the distinction between the equilibrium input flow of a resource and the actual input flow. It is clear that if resource demand is not adjusted to equilibrium in each period then the supply in each period is not the equilibrium supply. Thus, equilibrium supply is the planned output that would occur if equilibrium quantities of the inputs were used, and this differs from the actual planned supply because the actual input flows diverge from their equilibrium levels. Consequently, we may distinguish between the long run, or equilibrium, elasticity of supply with respect to product price and the short run, or actual, elasticity.

In order to derive these elasticities, let us first denote the equilibrium input flow of the ith resource by x_i^* and the actual input flow by x_i. We next define the aggregate production for agriculture by:

$$q = f(x_1, \ldots, x_k \mid \bar{x}_{k+1}, \ldots, \bar{x}_n) \tag{8.1}$$

where q is the value of the planned aggregate output flow (the value sum of individual product flows), $x_1, \ldots, x_k$ are the variable input flows from k resources and $\bar{x}_{k+1}, \ldots, \bar{x}_n$ are fixed input flows from $n - k$ resources. If farm-firms did use an equilibrium quantity of each input flow then planned output would be the equilibrium output (q^*) and we could write the aggregate production functions as:

$$q^* = f(x_1^*, \ldots, x_k^* \mid \bar{x}_{k+1}, \ldots, \bar{x}_n) \tag{8.2}$$

Let us denote product price by P. If we differentiate the aggregate production function (equation (8.1)) with respect to P we obtain:

$$\frac{dq}{dP} = \frac{\partial q}{\partial x_1} \cdot \frac{dx_1}{dP} + \cdots + \frac{\partial q}{\partial x_k} \cdot \frac{dx_k}{dP} \tag{8.3}$$

† This section is for more advanced students. A verbal summary of the theory which is derived in this section is given in the next section (III.2) together with some estimates of the aggregate supply elasticity for United Kingdom agriculture. This section represents, to some extent, a modification and extension of an article by Griliches: Zvi Griliches, The demand for inputs in agriculture and a derived supply elasticity, *Journal of Farm Economics*, vol. 41, 1959, pp. 309–22.

If we multiply (8.3) by P/q and multiply each ith term on the right-hand side by x_i/x_i $(i = 1, \ldots, k)$ we obtain:

$$\frac{dq}{dP} \cdot \frac{P}{q} = \frac{\partial q}{\partial x_1} \cdot \frac{x_1}{q} \cdot \frac{dx_1}{dP} \cdot \frac{P}{x_1} + \ldots + \frac{\partial q}{\partial x_k} \cdot \frac{x_k}{q} \cdot \frac{dx_k}{dP} \cdot \frac{P}{x_k} \quad (8.4)$$

Now $(dq/dP)(P/q)$ is the actual or short-run elasticity of aggregate supply with respect to product price and may be denoted by η_{qp}. Similarly, $(\partial q/\partial x_i)(x_i/q)$ is the elasticity of aggregate output with respect to changes in the input flow x_i and may be denoted by a_i. Similarly, $(dx_i/dP)(P/x_i)$ is the actual or short-run elasticity of aggregate demand for the input flow x_i with respect to product price and may be denoted by η_{ip}.

Therefore equation (8.4) may be written as

$$\eta_{qp} = a_1 \eta_{1p} + \ldots + a_k \eta_{kp} \quad (8.5)$$

Equation (8.5) therefore explains the actual or short-run elasticity of supply in terms of the production elasticities of the input flows and the short-run demand elasticities for the input flows. In the same way, we can derive an expression for the equilibrium or long-run elasticity of supply from the production function (8.2) which relates the equilibrium output flow to equilibrium input flows. We obtain:

$$\eta_{qp}^* = a_1^* \eta_{1p}^* + \ldots + a_k^* \eta_{kp}^* \quad (8.6)$$

where η_{qp}^* is the long-run elasticity of supply with respect to product price and η_{ip}^* is the long-run demand elasticity for the ith input with respect to product price. In addition, the magnitude of the production elasticity of the ith resource at the equilibrium input flow is denoted by a_1^*. If the magnitude of the production elasticity of the ith input changes as the quantity of input flow changes the a_i^* will differ from a_i.

So far, we have come to the conclusion that we can derive estimates of the short-run and the long-run elasticity of supply from estimates of the production elasticities of the inputs and the short-run and long-run elasticities of demand for the inputs. We have suggested in Chapter 2 that estimates of the short-run and long-run elasticity of demand for an input with respect to product price can be obtained as follows. Firstly, we suggested that the partial adjustment model provides a reasonable description of the adjustment of the demand for an input from one period to another, in a disequilibrium situation. Two versions of this adjustment model were suggested: one linear and the other logarithmic. In algebraic terms, these are:

$$x_{it} - x_{it-1} = \gamma_i (x_{it}^* - x_{it-1}) \tag{8.7}$$

$$x_{it}/x_{it-1} = (x_{it}^*/x_{it-1})^{\gamma_i} \tag{8.8}$$

In both models the adjustment coefficient γ_i is expected to have a value between zero and unity. If it has the value of unity then it implies that the demand for the ith input is adjusted to equilibrium in each period. Secondly, it was suggested that the partial adjustment model be combined with the demand function for the equilibrium input flow, to give a demand function for the actual input flow. From the latter, an estimate of the short-run elasticity of demand for the input with respect to product price can be obtained. In addition, the use of the adjustment model implies that the long-run elasticity of demand for the input with respect to product price is equal to the short-run elasticity divided by the adjustment coefficient, provided a suitable algebraic form is used to relate equilibrium demand to prices.

In other words:

$$\eta_{ip}^* = \eta_{ip}/\gamma_i \tag{8.9}\dagger$$

Two alternative procedures may be used to obtain estimates of the production function elasticities. In theory, we could estimate these elasticities directly by quantifying the aggregate production function relationship with the use of regression analysis and obtain estimates of both the a_i^*'s and the a_i's. Alternatively, we could estimate the production function elasticities indirectly from a knowledge of the cost structure of agriculture, with the assumption that at equilibrium there are zero profits, as defined from an economic standpoint. This indirect procedure takes the following form.

† This may be illustrated by the following model:

$$x_{1t}^* = (P_t/P_{1t})^{b_1} (P_{2t}/P_{1t})^{b_2} \tag{i}$$

where P_t is the price of x_t

$$x_{1t}/x_{1t-1} = (x_{1t}^*/x_{1t-1})^{\gamma_1} \tag{ii}$$

Therefore $\quad x_{1t} = (P_t/P_{1t})^{\gamma_1 b_1} (P_{2t}/P_{1t})^{\gamma_1 b_2} x_{1t-1}^{(1-\gamma_1)}$

Therefore $\quad \eta_{1p} = b_1\gamma_1 = \eta_{1p}^*\gamma_1$

In equilibrium, the marginal value product of any variable input flow will be equated to its opportunity cost,

i.e.
$$\frac{\partial q^*}{\partial x_i^*} = \frac{P_i}{P} \qquad (8.10)$$

where P_i is the price (opportunity cost) of a unit of the ith input flow.

Therefore the equation for the long-run supply elasticity (8.6) may be written as:

$$\eta_{qp}^* = \frac{P_i \cdot x_1^*}{P \cdot q^*} \cdot \eta_{1p}^* + \ldots + \frac{P_k \cdot x_k^*}{P \cdot q^*} \cdot \eta_{kp}^* \qquad (8.11)$$

In other words, the equilibrium elasticity of aggregate supply is derived from the equilibrium share of each input in total revenue (which is equal to the equilibrium production elasticity) multiplied by the equilibrium elasticity of demand for the input with respect to product price. The equilibrium input flow of the ith resource in any time period may be obtained from the partial adjustment model that was incorporated into the demand function for that input flow. For example, if the adjustment equation (8.8) were used to derive the demand function for the ith input flow, then the equilibrium input flow in period t would be given by:

$$x_{it}^* = x_{it}^{1/\gamma_i} \cdot x_{it-1}^{\gamma_i - 1/\gamma_i} \qquad (8.12)$$

However, the equilibrium output flow, q^*, cannot be obtained without empirical knowledge of the aggregate production function. If agriculture were a perfectly competitive industry, we could easily circumvent this problem. In equilibrium, we would be able to assume zero economic profits for firms in the industry and therefore in equation (8.11) one could replace the share of each variable input flow in equilibrium total revenue by its share in equilibrium total cost,

i.e.
$$\eta_{qp}^* = \frac{P_1 \cdot x_1^*}{T.C.^*} \cdot \eta_{1p}^* + \ldots + \frac{P_k \cdot x_k^*}{T.C.^*} \cdot \eta_{kp}^* \qquad (8.13)$$

where
$$T.C.^* = \sum_{i=1}^{k} P_i x_i^* + \sum_{m=k+1}^{n} P_m \bar{x}_m \qquad (8.14)$$

If we were to assume zero economic profits in agriculture in equilibrium then we could use equation (8.13) to estimate the aggregate supply elasticity for agriculture. However, there is not freedom of entry into and exit from agriculture and consequently, fixed factors may earn rents above or below their opportunity costs. Therefore, the procedure represented by equation (8.13) may overestimate or underestimate the "true" equilibrium supply elasticity to some extent. Clearly this criticism does not hold if all input flows are variable.

Equation (8.13) allows us to estimate the long run supply elasticity, at least approximately, without having to directly estimate the production elasticities. However, if we wish to estimate the short-run supply elasticity without directly estimating the production elasticities we have to make further assumptions. The assumption we make in the next section is to postulate that the production elasticities are constant over the range between the actual input flows and the equilibrium input flows. In other words, we assume $a_i = a_i^*$ $(i = 1, \ldots, k)$. We then replace the a_i's in equation (8.5) by our indirect estimates of the a_i^*'s which are based on the share of each input in equilibrium total costs. Finally, we estimate the short-run supply elasticity from this equation.

We have shown in the above discussion that it is possible to derive estimates of the aggregate supply elasticity from a knowledge of the demand elasticities for inputs with respect to product price. This indirect procedure necessitates quite a large amount of empirical estimation and it seems relevant to ask if it has any advantages over direct estimation of the supply elasticity. Direct estimation of the short-run and long-run aggregate supply elasticity would simply involve the estimation of an aggregate supply function which incorporated a partial adjustment model of supply. However, we can argue that there are some theoretical advantages to the indirect estimation method. To start with, the indirect method would seem to give a better description of the planning procedures of farmers. Thus farmers plan with regard to input quantities and adjust input flows from year to year in response to changes in relative prices. A partial adjustment model for each input may therefore describe in a fairly reasonable manner the adjustment of resource structure from year to year. Planned aggregate output is of course adjusted from year to year as a result of the adjustment of input flows. However, it seems probable that we need a fairly complex adjustment model to describe the adjustment of aggregate output, firstly, because it is unlikely that different input flows are adjusted at the same rate and secondly, because there are interaction effects between input flows in the production function. In other words, only in special circumstances will a simple partial adjustment model adequately describe the adjustment of aggregate supply over time, even if simple adjustment models give a reasonable description of the adjustment of inputs over time. This point may be illustrated as follows: if we replace each η_{ip} $(i = 1, \ldots, k)$ in equation (8.5) by equation (8.9) and divide equation (8.6) by the resulting equation, we obtain:

$$\frac{\eta_{qp}^*}{\eta_{qp}} = \frac{a_1^* \eta_{1p}^* + \cdots + a_k^* \eta_{kp}^*}{a_1 \gamma_1 \eta_{1p}^* + \cdots + a_k \gamma_k \eta_{kp}^*} \tag{8.15}$$

It is quite likely that the production elasticity and/or the demand elasticity of any resource will vary as the input flow of the resource varies. Therefore, it is probable that the proportionality between the short-run supply elasticity and the long-run supply elasticity will vary as output changes. Consequently, using the partial adjustment model to describe the adjustment of aggregate supply is likely to be inapplicable since it forces a constant proportionality between the two elasticities into the results.

If the production elasticities and the demand elasticities are constants then, from equation (8.15), we can see that the short-run supply elasticity is a constant proportion of the long-run supply elasticity. However, even in this situation, the partial adjustment model does not necessarily provide an apt description of the adjustment of supply over time. Indeed, the partial adjustment model is only theoretically applicable to supply adjustment if the adjustment coefficients for all the inputs are of equal magnitude. This may be illustrated as follows: let us assume that the aggregate production function may be described by a Cobb–Douglas algebraic form, so that the production elasticities are constants, and that there are only two variable inputs.

Therefore

$$q = x_1^{a_1} x_2^{a_2} \tag{8.16}$$

Furthermore, let the equilibrium demand functions for the inputs be logarithmic, so that the long-run demand elasticities are constants:†

$$x_{1t}^* = b_{10} \cdot P_t{}^{b_{11}} P_{1t}{}^{b_{12}} P_{2t}{}^{b_{13}} \tag{8.17}$$

$$x_{2t}^* = b_{20} \cdot P_t{}^{b_{21}} P_{1t}{}^{b_{22}} P_{2t}{}^{b_{23}} \tag{8.18}$$

where P_t is product price, P_{1t} is the price of x_1 and P_{2t} is the price of x_2, in period t.

Finally, let the adjustment equations for the inputs be logarithmic so that the short-run demand elasticities are constants:

$$x_{it}/x_{it-1} = (x_{it}^*/x_{it-1})^{\gamma_i} \tag{8.19}$$

Then the demand function for x_{it} ($i = 1,2$) is:

$$x_{it} = b_{i0} \cdot P_t{}^{\gamma_i b_{i1}} \cdot P_{1t}{}^{\gamma_i b_{i2}} \cdot P_{2t}{}^{\gamma_i b_{i3}} x_{it-1}{}^{(1-\gamma_i)} \tag{8.20}$$

Therefore we can derive that:

(i) $\quad q_t^* = x_{1t}^{*a_1} \cdot x_{2t}^{*a_2}$

$$= b_{10}{}^{a_1} \cdot b_{20}{}^{a_2} P_t{}^{a_1 b_{11} + a_2 b_{21}} P_{1t}{}^{a_1 b_{12} + a_2 b_{22}} P_{2t}{}^{a_1 b_{13} + a_2 b_{23}} \tag{8.21}$$

(ii) $\quad q_t = x_{1t}^{a_1} \cdot x_{2t}^{a_2}$

$$=: b_{10}{}^{a_1} \cdot b_{20}{}^{a_2} \cdot P_t{}^{a_1 \gamma_1 b_{11} + a_2 \gamma_2 b_{21}} \cdot P_{1t}{}^{a_1 \gamma_1 b_{12} + a_2 \gamma_2 b_{22}}.$$

$$P_{2t}{}^{a_1 \gamma_1 b_{13} + a_2 \gamma_2 b_{23}} \cdot x_{1t-1}{}^{a_1(1-\gamma_1)} \cdot x_{2t-1}{}^{a_2(1-\gamma_2)} \tag{8.22}$$

Equation (8.21) is the equilibrium supply function, whilst equation (8.22) is the actual supply function. *If* $\gamma_1 = \gamma_2 = \gamma$ we can derive from these two equations that:

$$q_t = q_t^* \cdot q_{t-1}{}^{(1-\gamma)} \tag{8.23}$$

and the adjustment of supply over time as well as the adjustment of input demands is therefore described by the logarithmic partial adjustment model. However, in general, it would seem unrealistic to assume that the adjustment rates for both inputs are the same. We can see from equations (8.21) and (8.22) that this implies that the adjustment

† This form of the demand function can be derived from the Cobb–Douglas production function, under the assumption of profit maximizing behaviour.

of supply over time is not described by the partial adjustment model. Therefore, we may conclude that it is *theoretically* more reasonable to estimate the short-run and the long-run elasticities of supply indirectly, using the procedure we have outlined, than it is to estimate them directly through the use of a partial adjustment model of supply.

III. 2. ESTIMATES OF THE DERIVED AGGREGATE SUPPLY ELASTICITY

In this section we illustrate the theoretical exposition of the last section by deriving some estimates of the aggregate supply elasticity for United Kingdom agriculture. In particular, we derive estimates for the years 1956/7 and 1965/6. It should be emphasized that we do not expect these estimates to be very precise, but we do expect them to be of the right order of magnitude. However, before presenting the estimates we summarize the theory behind their derivation.

As a starting point, we note that if actual input flows diverge from their equilibrium levels then actual supply will differ from equilibrium supply since supply is determined by input flows via the production function. Consequently, because we have distinguished between short-run and long-run elasticities of demand for inputs we must also distinguish between the short-run or actual elasticity of supply and the long-run or equilibrium elasticity of supply. It may then be shown that the short-run aggregate supply elasticity can be expressed as a weighted average of the short-run input demand elasticities with respect to product price. Similarly, the long-run supply elasticity may be expressed as a weighted average of the long-run input demand elasticities with respect to product price. The production elasticities of the input flows provide the appropriate weights;† in the case of the short-run supply elasticity the production elasticities are those of the actual input flows whilst in the case of the long-run supply elasticity the production elasticities are those of the equilibrium input flows. This derivation of the supply elasticity may be rationalized as follows: firstly, a change in product price, *ceteris paribus*, leads to a change in the demand for each input; secondly, the production function transmits the change in

† The production elasticity of an input flow is defined as the percentage change in output resulting from a 1 per cent change in the input flow, *ceteris paribus*.

the demand for each input into a change in output.† The *ceteris paribus* assumption implies that input prices are held constant and therefore that the supply elasticity which we are deriving is the partial elasticity or the elasticity with respect to "real" product price.

Derivation of the short-run and the long-run aggregate supply elasticity therefore requires us to obtain estimates of the short-run and long-run input demand elasticities and of the production elasticities. It was shown in Chapter 2 how we could theoretically obtain estimates of the short-run and long-run input demand elasticities by incorporating a partial adjustment model into the input demand function. In addition, this procedure was utilized in two of the empirical chapters. The production elasticities may be obtained directly by using regression analysis to estimate the aggregate production function. However, the estimation of the production elasticities in this way has several drawbacks attached to it. One important difficulty is that only a few separate and very aggregated input categories may be considered as independent variables in the production function whereas for our purposes we wish to obtain production elasticities referring to many disaggregated input categories to correspond with the estimated demand elasticities. This difficulty will be illustrated shortly when we discuss the derivation of the supply elasticity for United Kingdom agriculture using production function estimates of the production elasticities. An alternative approach toward obtaining the production elasticities is to use the indirect factor share method as described in the last section. With this method we assume that *in equilibrium* the opportunity cost of any input flow will be equal to the value of its marginal product. The production elasticity of any input flow is equal to the marginal product of that input flow times the ratio of the input flow to output flow. Therefore in an equilibrium situation, the marginal product element of the production elasticity may be replaced by the ratio of the opportunity cost of the input to product price. In other words, the production elasticity may be replaced in *equilibrium* by the cost of the input as a proportion of total

† Thus, if we differentiate the aggregate production function $q = f(x_1, \ldots, x_k)$ with respect to product price P, we obtain:

$$\frac{dq}{dP} = \frac{\partial q}{\partial x_1} \cdot \frac{dx_1}{dP} + \cdots + \frac{\partial q}{\partial x_k} \cdot \frac{dx_k}{dP}$$

Multiplying this equation through by P/q gives the elasticity result mentioned above.

revenue. If we make the further assumption that in equilibrium there are zero economic profits we may replace the production elasticity by the cost of the input as a proportion of total costs—that is, by the factor share of the input. This procedure only applies as we have stressed in equilibrium and therefore only provides an estimate of the production elasticities to be utilized in calculating the long-run supply elasticity. However, if we make the assumption that production elasticities are approximately constant over the range between actual and equilibrium input flows we may utilize the factor share estimates of the production elasticities to calculate the short-run supply elasticity. This assumption was made in calculating estimates of the short-run aggregate supply elasticity for United Kingdom agriculture.

Both the long-run and the short-run supply elasticities were calculated using the equilibrium factor share approach for the two years 1956/7 and 1965/6 (May–June years). Before the factor shares could be calculated the opportunity cost of the equilibrium flow of each resource had to be obtained. These costs were obtained as follows: firstly, the demand for each input flow for the particular year with which we were concerned was adjusted to its equilibrium level using the particular partial adjustment model that was utilized in estimating the demand function for that input flow. For example, if the linear partial adjustment model were used in estimating the demand function for the ith input, then the equilibrium input flow of the ith resource in year t $(x_{it})^*$ is given as a function of the actual input flow in year $t(x_{it})$ and the actual input flow of the previous year (x_{it-1}):

$$x_{it}^* = \frac{x_{it} + (\hat{\gamma}_i - 1)\, x_{it-1}}{\hat{\gamma}_i} \qquad (8.24)$$

where $\hat{\gamma}_i$ is the adjustment coefficient which was obtained when the demand function for the ith input was estimated. Clearly, this adjustment procedure was not needed for those resources whose input flows were assumed to be adjusted to equilibrium in each year. Secondly, the opportunity cost of the equilibrium flow of each resource was estimated using the methodology outlined in section I of this chapter. The derived equilibrium factor shares for the two years are given below, along with the input demand elasticities, in Tables 8.3 and 8.4. Estimate B of the factor shares assumes a higher opportunity cost for landlord's capital

TABLE 8.3. DERIVED AGGREGATE SUPPLY ELASTICITY FOR 1956/7 USING THE
EQUILIBRIUM FACTOR SHARE APPROACH

*	Resource flow	Elasticity of demand with respect to product price		Equilibrium factor share of total costs (%)	
		Short run	Long run	Estimate A	Estimate B
1	Hired labour	0·83	0·83	23·8	22·6
2	Fertilizer	1·00	1·43	5·1	4·8
3	Feed and seed and sundries	0·30	0·30	28·8	27·4
4	Machinery	0·24	0·35	18·4	17·5
5	Cattle and sheep	0·21	0·63	3·6	3·4
6	Pigs	1·09	1·55	0·22	0·21
7	Poultry	0·34	3·10	0·08	0·08
8	Land	0·00	0·00	4·0	7·6
9	Buildings	0·25	0·62	1·5	2·8
10	Labour of farmer	0·00	0·00	14·5	13·6
	Derived aggregate supply elasticity:				
			Short run	0·39	0·38
			Long run	0·46	0·44

* For legend, see Table 8.4.

than estimate A—along the lines discussed in section I. The factor
share estimates are presented as percentages so that, for example, the
equilibrium factor share for hired labour, in Table 8.3, of 23·8 per cent
implies a production elasticity for the equilibrium input flow of hired
labour of 0·238. The supply elasticities for the two years were then
calculated from the data in the tables and are entered below in the
tables.

The short-run supply elasticity is defined, for our purposes, as the
percentage adjustment of supply that is completed within one year in
response to a 1 per cent change in product price, *ceteris paribus*. The
derived results indicate that the short-run supply elasticity for United
Kingdom agriculture was of the order of 0·35 to 0·40 for 1956/7 and
1965/6 with very little difference between the two years. The long-run
supply elasticity—the full or equilibrium adjustment to a 1 per cent
price change—was estimated to be only slightly higher than the short-
run elasticity. As a check on the factor share derivation of the supply

TABLE 8.4. DERIVED AGGREGATE SUPPLY ELASTICITY FOR 1965/6 USING THE
EQUILIBRIUM FACTOR SHARE APPROACH

*	Resource flow	Elasticity of demand with respect to product price		Equilibrium factor share of total costs (%)	
		Short run	Long run	Estimate A	Estimate B
1	Hired labour	0·86	0·86	20·1	18·4
2	Fertilizer	0·70	1·00	3·8	5·3
3	Feed and seed and sundries	0·30	0·30	29·5	27·0
4	Machinery	0·24	0·35	18·2	16·7
5	Cattle and sheep	0·21	0·63	3·2	3·0
6	Pigs	1·09	1·55	0·33	0·3
7	Poultry	0·34	3·10	0·18	0·16
8	Land	0·00	0·00	5·8	10·6
9	Buildings	0·25	0·62	3·3	6·7
10	Labour of farmer	0·00	0·00	13·6	11·8
	Derived aggregate supply elasticity:				
			Short run	0·36	0·34
			Long run	0·43	0·42

* *N.B.* Estimates of the input demand elasticities were obtained from:
  1. Chapter 3, table 3.2, equation (3).
  2. Chapter 5, table 5.6, equation (4).
  3. Guess based on some work by D. R. Colman, An econometric study of the U.K. cereals market, 1954–67, Ph.D., Manchester, 1969.
  4. Assumed equal to the tractor demand elasticity: Chapter 4, Table 4.1, equation (4c).
  5–7. Colman, *op. cit.*
  8. Assumed zero.
  9. Pure guess.
  10. Assumed zero for small changes in product price.

elasticity an attempt was also made to estimate the supply elasticity using production function estimates of the production elasticities. As described in Chapter 2 (section III.1a), Rasmussen† estimated an aggregate production function for British agriculture using cross-section data on farm accounts, over the years 1954/5 to 1957/8. Only

† Knud Rasmussen, *Production Function Analyses of British and ~~Farm Accounts~~*, University of Nottingham, Agricultural Economics Department, 1962.

TABLE 8.5. DERIVED AGGREGATE SUPPLY ELASTICITY USING RASMUSSEN'S
PRODUCTION FUNCTION ESTIMATES OF THE PRODUCTION ELASTICITIES

Resource flow	Elasticity of demand with respect to product price		Production* elasticities
	Short run	Long run	
Landlord's capital	0·07	0·17	0·078
Tenant's capital	0·24	0·42	0·179
Labour	0·52	0·52	0·283
Current capital inputs	0·41	0·47	0·456
Derived aggregate supply elasticity:			
		Short run	0·38
		Long run	0·45

* *Source*: Knud Rasmussen, *op. cit.*, p. 12, group 3.

four very aggregated input categories were identified in this analysis—landlord's capital, tenant's capital, labour and current capital inputs. This is many fewer than the input categories identified by the factor share derivation of the supply elasticity as described in Tables 8.3 and 8.4. The input demand elasticities corresponding to these four input categories therefore had to be derived as weighted averages of the separate demand elasticities set out in Table 8.3. The weights used were the proportionate factor shares of the separate input categories. Short-run and long-run supply elasticities were then derived and the results are set out in Table 8.5 below.

The results derived by this approach are very similar to those derived by the factor share approach. Therefore, we may conclude that the short-run supply elasticity of United Kingdom agriculture was of the order of 0·35 to 0·40 between 1955/6 and 1965/6 and the long-run supply elasticity slightly higher. Whilst we believe these estimates to be of the right order of magnitude, it must be remembered that they have been derived mainly for illustrative purposes since some of the figures which were used in the derivation were based on very scanty evidence. However, we should also remember that this indirect method of estimating the supply elasticity does have some theoretical advantages over direct estimation using a partial adjustment model of supply. To start with, it is more akin to the planning procedures of farmers—they plan input quantities and only implicitly do they plan supply. Consequently, a partial adjustment model of the adjustment of the demand for each input over time may reasonably describe their planning procedures. If all input demands are adjusted at the same rate then clearly the adjustment of supply will be carried out at the same rate also, because of the connection of supply and input flows through the production function. However, we might normally expect that input demands will be adjusted at different rates, and given the interaction of input flows in the production function, this will lead to a fairly complex model of supply adjustment.

IV. Future Pattern of Resource Use and Technological Change†

From our analyses of resource demand in the post-war period we may detail three major influences on future resource use in agriculture. Firstly, trends in the prices of inputs will determine whether or not present trends in resource use are consolidated. Secondly, governmental policy toward agriculture will influence both these trends in resource structure and the level of agricultural output. Thirdly, the future resource structure will be partly determined by the development of new technology. These influences represent pressures which are mainly generated from outside the farm sector. However, if farmers raise their bargaining power *vis-à-vis* other sectors of the economy, then forces internal to agriculture will also play some role in determining the future resource structure.

If we project present trends into the future then it is clear that the substitution of capital services, in aggregate, for labour will continue. At present, many farmers are still adjusting their resource structure in response to past changes in the ratio of the cost of capital services to labour costs. In addition, this cost ratio is likely to continue to fall under the stimulus of technological innovations. Consequently, we are

† The authors wish to thank Mr. C. H. Mudd, Director of the Helmshore Experimental Farm, for helpful advice with regard to future technological developments. Any errors or omissions are of course the responsibility of the authors.

likely to see a continuous trend toward the automation of many farming tasks such as the feeding of livestock. More complete mechanization of many tasks, such as the harvesting and handling of forage crops, is also likely.

Whilst an increase in capital services for "capital deepening" of the resource structure is almost certain to occur in the future, an increase in capital services for "capital widening" is not so certain. Under the United Kingdom agricultural support system the level of agricultural output is very dependent upon governmental policy toward agriculture. Consequently, if the government gives price incentives to encourage output expansion, some capital widening, particularly through inputs such as livestock and buildings, can be expected. Whether or not output expansion will be encouraged is uncertain at the present and the matter is discussed in the next chapter.

We turn now to look at future trends in input use on a less aggregated basis. We have already indicated that the drift from the land is likely to continue as a result of the "push" of the falling price ratio of capital services to labour. However, the rate of outflow will depend partly on governmental policy, as previously outlined, toward agricultural expansion. The structure of this outflow is also likely to depend on governmental policy. For example, governmental incentives in the form of amalgamation schemes and retirement policies should help to accelerate the mild trend in the number of farmers leaving agriculture. On the other hand if an output expansion policy relieves the squeeze on farmers' incomes to some extent then this will tend to deaccelerate this trend. However, as the stock of purchased durable inputs increases on farms this creates internal pressure toward farm amalgamation and increasing farm size, thus counterbalancing the latter effect.

If we refer back to Chapter 4, we can see that the stocks of many farm machines have reached a ceiling level. Consequently, gross investment in these machines is likely to be mainly for replacement purposes only. However, it is likely that quality improvement in some of these machines will continue and that stocks, measured so as to allow for quality change, will continue to grow although at a slower rate than previously. Whilst mechanization in the production of arable crops has reached a fairly "mature" stage, this is not the case in livestock farming. Clearly, developments in this sector depend upon the availability of new technology at the "right" price, but it seems reasonable to predict substantial mechanization of many tasks in this sector.

The demand by agriculture for chemicals is more closely associated with the level of agricultural output than is the demand for machinery. Hence, the demand for chemicals will be more affected by the extent to which the government encourages the expansion of agricultural output. However, the adoption of chemicals in agriculture has not reached such an advanced stage as the trend in mechanization, and the potential for further expansion is substantial. In fact, chemicals may begin to replace machinery services to some extent. For example, on many soil types, chemical sprays may replace mechanical cultivation in the preparation of arable land for sowing. However, in the immediate future, much of the future expansion in the demand for chemicals is likely to be for nitrogenous fertilizers provided that the "real" price of fertilizer continues to fall. Looking further ahead into the future, it is likely that there will be new developments in the use of chemicals in livestock husbandry as well as in crop husbandry. For example, it is suggested that simple organic forms of nitrogen, such as urea, and mineral "bullets" will be used to supplement natural herbage on poorer land as feed for livestock rearing. Also, intensification in the production of livestock, particularly pigs and poultry, is likely to continue with a consequent increased demand for pharmaceuticals.

In recent years, there has been a substantial increase in gross investment in buildings. This trend seems likely to continue under the pressure of rising labour costs and also if output expansion in agriculture is encouraged. In addition, a breakthrough in technology—particularly in the development of new building materials and methods—would help to stimulate this investment.

Finally, we should mention future technical possibilities which do not fit into the above categories. Firstly, developments in the biological sciences have been rapid in recent years and these are likely to impinge on agriculture in the not too distant future. For example, two developments which may soon offer commercial prospects are (i) breeding sheep out of season, (ii) using hormones to induce larger litters in pigs. Secondly, the slurry-pollution problem is one that is increasing and methods need to be developed to solve this satisfactorily at a reasonable cost. Thirdly, we may find an increased use of aircraft in agriculture and forestry.

In fact, it has been suggested that a breakthrough in forestry technology may occur by using aircraft firstly, to spray herbicides to clear the land of vegetation and, secondly, to "seed" trees from the air. In this way, the initial cost of the establishment of a forest could be considerably reduced, enabling forestry to be much more of a commercial venture.

CHAPTER 9

IMPLICATIONS OF PUBLIC POLICY

I. Introduction

The aim of this chapter is to bring together, in terms of policy implications, some of the material presented in earlier chapters. Essentially, we wish to know how government policy impinges on the factor markets.† A major problem in outlining the effect of government policy on aggregate resource demand is where to stop. Thus some policies have a direct and obvious impact: for example, fertilizer subsidies will, *ceteris paribus*, increase the quantity demanded of chemical fertilizer. Other policies have a direct but less obvious effect: for example, an incomes policy which allowed increases in the pay of low paid workers would raise agricultural earnings relative to industrial wage earnings. This would reduce the pull of the non-farm sector from the viewpoint of the potential migrant, and encourage the farmer to substitute capital for labour. Other policies have an indirect but possibly important impact: for example, a vigorous anti-trust policy which kept down the price of steel and other components which go to make up agricultural machinery would, *ceteris paribus*, lower the price of that machine and so increase the quantity demanded of it. This list could be extended.

One solution to this problem would be to take each input in turn and document just about every conceivable variable which might influence the market for that input. However, such an approach would not be very interesting: it would merely add more explanatory variables to those already suggested in the respective chapters. Rather, a better approach is to indicate the policy instruments used by the government and see how manipulation of these instruments affects the agricultural

† Mainly in terms of how policy affects the demand for inputs, but in the case of the labour input also the effects on the supply of labour.

factor markets. Whilst this approach may not pick up some of the more indirect influences on the factor markets, it will, painting broad strokes, outline the policy problems confronting the government and suggest how the decisions taken to resolve or mitigate these problems impinge on the agricultural factor markets.

Broadly we can divide the policy instruments which might be hypothesized to influence the resource markets of the agricultural sector into two types—agricultural and macro. We start with a discussion of agricultural policy: this includes a brief historical review and a description of current policy. We suggest the ways in which agricultural policy affects the demand for inputs. Finally, we indicate the magnitude of agricultural product price change necessary to get a given increase in agricultural output.

II. Agricultural Policy

We begin this section with a highly synoptic historical survey of government intervention in agriculture and a description of present policy.

Agricultural policy may be thought of as a hierarchy of goals and instruments. Thus the goals may, for example, be improving farmers' incomes and improving the balance of payments; the instruments to attain either or both of these goals are numerous, for example structural change, deficiency payments, variable levies, input subsidies and so on. It is not the purpose of this section to construct a hierarchy of agricultural goals and instruments, nor to discuss the merits of deficiency payments versus variable levies, nor to go into policy conflicts.†
Rather, here we accept that agricultural product prices can be changed by a variety of methods and go on to indicate the effect of changing agricultural product prices on factor markets. We also indicate the effect on the mix of factors demanded of changes in factor prices. Finally, we survey a number of other factors, for example, the Agricultural Training Board, which impinge on the various input markets.

† For a lucid discussion of these problems see T. Josling, A formal approach to agricultural policy, *Journal of Agricultural Economics*, 1969. See also R. Spitze, Economic redirections in U.S. agricultural policy, *Journal of Agricultural Economics*, vol. XIX, 3, Sept. 1968.

II.1. HISTORY

Between 1846, when the Corn Laws were repealed, and the early 1930's British agricultural policy was virtually a *laissez-faire* policy: imports entered duty free and domestic prices adjusted accordingly. In the 1870's North American grain supplies increased substantially and wheat price fell by half between 1870 and 1890 and the price of barley and oats fell by one-third: this led to an increase in the amount of land used for permanent pasture. Grain prices were stable between the 1890's and World War I. They rose during World War I then declined sharply. This latter fall led to the first major planned intervention: the 1920 Agriculture Act planned to give guaranteed minimum prices of wheat and oats for 4 years ahead: however, the act was repealed before it came into force. Despite representations by both farmers' and agricultural workers' organizations successive 1920's governments declined to introduce agricultural support measures—whether via tariffs, subsidies or other instruments.

In the early 1930's the *laissez-faire* policy was abandoned. The Agricultural Marketing Acts of 1931 and 1933 established producer controlled marketing boards for certain commodities (for example, milk). The Wheat Act of 1932 introduced a standard price of 10s. per cwt. for millable wheat. If the market price fell below 10s., the difference between the market and standard price was made up by a deficiency payment. The Act also introduced standard quantities: the deficiency payment was made on 1·35 million long tons. The 1937 Agriculture Act introduced acreage payments, for oats and barley.

Measures which interfered more directly with international trade were undertaken in the Ottawa Agreements Act of 1932: first, tariffs were imposed on certain non-Commonwealth produced grain products —for example wheat. Second, some meat imports were subject to quantitative restriction: in the case of bacon the restriction of imports resulted in the U.K. price being 50 per cent above the Danish (free) market price in 1936. (The government had undertaken not to impose a tariff on meat imports. It therefore imposed import controls!)

The advent of World War II resulted in efforts to increase production of cereals. Subsidies for ploughing up grassland were introduced in 1939. Fertilizer subsidies, introduced in 1937, were maintained. Cereal acreage rose from 5·3 million acres in 1939 to 9·6 million acres in 1943, an increase of 80 per cent. Correspondingly, livestock production declined.

The basis for post-war agricultural policy was provided by the 1947 Agriculture Act. This provided for guaranteed prices. The stated aim was to "attain a stable and efficient agricultural industry capable of producing such part of the nation's food and other agricultural produce as is in the national interest it is desirable to produce in the U.K., and of producing it at minimum prices consistently with proper remuneration and living conditions for farmers and workers in agriculture and an adequate return on capital invested in the industry".

II.2. CURRENT POLICY

Currently the government intervenes in the agricultural product markets through deficiency payments, production grants and other grants and subsidies. In 1967/8 the total estimated cost of agricultural support was £270 million of which deficiency payments made up a little over a half. Originally, imports were allowed into the U.K. at world (free market) prices, the government making up the deficit between the guaranteed price and market price by a *deficiency payment*.† The open ended nature of these subsidies and the resulting drain on the exchequer led the government to attempt to cut down on the magnitude of the deficiency payments. First it now pays the deficiency payment only on *standard quantities* of output in the case of some commodities (for example pigs). This system was introduced in 1964. Second, it negotiated *minimum import prices* with suppliers of some commodities (for example some cereal crops), such that they agree not to export their agricultural products to the U.K. below a specified price.‡

The effect of the modifications to the original scheme is such that the only commodities without schemes for supply management are beef, cattle and sheep.

The aims of U.K. agricultural support policy are complex. The above

† Milk imports are not allowed. Also some home producers, mainly of horticultural products, are protected by tariffs. The U.K. has also imposed quotas on the import of certain commodities, e.g. butter (since 1962) and bacon (since 1963).

‡ This system was negotiated at the time that the U.K. balance of payments was in serious adverse disequilibrium. For a discussion of minimum import prices see G. Peters, A note on minimum import prices, *Farm Economist*, vol. X, 11, 1965.

quotation from the 1947 Agriculture Act does not indicate concise goals. Probably the two main aims currently are first to increase the returns to the resources in agriculture and second to expand domestic food output to save food imports. Thus the first main goal of support policy is to increase *per capita* farm incomes: this raises the question as to whether or not there are better instruments to raise farm incomes. Insofar as the deficiency payments are designed to support the incomes of "small" farmers (i.e. those having a low value of total output) the goal is not achieved: the bulk of the payments must inevitably go to those farmers having high output—possibly the least likely to need income support. The incomes of small farmers are better raised by, for example, a cash handout rather than through the deficiency payments system.

The main controversy with respect to the aims of agricultural policy concerns the import saving role of agriculture. No one denies that by expanding domestic agriculture the U.K. could cut down on food imports. However, the relevant question concerns the opportunity cost of the extra (marginal) resources used to expand agriculture. This is not the place to enter the controversy: however, the economic analysis of Josling indicates that "present support levels begin to look extremely expensive in terms of import substitution".[†] However, see also the work of Peters who concludes "the accumulation of fixed capital within the agricultural sector results in an output gain and a freeing of valuable labour, which is in no sense inferior to the contribution made by investment in other sectors of the economy".

II.3. PRODUCT AND INPUT PRICES AND THE DEMAND FOR INPUTS

(a) *Factor/Product Price Ratio*

In Chapter 2, which outlined the theory of resource demand, it was suggested that the real price of a factor (i.e. price of the factor relative to the price of the agricultural output it goes to produce) is likely to be important in explaining variations in the demand for factors. This

[†] T. Josling, A formal approach to agricultural policy, *Journal of Agricultural Economics*, 1969; G. Peters, Capital and labour in British agriculture, *Farm Economist*, vol. XI, 6, 1967.

hypothesis was tested using the statistical material presented in Chapters 3–6, and was generally substantiated. Thus fertilizer subsidies, investment allowances and increases in agricultural product prices reduce the real price of the factors and stimulate demand. For example, the analysis of fertilizer consumption indicated that the short-run elasticity of demand with respect to changes in the real price of fertilizer was, in 1965, $-0·6$. Similarly, the statistical evidence of tractor demand indicated that the short-run stock elasticity of demand with respect to changes in the price of agricultural output was $+0·23$.

(b) *Product/Product Price Ratio*

The mix of inputs used may be changed by the mix of agricultural products produced; this latter will be determined by the structure of agricultural product prices. For example, a rise in the relative price of beef and milk might encourage farmers to switch out of cash crops and into livestock production. This would result in an increase in the demand for farm buildings and a decrease in the demand for tractor services. It may also result in an increase in the quantity of labour demanded.

(c) *Factor/Factor Price Ratio*

In Chapter 2 it was stated that one important influence on the demand for a particular factor (X_1) is the price of substitute (X_2) and complement (X_3) factors. Thus (for a constant output) if the price of X_2 goes up this is likely to cause an expansion in the demand for X_1 (X_1 and X_2 are substitutes); if the price of X_3 rises, this causes a reduction in demand for X_1 (X_1 and X_3 are complements). Such factor price ratios were included as relevant explanatory variables in the statistical sections of Chapters 3–6. The factor price ratio which has had the most obvious impact on demand is the agricultural wages/tractor price ratio. Over the period 1948–65 agricultural labour earnings increased by over 130 per cent whilst (constant quality) tractor prices increased by 25 per cent. This encouraged capital deepening—the substitution of capital for labour. This price ratio was the dominant explanatory variable in the regression equations explaining the demand for tractors. This suggests, therefore, that if the Agricultural Wages Board continues to grant, and the government continues to sanction, annual wage increases of greater magnitude than tractor price increases, then farmers will continue to substitute capital for manpower. This poses an interesting problem for the National Union of Agricultural Workers, viz.: what is the *objective function* of that union? If, for example, it is trying to maximize its membership, then maybe it should not press for wage increases as this encourages farmers to push labour out of the industry. (Although if it does not press for wage increases, the members may leave the union because of discontent with its policies.) Alternatively, is the union trying to maximize the wage bill paid by the industry?† Another factor price ratio tested in the statistical sections was the feedingstuff/fertilizer price ratio. However, the results were inconclusive.

II.4. OVERALL IMPACT OF PRODUCT PRICE CHANGES

In Chapter 8 the estimates of the elasticity of demand for inputs with respect to changes in their real price was used to indicate how farmers *plan* to change output in response to price changes. This in turn allows an estimate of the aggregate supply elasticity of the agricultural sector with respect to product prices. They are

	1956–7	1965–6
Short run	0·38	0·34
Long run (equilibrium)	0·44	0·42

These estimates indicate how large an aggregate price change is necessary to get a specified change in the aggregate quantity of output supplied. Say the government decided, rightly or wrongly, that for balance of payments reasons it desired a 2 per cent increase in the quantity of output supplied compared with what it would have been in the absence of product price changes. The 1965–6 short-run supply elasticity indicates that agricultural product prices would have to rise,

† For a discussion of possible union objectives see J. Dunlop, *Wage Determination Under Trade Unions*, chapter 3, Macmillan, New York, 1944.

in aggregate, by 6 per cent to attain the desired output increase. This 6 per cent price change would in the long run induce a 2·5 per cent increase in output. The estimates of the elasticity of supply cannot really be used to indicate what would happen to agricultural output if, for example, the U.K. were to join the European Economic Community or if the government were to abandon all subsidies and other forms of supply control and let imports in freely: in these cases the product price changes would be relatively large. The above supply elasticity estimates refer to small price changes. Nevertheless it may be interesting to speculate on one of the above possibilities: agricultural subsidies are equivalent to a 14 per cent rate of protection (in 1967–8 sales of agricultural products were estimated to be £1933 million and subsidies £270). Assume that the other methods of protection, such as an artificially high price to liquid milk consumers and import quotas, push up the overall rate of protection to 20 per cent. If this protection were withdrawn the above estimates suggest that in the long run the quantity of output supplied would decline by 8 per cent. Whether in fact the farmers' response would be more or less elastic we do not know: it depends on such factors as how far the product price changes get transmitted to the prices of the resources, whether farmers produce more in an attempt to offset the price reduction, etc.

II.5. AGRICULTURAL TRAINING BOARD†

In March 1964 the Industrial Training Act was passed "to make further provision for industrial and commercial training" as an umbrella under which training boards could be set up for individual industries. The aims of the Industrial Training Act are: first, to ensure an adequate supply of properly trained men and women at all levels in British industries. Second, to improve the quality, quantity and efficiency of training. Third, to share the cost of training more equitably.

The basis of the Industrial Training Act rests on the welfare argument that without the levy the socially optimum amount of industrial training will not be attained: each employer will prefer to let other employers undertake the training costs and then bid away the trained people by

† See Agricultural, Horticultural and Forestry Industry Training Board, *Background Facts and Figures*, Feb. 1969, on which this section is based.

offering them slightly higher wages than they would receive in the firm which financed their training.

The Agricultural, Horticultural and Forestry Industry Training Board was established in August 1966. It was authorized originally to collect from employers a levy of £6 per full-time employee for the year 1967–8. Subsequently, the levy was reduced to £3. The proposed levy for 1968–9 is £3 10s. 0d. per full-time employee. This is equivalent to 0·47 per cent of the agricultural wage bill, which is substantially lower than the percentage levied by most other Industrial Training Boards. There are 92,000 leviable employers with over 280,000 employees.†

The Board, after studying the training requirements of the industry established the following priorities:

1. To continue the policy of developing training in co-operation with education authorities and other organizations that are able to make a contribution.

2. To support the existing apprenticeship schemes whilst, at the same time, working on new proposals for training entrants to the industry.

3. To train key men from the industry as instructors.

4. To develop training for established workers at, or where more convenient, away from their place of work.

5. By means of the Grant Scheme and the Board's field staff, to encourage more employers to become involved in training.

6. To plan and develop new training schemes ahead of changes in farming techniques.

It remains to be seen whether the Board will attain its aims successfully. For example, it has not yet produced any forecasts of different occupational requirements for the coming years. If it is successful, the activities of the Board will supplement the stock of human capital in the agricultural industry, and will favourably affect the quality of the manpower supplied to the industry. Evidence suggests that, for the economy as a whole, the payoff to education and training, both private (to the individual) and public (to the community) is in excess of the rate of return on a large number of other projects.‡ As yet, no calcula-

---

† The levy is the Board's only regular source of funds. However, in 1968 the Department of Employment and Productivity gave the Board a grant of £450,000.

‡ See, for example, M. Blaug, The rate of return on investment in education, *Manchester School*, vol. 33, 3, 1965.

tions have been made specifically for the U.K. agricultural industry comparing the costs and benefits of industrial training with (say) those of bigger investment allowances on capital equipment; an evaluation of the agricultural training programme awaits such calculations. It may be pertinent to remark, however, that, given the persistent downward trend in the ratio of capital price to labour earnings and the resulting push of hired labour from agriculture as farmers reduce the quantity of hired labour they demand, estimates of the impact of industrial training on, on the one hand, earnings in agriculture and, on the other hand, the rate of outmigration are important in evaluating the future farm income problem.

II.6. AGRICULTURAL MORTGAGE CORPORATION

The Agricultural Mortgage Corporation Limited, a semi-public institution, provides a source of funds for farmers. Loans are made to owners of freehold properties in England and Wales, but if the applicant is not at present the owner, he can apply for a loan to enable him to buy the property. The loan will be up to two-thirds of the value of the freehold property. The activities of the A.M.C. can be shown from the following table.

TABLE 9.1. ACTIVITIES OF THE A.M.C.

	1968 £m	1967 £m	1966 £m
Total of loan applications	48	44	35
Loans completed	21	20	11
Net lending	16	16	7
Total loans outstanding	103	87	71

Source: A.M.C. Ltd., *Report of Directors and Accounts*, 1968.

The proceeds of a loan may be used for many purposes: for example, the purchase of a farm; capital improvements such as the reconstruction or provision of new cottages or farm buildings, electricity or water supplies, drainage, farm roads. The operation of the A.M.C. is therefore likely to increase the demand for agricultural inputs which make for farm improvements.

II.7. LONG-TERM GUARANTEES

In the 1957 Agriculture Act the Government set out long-term guarantees for agricultural product prices. Under this system the agricultural support price will, in any one year (a) in aggregate not fall below $97\frac{1}{2}$ per cent of the previous year's level; (b) for any commodity not fall below 96 per cent of the previous year's level. For livestock there is the additional guarantee that the support level will not fall by more than 9 per cent in three years. This system has substantially reduced the degree of uncertainty in the industry. Minimum prices are now known with certainty (although *revenue* also depends upon the *quantity* produced).

It was suggested in the empirical chapters that the adoption of long-term minimum price guarantees has had an important impact on some factor markets. In the case of the tractor market this system encourages a fairly rapid adjustment towards the equilibrium stock of tractors, two-thirds of the adjustment towards equilibrium being undertaken in any given year. In contrast, in the U.S.A. where there are no such long-term price guarantees, the adjustment towards equilibrium takes much longer—only one-fifth of the adjustment towards the equilibrium tractor stock being made in the current year.

Similarly, the analysis of the causes of the rise in the price of agricultural land suggested that a main reason for the spurt in land prices after 1957 was the adoption of the long-term guarantees in that year. It was surmised that this legislation had a favourable effect on farmers' future income expectations, which encouraged them to attempt to enlarge their farms thereby shifting the demand function for farm land rightwards.

II.8. STRUCTURAL CHANGE

The government is currently actively engaged in a campaign to increase average farm size; it is particularly concerned to produce farms of "commercial size" (defined as 600 man-days a year). A number of measures have been adopted to attain larger farms.† For example, (a) the government gives grants of up to 50 per cent of the cost of private amalgamations on condition that the farm produced is of commercial size (defined above) and under single ownership; (b) an occupier can sell his land to the state for amalgamation purposes; (c) the government provides grants or pensions to outgoing occupiers. The cost of these schemes together with the exchequer payments under the Farm Improvement Scheme and payments to encourage the establishment of co-operatives is around £30 million per annum.

The relevant question for us is what effect increasing farm size has on the demand for inputs. Take the case of farm building. Will increasing farm size encourage farmers to utilize existing buildings more intensively or will it encourage a more capital intensive method of production? The former case would dampen demand for farm buildings, the latter stimulate that demand. Similar questions can be framed concerning the demand for other inputs. The empirical evidence on these questions is, as yet, inconclusive.

III. Macro-economic Policy: Goals, Instruments and Impact on Agricultural Factor Markets

The government's macro economic policy may be viewed as a hierarchy of ends and means. A suggested hierarchy is:

Final goals	Economic growth; Equity
Intermediate goals	Full employment; Balance of payments Equilibrium; Price Stability
Instruments	Fiscal; Monetary; Prices and incomes; Regional; Agricultural; Tariff; Exchange rate, etc.

The essential element in the construction of this hierarchy is the distinction between policy *goals* and policy *instruments*. Manipulation of the instruments helps us to attain the goals we (as a community) desire. Whether the goals are called *intermediate* or *final* does not matter so much as the distinction between goals and instruments. The distinc-

† See Ministry of Agriculture, *The Development of Agriculture*, Cmnd. 2738, H.M.S.O., 1967.

tion between policy instruments and intermediate and final policy goals is indeed difficult: different writers would probably draw up different hierarchies but the above probably represents an adequate synthesis of both what people want and what our society is currently striving for. However, one can raise numerous questions. For example (a) is the prestige of the pound a final goal? (b) would an old age pensioner view price stability as more important than economic growth? (c) would a politician in Northern Ireland view full employment as more important than economic growth? (d) is it true to say most people desire greater equity as a final goal?† Thus we have a prices and incomes policy to get price stability and balance of payments equilibrium, a regional policy to help in the quest for full employment, and so on. What we are concerned with here is not the impact which manipulation of the macro economic instruments has on the macro economic goals, but the effect, direct or indirect, such manipulation has on the markets for inputs in agriculture.

The overriding macro policy problem of the last decade has been that of the balance of payments. We do not really desire balance of payments equilibrium for its own sake (although pronouncements by bankers and politicians would sometimes suggest that we do). Rather we have to correct any adverse equilibrium in our balance of payments because foreigners will not lend to us indefinitely and because we do not wish to reduce our gold and foreign currency reserves to zero. If therefore our pursuit of faster economic growth leads to a balance of payments deficit, this must, in time, be corrected. Now there is a number of methods of correcting the balance of payments. Many economists would suggest that the most sensible balance of payments instrument is freely floating exchange rates. However, this is a political non-starter, mainly, we surmise, because it would reduce the "importance" of bankers and politicians—for they would no longer have to scurry round the globe solving international monetary crises.‡ Under a system of

---

† For a lucid discussion of macro goals and instruments in the U.K. see R. E. Caves *et al.*, *Britain's Economic Prospects*, Brookings Institution Study, Allen & Unwin, 1968.

‡ For a discussion of the case for flexible exchange rates see M. Friedman, The case for flexible exchange rates, in *Essays in Positive Economics*, University of Chicago Press.

freely floating exchange rates there would be no balance of payments deficit or surplus to correct. The main argument advanced against freely floating exchange rates is that they would lead to disruption in international trade. However, to maintain fixed parities we resort to deflation, import controls, border taxes, etc.! Therefore, governments have tended to adopt other methods of curing deficits on the payments balance. The three main instruments are deflation, prices and incomes policy and devaluation. Let us therefore start our assessment of the impact of macro instruments on agricultural factor markets by an examination of these three instruments.

III.1. DEFLATION

Deflation, i.e. reducing the magnitude of the circular flow of income, is generally carried out via the instruments of fiscal and monetary policy, for example, reducing government expenditure and/or increasing taxation; reducing the money supply and availability of funds and increasing the cost of borrowing. If successful, deflation will reduce home aggregate demand, slow down the rate of increase in prices and reduce import requirements. Typically, deflation results in a higher level of *aggregate unemployment*. In Chapter 3 we saw that higher aggregate unemployment was associated with a reduction in off-farm migration: labour "backs-up" on the farm because of the increased difficulty in finding alternative employment. This is especially so in high labour demand areas (i.e. regions of low unemployment) where outmigration is very sensitive to variations in the level of unemployment. In areas of low labour demand, however, it is less responsive to local unemployment levels: probably indicating that national unemployment is more relevant in determining the magnitude of outmigration in these regions than local unemployment.

A higher level of industrial unemployment may also reduce the pull of the non-farm occupations through its effect on industrial wages. Some evidence suggests that when industrial unemployment rises, the rate of increase of *industrial earnings* declines. Providing the rate of increase in agricultural earnings does not decline similarly the differential between agricultural and industrial earnings will be narrowed, so reducing the pull of the non-farm occupations.

The use of fiscal and monetary instruments in deflating the economy affects agricultural factor markets in other ways too. For example, first: *farm incomes*, like those of any other group of workers, will be affected by tax changes. If their incomes are reduced we would hypothesize that this would shift the supply of labour schedule to agriculture leftwards: farmers will encourage their children to enter non-agricultural occupations rather than remain on the farm-firm.

Second, if the government pursues a tight monetary policy, then *interest rates* will rise and availability of funds for lending fall. The interest rate was included in Chapter 4 as a variable to explain the demand for tractors. The statistical results, however, cast doubt upon its importance—at best the elasticity of demand with respect to changes in interest rates is very low. A tight monetary policy may also result in a slowing down of the rate of increase in the prices of land and capital goods.

III.2. PRICES AND INCOMES POLICY

Another prong in the attempt to correct the balance of payments disequilibrium has been prices and incomes policy.† A prices and incomes policy may impinge on agricultural factor markets in a number of ways. First, it may have a direct effect on agricultural earnings and therefore on the amounts supplied and demanded of hired agricultural workers. For example, the National Board for Prices and Incomes (N.B.P.I.) recently (Feb. 1969) approved a 17s. pay award for agricultural workers, equivalent to slightly over 7 per cent. The N.B.P.I. stated that although the increase of 7 per cent granted by the Agricultural Wages Board was in excess of the overall norm of $3\frac{1}{2}$ per cent, the increase was justified (a) because agricultural workers are amongst the lowest paid in the country, and (b) because the N.B.P.I. recognized the contribution made by agricultural workers to the increased produc-

---

† A prices and incomes policy may also have other beneficial effects. For example, greater equality of pay and less hardship for those on fixed incomes, but its aim in the U.K., as yet, has been the short-run one of eliminating the balance of payments disequilibrium by keeping aggregate money earnings increases in line with the increase in aggregate productivity. For a discussion of the mechanics, economics and success of U.K. incomes policy, see D. C. Smith, Incomes policy, chapter 3 in R. E. Caves, *op. cit.*

tivity of the sector.† The estimates presented in Table 3·4 of Chapter 3 suggest that, *ceteris paribus*, this will result in an increase in the quantity of labour supplied to agriculture of 3·5 per cent (7 per cent × 0·499) and a decrease in demand of 1·5 per cent (7 per cent × − 0·215), possibly (i.e. assuming that the labour market was in equilibrium to start with) resulting therefore in unemployment of agricultural workers. Second, prices and incomes policy may affect the demand for inputs through allowing or not allowing price rises in those inputs. For example, in March 1967 the N.B.P.I., in its adjudication of the fertilizer manufacturers' case for a price rise allowed price rises for compounds but not for straight nitrogen fertilizers.‡ This may shift the mix of fertilizers demand in favour of straight nitrogen and/or may, *ceteris paribus*, reduce aggregate fertilizer demand.

III.3. DEVALUATION

In November 1967 the pound was devalued by 14·3 per cent. This was a belated recognition of the fact that deflation and prices and incomes policy were likely to continue to be insufficient to cure the underlying balance of payments disequilibrium. The effect of a devaluation of the pound is to make imports into the U.K. dearer (i.e. the importer in the U.K. has to pay out *more* pounds than prior to devaluation to get the given amount of foreign exchange necessary to purchase a specific quantity of imports) and exports from the U.K. cheaper (the importer in the foreign country has to pay out *less* foreign currency than before to purchase the given amount of pounds necessary to get a specific quantity of U.K. exports). The problem of assessing the impact of devaluation on the demand for agricultural imputs is complex. We divide the effect of devaluation into, first: its impact on the agricultural product market, and therefore on the derived demand for inputs; and second: its impact on factor supply and therefore directly on price.

The effect of the devaluation of the pound on the agricultural product market, from the viewpoint of the farmer, was relatively unimportant. For those products having deficiency payments the magnitude of those

---

† See N.B.P.I., *Pay of Workers in Agriculture in England and Wales*, Rept. No. 101 Cmnd. 3911, Feb. 1969.

‡ N.B.P.I., *Prices of Compound Fertilizers*, Rept. No. 28, Cmnd. 3228, March 1967.

payments was such that prices received by domestic producers remained greater than the world price (in sterling terms) even after devaluation: therefore devaluation had little effect on the derived demand for inputs. However, devaluation has the effect of narrowing the gap between market price and guaranteed price, thereby lowering the unit deficiency payments and (potentially) lowering the cost of support. This effect is dampened, however, as some of our main suppliers (for example, New Zealand, Ireland, Denmark) devalued simultaneously with the U.K.

Similarly, the devaluation of the pound is unlikely to have had much direct effect on the price of most inputs and therefore on the demand for them. This can be shown, in extremely broad terms, by the following calculation. Assume that the import content in fertilizer (for example sulphur) and tractors (for example steel) and other inputs ranges from 0–20 per cent. Therefore a 15 per cent devaluation should have an effect on the final price of the input of, at most, between 0 and 3 per cent. The statistical estimates presented in the earlier chapters suggest that such a price change will have only a minor effect on the quantity of inputs demanded. However, devaluation may have made a bigger impact on one particular area: the production of some commodities, for example pigs and poultry, requires substantial imported feedgrain inputs. This may encourage producers of these products to switch to alternative products and therefore lessen the aggregate quantity demanded of feed inputs. (In the event, feed prices did not rise very much as the trend of world prices has been downwards, offsetting at least partially the impact of devaluation.)

We have now viewed the effect on input markets of manipulation of the three main instruments used to correct the balance of payments. However, other instruments will also affect the agricultural resource markets, and it is to an examination of these other instruments that we now turn.

III.4. INVESTMENT ALLOWANCES

An additional fiscal variable which evidence suggests is important in determining demand for capital inputs is that of investment allowances (changed in 1966 to investment grants). An investment allowance enabled the farmer to offset part of the cost of a new machine or new building against profits for taxation purposes. An investment grant is a cash grant towards part of the cost of the capital input. Currently, the government provides a grant of one-tenth towards the cost of all fixed equipment in agriculture. The effect of these investment allowances/ grants is to lower the real price of the capital equipment to the farmer. Chapter 4 suggested that investment allowances are an important factor in explaining the demand for tractors. For example, there was an increase in the allowance from 20 to 30 per cent during the period studied (i.e. a 50 per cent increase in the allowance) and the results indicated that *ceteris paribus* this raised the level of the stock of tractors by 0·5 per cent.

III.5. OTHER INSTRUMENTS

A number of other policy instruments may also be hypothesized to impinge on agricultural factor markets. We cannot present an exhaustive analysis of these influences but the following provide some examples.

(a) *Tariffs*

The U.K. protects many of its industries by tariffs. Over the last few years the structure of the tariffs has undergone significant changes. For example, they have been reduced between EFTA countries, and the Kennedy Round has encouraged more general reductions. A tariff reduction may shift the mix of inputs demanded and/or may increase the aggregate quantity of factors demanded in the manner examined under devaluation.

(b) *Regional*

The government has, especially since 1964, been pursuing policies designed to even out regional employment levels. For example, in 1967 a Regional Employment Premium was adopted.† This premium subsidizes the employment of labour in the Development Areas. If

† D.E.A./Treasury, *The Development Areas: A Proposal for a Regional Employment Premium*, H.M.S.O., April 1967.

unemployment is made more even amongst these regions this, as was indicated in Chapter 3, will affect agricultural labour supply in the different regions: if unemployment rises in the current low unemployment regions, then the incentive to leave agriculture will be lessened, and conversely in the current high unemployment regions.

(c) *Urban Planning*

It was suggested in Chapter 6 that an important factor explaining the rise in the price of agricultural land in the post-war period has been urban development. For example, new towns and more liberal housing densities increase the demand for land for urban use. This itself partly causes a rise in the price of agricultural land: but the rise in land price is accentuated because farmers who sell their agricultural land to urban developers frequently re-enter the land market quickly.

(d) *Education*

In Chapter 3 it was suggested that higher educational levels would make it easier for agricultural workers to transfer to alternative occupations. Thus a rising of the school-leaving age to 16 (proposed for 1971) may reduce the supply of agricultural manpower. Similarly, the raising of the school-leaving age will have the effect of keeping one complete cohort off the labour market, which will again reduce labour supply to agriculture.

(e) *Anti-trust Policy*

A vigorous anti-monopoly and anti-restrictive practices policy may encourage more efficiency in the economy and help keep down price rises. Chapters 4 and 5 suggested that the real price of tractors and fertilizers are important determinants of the demand for those factors: an anti-trust policy which succeeds in reducing the magnitude of price increases of these factors would probably therefore lead to an increase in the quantity demanded of these factors.

IV. Conclusion

In this chapter we have attempted to draw together and summarize the impact of public policy on the agricultural factor markets. It has been shown that a wide range of macro-economic and agricultural policy instruments influence the supply, demand and price of the various agricultural inputs. We may conclude the chapter by returning to the balance of payments question. It was indicated in the discussion of macro-economic policy that much of Britain's recent economic policy has been directed to improving our balance of payments. Similarly, much of our agricultural policy is based rightly or wrongly on the idea that expansion of agriculture contributes an improvement in the balance of payments by saving imports.

Thus we have indicated how deflation, prices and incomes policy, agricultural price guarantees, etc., impinge on factor markets. However, we have not raised the question as to whether the distortions introduced into the economy by these measures to improve the balance of payments are worthwhile. It may well be that the adoption of a floating exchange rate, which would eliminate these distortions caused because of our attempt to maintain fixed parities, would distribute economic resources according more to economic efficiency criteria: this may in turn result in a smaller agricultural sector and a reduction in the aggregate demand for inputs by agriculture.